DEEP DIVE INTO FINANCIAL MODELS

Modeling Risk and Uncertainty

DEEP DIVE INTO FINANCIAL MODELS

Modeling Risk and Uncertainty

Mathieu Le Bellac
BRED Bank, France

Arnaud Viricel
Natixis, France

edp sciences

World Scientific

Published by

EDP Sciences
17, av. du Hoggar F-91944 Les Ulis
France

and

World Scientific Publishing Co. Pte. Ltd.
5 Toh Tuck Link, Singapore 596224
USA office: 27 Warren Street, Suite 401-402, Hackensack, NJ 07601
UK office: 57 Shelton Street, Covent Garden, London WC2H 9HE

British Library Cataloguing-in-Publication Data
A catalogue record for this book is available from the British Library.

DEEP DIVE INTO FINANCIAL MODELS
Modeling Risk and Uncertainty

ISBN 978-981-3143-71-5
ISBN 978-981-3142-10-7 (pbk)

Desk Editor: Jiang Yulin

Typeset by Stallion Press
Email: enquiries@stallionpress.com

Contents

*The sections marked with a (*) are mathematically more demanding; they can be skipped at first reading.*

Preface

For 40 years, financial engineering has suffered from an excess of axiomatization, from useless theorems and from models sometimes so unfit that they become a source of systemic instabilities. The perfection of the mathematical tool clouds the intuition for mechanisms, the beauty of formulas hides the complexity of phenomena, and reality vanishes behind formalism. The students who will become financial engineers, risk managers or traders are often lost in the demonstrations of theorems and are fascinated by the aesthetics of results, at the expense of a critical view of the assumptions and of the intuitive understanding of models and of their limitations.

Even more than in other domains, modeling in finance should be guided, and even curbed, by empirical observations. Of course, dynamics of markets evolution are complex, but that is not a reason to give up inventing models well-suited to observations, rather than forcing mathematical models, convenient but implausible, to match financial data. As said by psychoanalyst Gerald Haddad: "One must enter the patient's views, and not attempt to impose ours."

Nevertheless, most textbooks dealing with financial mathematics — even those published after the 2008 crisis — pursue with business-as-usual Brownian motion and Black-Scholes model, carry on invoking "perfect replication" and zero risk, or even the "fundamental theorem of finance", while failing to display empirical data and to compare models with reality. One jumps into the calibration of models, meaningless but so flexible that they could "reproduce an elephant", as one usually says.

In this context, the book written by Mathieu Le Bellac and Arnaud Viricel is particularly valuable. They demystify the standard models of finance, by focusing on their interpretation and on their limits, while using only a minimum of mathematical formalism. Their arguments are very carefully illustrated by graphics based on empirical data, which allows them to highlight some theoretical aberrations in a blatant way. They attempt to induce in the reader the desire to understand in depth the mechanisms of financial markets, and to develop a direct intuition, an almost sensual one, before proceeding to quantitative modeling. For those who allow themselves to follow it, this pedagogy of risk will certainly be useful in any crisis environment. Indeed, as implied by the book subtitle "Modeling risk and uncertainty", the main limitation of present financial engineering — and the real challenge for the years to come — is really the drastic uncertainty, the "unknown unknowns" and the Black Swans, which we must, in one way or another, tame some day.

Jean-Philippe Bouchaud
Founder and Chairman,
Capital Fund Managment (CFM)
Professor of Physics, École Polytechnique

Foreword

Financial mathematics has been blamed by a number of experts and laymen for being responsible for the latest financial crisis. The arguments supporting or not this thesis often stem from a misunderstanding of what financial mathematics really is. This is why we propose to go back to the foundations and the rationale of the discipline. Our aim is to go beyond a purely descriptive presentation, and to invite the reader to fathom our domain from inside: to understand its objects, the tools it uses, the questions it raises, as well as its problems and difficulties.

At the roots of financial mathematics are financial products; we shall introduce them as we proceed through the various chapters. The simplest products are ownership and property titles, such as shares, gold, oil, real estate etc. Other financial products may be seen as a set of future cash flows, guaranteed or not. For example, debt securities such as bonds are nothing else than loans granted to companies or governments. Derivatives are more complex products, whose cash flows depend on a predetermined event according to conditions which have been agreed in advance between the parties. For example, cash flows exchanged within a credit default swap are linked to a possible failure of some reference entity. Another example, equity options are financial products whose payoff is linked to the price evolution of some reference stock. The financial markets are the marketplaces where these financial products may be traded.

Three main issues may be raised before initiating an operation on a financial market:

➲ How may we determine the prices of financial products?
➲ What investment strategies should we follow?
➲ What are the risks at stake and how should they be managed?

Mathematicians and economists have built, mainly since the second half of the 20th century, a number of methods, models and mathematical theories in order to give rudiments of answers to these questions. This collection of mathematical tools developed around financial products is what is nowadays called financial mathematics or quantitative finance. Our goal is to get the reader familiar not only with the theoretical notions of martingale, correlation structure or implied parameters, but also with the practitioners' methods and tools.

Understanding concepts also clearly entails knowledge of their limitations. We shall devote a particular attention to the model assumptions and to their validity domain. The main responsibility of quants — as are referred to people in charge of mathematical modeling within financial institutions — is precisely to master the qualities and the flaws of their models and to precisely know what they account for and what they do not.

This is a popular science book. The principles which underlie the calculations will be explained in detail, but not the calculations themselves; we shall spend time on the implications and interpretations of the equations, and not on the equations. As far as possible, we shall provide an intuitive or physical representation of phenomena and models while attempting to extricate ourselves from the mathematical formalism. The book should be accessible to non-experts; the prerequisites in taking up this book are a knowledge of elementary mathematical functions (logarithms, exponentials) and some elementary notions of probability theory.

We would like to give our special thanks to Joanna Kubar and Michel Le Bellac for their tremendous help, their heavy involvement and their tireless support.

Mathieu Le Bellac
Chief Risk Officer, BRED Bank
Arnaud Viricel
Head of Counterparty Risk, Natixis

Chapter 1

Interest Rates

Benjamin Franklin stated "Time is money". This applies in particular to the financial world, where it is materialized by interest rates. It seems indeed natural that all loaned money must have some payment as a counterpart: we shall consider that the payment of interests is aimed at compensating the loss, by the lender, of other profitable investment opportunities or of consumption capacities. Interest rates also take into account the risk that the loaned sum is not reimbursed. This risk is called the credit risk and it will be addressed in the next chapter.

In the present chapter, we shall introduce the notions of interest rates and of present valuation (section 1) and we shall demonstrate the existence of a term structure of interest rates (section 2). We shall finally study in section 3 the time evolution of the interest rates curve by relying in particular on the Principal Component Analysis introduced by [Litterman and Scheinkman 1991].

1.1 Present valuation

The purpose of interests is to pay the lender, or the creditor, for having made available some amount of money to the borrower, during a time period and according to specific terms of payment. The range of available options is quite large: the duration of the loan, generally called the *maturity*, may vary from 24 hours to half a century; the capital may be reimbursed progressively, as in a retail real estate loan, or fully at maturity. Whatever the type of loan, the borrower must be able to compute an interest rate in order to assess the cost of the loan and to compare the different configurations which may be offered.

When we put money on a savings account, we lend money to our bank and we are entitled to a payment as a counterpart. Thus, \$100 invested at a yearly interest rate of 2% capitalize and become \$102 at the end of the year. If the sum is fully reinvested into a savings account under the same conditions, after a second year of bearing interest, it will be worth $102 \times (1 + 2\%) = \$104.04$, then $\$100 \times (1+2\%)^3$ in the third year, ..., and $\$100 \times (1+2\%)^n$ in the nth year. This calculation shows that after 10 years, we own about \$122: the 2% interest rates have brought us more than 10 times the yearly interest rate, as all the interests have been reinvested and have capitalized in turn. This is the convention on which all our calculations will be grounded: the interests unpaid to the lender at the end of the period during which the rate is applied generate further interests at the same rate.

With this convention, an amount M which capitalizes at the yearly interest rate r will be worth $M \times (1 + r)^T$ after T years. Thus, theory implies that, had Platon invested \$1 in 400 BC at a 1% yearly rate, he would own $\$(1.01)^{2416}$ today in 2016, namely more than \$25 billion.

Let us reverse our viewpoint and assume that we would like to own \$100 in 10 years: what amount of money should we invest? The calculation is very simple: the answer is $\$100/(1 + r)^{10}$, which is about \$82 given an interest rate $r = 2\%$. This property may be conceptualized the following way:

- It is equivalent to own \$82 today or to own \$100 in 10 years.
- What we must pay today to own \$100 in 10 years is \$82.
- The present value of \$100 in 10 years is \$82 today.

We have just introduced the fundamental notion of *discounted value*, also called the *present value.* This value is simply the price to be paid today in order to receive a future cash flow. In our example, the present value of \$100 to be collected in 10 years is \$82. When one uses an interest rate to compute the present value of a payment, then this rate is called the *discount rate.* A large part of financial mathematics which we are going to uncover in the following chapters addresses the calculation of the present value of future cash flows, known or unknown. This value is today's market price of those future cash flows, that is, the price at which traders are ready to buy or to sell these cash flows.

Box 1.1. Present valuation, or discounting. Discounting is the computation of today's value of a future cash flow. This computation depends on the level of interest rates: if the yearly interest rate is 5%, the present value of a \$105 cash flow to be collected in one year is \$100. Therefore, present valuation allows one to compare the value of cash flows paid at different dates.

Let us summarize where we stand using a slightly more sophisticated example. Assume you are the representative of a Government and you wish to borrow on financial markets. You are ready to pay \$5 M for the first two years and reimburse \$105 M at the end of those 3 years. Given a 2% discount rate, how much will you be lent? In other words, what is the present value of the cash flows? The answer is readily computed:

$$\frac{5}{1+2\%} + \frac{5}{(1+2\%)^2} + \frac{105}{(1+2\%)^3} \simeq \$108.65\,\text{M} \tag{1.1}$$

Indeed, each cash flow to be collected has a price: the first one is worth $5/(1+2\%) \simeq \$4.9\,\text{M}$, the second one $5/(1+2\%)^2 \simeq \$4.8\,\text{M}$ and the last one $105/(1+2\%)^3 \simeq \$98.95\,\text{M}$. The total cost is the sum of the prices of each cash flow.

It is very important to be able to compute at any time this present value of the cash flows which the Government pays, as the loan granted may be resold by the lender on financial markets to another market participant wishing to own a Government debt. In order to do so, the Government loan often takes the form of a *bond*. A bond operates exactly as a loan whose advantage is that it can easily be exchanged on financial markets: it is the holder of the bond who collects the reimbursement flows from the borrower who issued the bond. A whole jargon was developed around these bonds: the amount of capital is called the *face value* of the bond and the interests which are paid, the *coupons*. In general, the coupons are known in advance and fixed as a percentage of the face value of the bond: one then speaks of fixed rate bond. The face value of the bond is then reimbursed together with the last coupon at maturity.

Box 1.2. Bonds. A bond is a security, that is an asset tradable on financial markets, which represents the debt of a Government or of a company towards the holder of the bond. Thus, the owner of the bond, the bondholder, is the creditor of the debt. He is entitled to receive at fixed intervals of time some amount of interests called a *coupon*, computed as a percentage of the capital (also named the face value, or the nominal) which the borrower must reimburse at maturity.

In the example of equation (1.1), we computed the present value, that is, the price of a bond reaching its maturity in 3 years, whose face value is \$100 M and with yearly coupons of 5%. If the interest rates are 2%, an investor will therefore buy the bond at a price of \$108.65 M.

Our presentation may puzzle the reader who attempts to link bonds with retail real estate loans. In our example:

- The amount paid by the investor to buy the bond, \$108.65 M, is not the face value, which is \$100 M.
- The coupon rate, 5%, which is the interest paid to the bondholder, is different from the interest rate used for discounting, which is 2%.
- In our presentation of the bonds, the face value is reimbursed at the end of the loan only, in other words, it is not amortized over the lifetime of the loan.

If the interest rates matched exactly the coupon rate, 5%, the price of the bond would match the face value of $100 M. However, in practice, interest rates vary constantly on the markets (similarly to the rate of a savings account which varies during the year). Let us assume that the sovereign bond was issued at a time when the interest rate was 5%. In our example, the interest rate then went down to 2%. The sovereign bond brings now more interests than the market's interest rate: it is logical that its price has risen and that it is worth more than its face value. The fall in interest rate has therefore increased the price of the bond. Conversely, it seems clear that the right to receive fixed interests is less interesting when the rates increase and market participants have the opportunity to invest into products which take this rise into account. This explains the famous rule according to which the price of bonds falls when interest rates rise, and conversely (Figure 1.1).

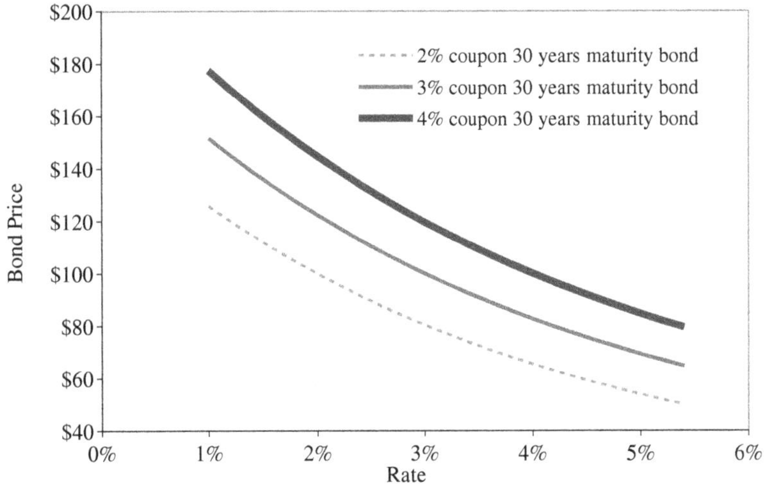

Figure 1.1: Variation of bond prices as a function of the interest rate. One must notice that (i) for the same rate and the same maturity, the bond prices rise with the value of the coupons; (ii) the bond prices decrease with the level of the interest rates; (iii) the curves giving the bond prices are not straight lines and they are steeper as the interest rates decrease.

More formally, the equation which links the discount rate, the price, the coupons, the maturity and the face value of a bond is:

$$\text{Price} = \sum_{t=1}^{\text{maturity}} \frac{\text{coupon}}{(1+\text{rate})^t} + \frac{\text{face value}}{(1+\text{rate})^{\text{maturity}}} \tag{1.2}$$

If all parameters of this equation but the discount rate are fixed, then there is only one rate which satisfies equation (1.2). This rate is called the *yield* of the bond. From the very way the equation is built, the yield represents the true return of the bond, since it is strictly equivalent to buying the bond or to investing money on a savings account which capitalizes at this precise return rate. Indeed, as we have seen, it is strictly equivalent to receive today $1/(1+\text{rate})^t$ or 1 at time t.

In order to be really convinced by the concept of yield, let us compute the money which is available at the maturity of the bond. If we deposited the money corresponding to the price of the bond on a savings account which offers the same return rate, we would obtain at maturity the amount: $\text{price} \times (1+\text{rate})^{\text{maturity}}$. If we bought the bond and decided to invest each of the received coupons on the same savings account, we would obtain at maturity the amount: $\sum_{t=1}^{\text{maturity}} \text{coupon} \times (1+\text{rate})^{\text{maturity}-t} + \text{face value}$. Equation (1.2) precisely states that these two quantities are equal; this is why the discount rate of this equation is also termed “yield”.

One can equally well compute the price of a bond from its yield or deduce the yield from the price of a bond. An investor will buy a bond at a given price only if this bond guarantees a yield which aligns with the return rate of other similar investment opportunities. It is credited to this fact that there is a kind of equilibrium on the general level of interest rates at a given time, and that all investments must align with this general interest rate level.

The notion of inflation has not been addressed in this chapter while it would seem to be, at first sight, closely linked to interest rates. Inflation expresses the evolution of the value of money, and it is generally measured as the evolution of the number of monetary units necessary to buy consumer goods and services. Thus, it is a notion which links a world where the absolute reference is the monetary unit with a world where the reference is the ability to purchase goods and services. A positive inflation rate means that the value of money decreases with time, that is, with the same amount of money, the consumption opportunities decrease. The same logic implies that, if the interest rate of a financial investment is exactly equal to the inflation rate, the value of this investment expressed as a capability of consumption will be constant over time. This explains why inflation and interest rates may appear to be correlated. However, the two concepts are fundamentally different, and they may evolve in opposite directions. In fact, interest rates reflect the price of liquidity; in other words, interest rates account for the fact that we have at our disposal a sum of money today and not tomorrow. It is rather clear that even in a world without inflation, it is more interesting to use a sum of money right now rather than 10 years from now. Generally speaking, loans are subject to interests, even in the absence of inflation. The link between inflation and interest rates is known to exist, but is not systematic; economic theories which conceptualize those interactions lie beyond the classical scope of financial mathematics and will not be dealt with in this book.

Although the concept of interest rate might appear intuitive, this first section shows that it uncovers in fact different meanings:

- The rate used to calculate the interests due by a borrower to its creditor is called interest rate for a retail loan but is called coupon when the debt is a bond. In this case, recall that the borrower is named issuer and the creditor is the bondholder.
- The rate used to calculate the present value of cash flows, that is today's price of an amount of money to be received in the future, is the discount rate.
- The rate of return offered by a financial product on the market is its yield. We showed that the yield of a bond is the discount rate that should be used to calculate the market price of the bond.

1.2 Building the interest rates curve

At this point, we do not know how to compute in practice these interest rates: how can we determine the interest rates to be used in order to discount a cash flow? The observable quantities on financial markets are prices: prices of transactions on most exchange-traded markets are public; for example, one may access all the stock prices of the Dow Jones Index on the Internet. Bond prices are more difficult to obtain for individuals, but a large number of bonds are exchanged daily between financial institutions, with conditions that are disclosed to professional market participants. Thus, we can deduce the levels of interest rates from these reference bonds. Let us study the result of such an analysis on the Government bonds of Figure 1.2.

This figure displays the fact that yields increase globally with maturity. This observation seems rather natural, if one considers that the longer the maturity, the longer cash invested will not be available to the investor. It is thus logical that the investor should be paid for

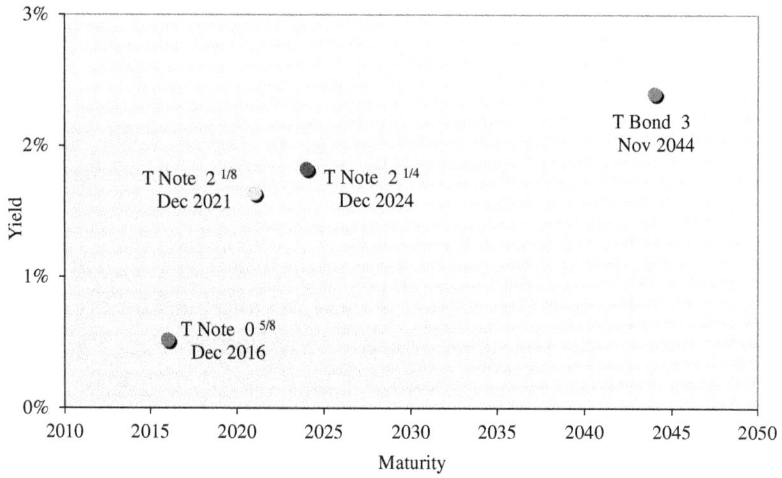

Figure 1.2: The graph displays the yields of different US Government Bonds ("T-Note") depending on their maturity. The yields seem to be all the higher as the maturity is longer. This phenomenon is often observed, but is not a general law (see the different shapes of the interest rates curve in Figure 1.5).

the corresponding risk, the so-called *liquidity risk*, which is all the higher as the duration of the investment is longer.

As a consequence, the discount rate that should be used to calculate bond prices depends on the maturity of the bond. This fact is true for all financial investments; the interest rate associated with a six-month loan is not the same as that associated with a 25-year loan. It explains why we speak of the *interest rates curve*: this curve is the function which links each maturity with the corresponding level of interest rates.

Building the interest rates curve is worth our attention, and the present section will be devoted to it. First of all, we should be careful about the definitions: we shall denote $r(t)$ the discount rate associated with the date t. By definition, when we compute the present values, each cash flow will have to be discounted at the discount rate associated with the date at which this flow is paid. The price of a bond is then, by definition, adapting equation (1.2):

$$\text{Price} = \sum_{t=1}^{\text{maturity}} \frac{\text{coupon}}{(1+r(t))^t} + \frac{\text{face value}}{(1+r(\text{maturity}))^{\text{maturity}}} \tag{1.3}$$

This equation is important as it shows that the price of a bond, and hence its yield which is still defined by equation (1.2), is sensitive not only to the rate $r(\text{maturity})$ associated with the maturity date, but also to all the rates $r(t)$ associated with the intermediate dates t when coupons are paid. The only case in which the yield of a bond is equal to the rate $r(\text{maturity})$ is when the bond does not bear coupons (coupon rate $= 0\%$). These bonds are called Zero Coupon and they do exist on financial markets. For this reason, these discount rates $r(t)$ are called Zero Coupon rates, which we shall denote ZC rates in all that follows.

Given the price of a bond, knowing the ZC rates at dates strictly preceding its maturity and using equation (1.3), we can build the ZC rate associated with the maturity date of the bond. In other words, we shall remember that, from a set of bonds with different maturities, we can recalculate step by step the ZC rates, starting with the most recent maturities and ending with the longest ones.

Box 1.3. Zero coupons, ZC rates. A zero coupon is a bond whose coupon rate is 0%, hence its name. Thus, the only payment is the face value at the maturity of the bond. The yields of zero coupons are termed the zero coupon rates, or ZC rates; they depend on the maturity of the bond. They are very important rates as the ZC rate of maturity t is the discount rate that should be used to calculate the present value of a cash flow paid at date t.

Let us illustrate the preceding considerations with an example. Assume that the price of two bonds, bond A and bond B, are known. Each bond has a face value of $100:

- Bond A, of maturity 1 year and with a yearly coupon of $5 is worth $102.
- Bond B, of maturity 2 years and with yearly coupons of $6 is worth $104.

Equation (1.3) applied to bond A leads to $r(1) \simeq 2.94\%$. When applied to bond B, this same equation allows us to compute in a second step $r(2)$ from the value of $r(1)$, with the result $r(2) = 3.91\%$.

At this point, the goal which we set to ourselves, building the interest rates curve, seems to be achieved since we can observe the price of some reference bonds and afterwards deduce from them the ZC rates, as we proceeded in the preceding example. However, we have neglected many important points. First, the construction of the ZC curve relies on a limited number of bonds whose maturities are not necessarily well distributed: the question is then how to build ZC rates for a maturity which lies between two consecutive bonds for which prices are available. Second, the Government bonds are market products whose prices are, of course, sensitive to the level of interest rates, but also to other factors such as the risk of default, the impact of taxes, the scarcity of a maturity affecting the prices through the supply and demand equilibrium, the difficulty of finding sellers or buyers for some illiquid bonds etc. In fact, most of the financial products which require ZC rates for valuation are products traded among banks. As a consequence, the ZC rates curves to be used should reflect the level of interbank rates, that is, the rates at which banks lend money between themselves, and not the rates of Government bonds. However, the reader should be aware that the selection of interest rates to be used is in fact a very sensitive question, with no obvious answer, and that has a tremendous impact on the valuation of financial products.

In order to build the ZC rates curves, banks generally use other financial products, negotiated on the interbank markets, but we shall not linger over these aspects.[1] We shall remember that these products have many advantages:

- Their available maturities are numerous and well distributed.
- The quotes of their prices are frequent and shared by all the market participants.
- These products are not securities and can thus be generated ad infinitum; they are less subject to liquidity constraints than bonds. In this sense, their listings have the reputation of being purer.

As is illustrated in Figure 1.3, the ZC computation methods applied in the framework of interbank products lead to a consistent and granular enough meshing of ZC rates, while their application to bonds may generate a cloud of points which is more difficult to interpret and to manipulate.

Whatever the meshing density obtained, it is necessary to develop methods of interpolation and smoothing in order to compute ZC rates between two observed ZCs. The interpolation methods will aim at connecting the dots between two observed ZC rates, while the smoothing methods will not require that the interest rates curve exactly matches the observed ZC rates.

[1]In order to explore this subject further, the interested reader may look into short-term interbank deposits, futures and interest rate swaps: these financial products are introduced, for example, in [Hull 2011].

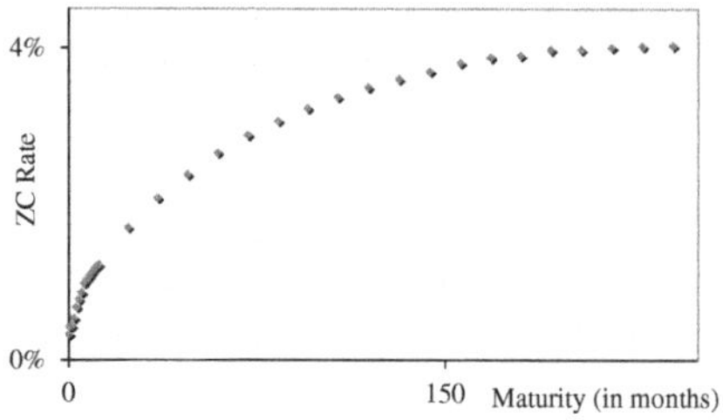

(a) Sample of ZC rates observed on the interbank market

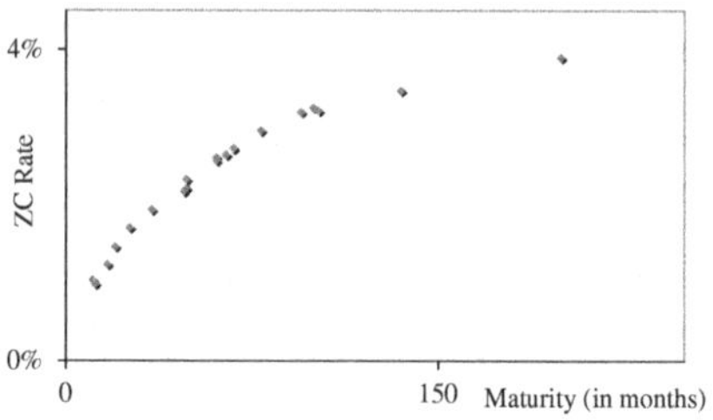

(b) Sample of ZC rates deduced from bond prices

Figure 1.3: An example which illustrates the use of some basic samples in order to build the ZC rates curve. The data which can be observed on the interbank market are more numerous and regular.

It is in general impossible to find a unique simple function that will exactly connect all the dots on an observed sample. Indeed, either the function does not have enough degrees of freedom and interpolation is not possible, or the number of degrees of freedom is sufficient, but the constraint of going through compulsory points leads to an erratic shape to the curve. The methods which are usually applied use piecewise continuous functions. For each interval of maturity, that is, between two maturities of observed ZC rates, we build a function which is defined on this interval only; generally speaking this function is chosen thanks to continuity and differentiability constraints. The resulting interpolating function is the juxtaposition of the piecewise individual functions.

Smoothing techniques may also be used. In this case, the question in general is to obtain the best possible coincidence of the curves, called parametric curves, with the observed ZC rates. The shapes of these curves are:

➲ either built in order to replicate as well as possible the various configurations of the rates curves (parametric curves of Nelson-Siegel and augmented Nelson-Siegel);
➲ or deduced from models used to simulate the evolution of interest rates (models of Vasiseck, Cox-Ingelson-Ross and so on). These models define implicitly the admissible shape that the interest rates curve may take.

The choice of any of those methods must be consistent with the desired goal, for example:

- a bank which uses ZC interest rates curve to value its financial products that will be bought or sold to other market participants will turn to an interpolation method in order to ensure that the observed ZC rates are preserved in the final curve. Indeed, the prices of products which are bought or sold must be consistent with the prices recalculated with the constructed interest rates curve.
- a company managing assets which wishes to identify underpriced bonds in the perspective of an investment decision will rather attempt to find a smoothing method able to give an economic meaning to the constructed interest rates curve. Actually, in this case, duplicating perfectly the prices of the bonds would not provide the company with any information useful for the identification of underpriced bonds.

Figure 1.4 presents the construction of ZC rates curves from observed interest rates. The left-hand graph uses rates with monthly spaced maturities between 1 month and 6 months, and a yearly spaces between 1 year and 20 years. The right-hand graph uses the same

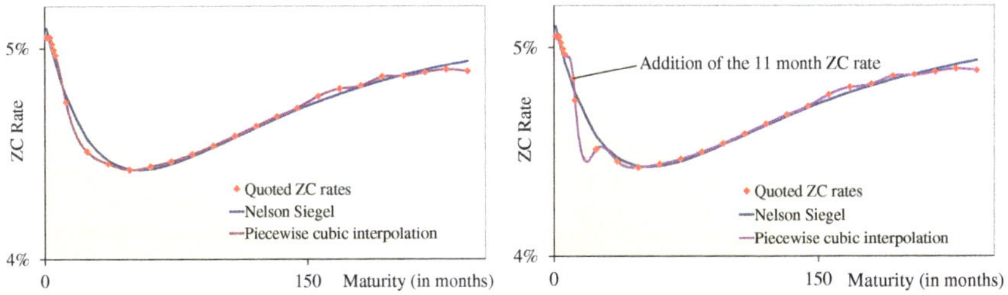

(a) Interpolation and smoothing from a sample of observed rates

(b) Interpolation and smoothing from the same sample plus another observed rate at 11 months

Figure 1.4: Examples of interpolation and smoothing of ZC rates. The piecewise interpolation may create unwanted technical perturbations, such as the trough observed on the (b)-graph. Parametric interpolations [Nelson and Siegel 1987] are more robust (blue lines), but they have the drawback of not going through all the observed points (red points).

observed rates to which we have added a ZC rate of 11 months maturity. This example is instructive, as it shows that the parametric method is insensitive to the addition of the 11 months ZC rate, while the piecewise interpolation method is very sensitive to it. We may rightfully consider that the addition of the 11 months ZC rate has altered the economic meaning of the interpolation: the trough observed between the first and second year has no economic meaning, as it is the sole result of the arbitrary choice of an interpolation method. The selection of an interpolation method is far from harmless, and these methods should be carefully controlled before being used.

The construction of the ZC rates curve is the preliminary step for any financial modeling, because it defines the rates at which cash flows shall be discounted. At this early stage of our journey in financial mathematics, choices are already mandatory: the selection of financial products to be used in order to put points on the curve, as well as the rules for building a continuous curve, lead to different prices, among which none will be intrinsically more accurate than the others, but which will turn out to be more or less adapted to the final goal of the modeling.

1.3 Dynamics of the interest rates curve

In this chapter, we introduced interest rates and the fundamental principle of present valuation. We then noticed that there is no unique interest rate, but a rate associated with each maturity, the set of these rates building the interest rates curve. In this third section, we shall see that this curve evolves over time and attempts to identify the main components of this motion. As a first element of this study, let us look at the sample of interest rates curves in Figure 1.5; it shows that the hectic history of modern financial markets has resulted in various configurations of interest rates.

Financial markets experienced many different interest rates curves:

- A rising curve: interbank euro curve of February 2010.
- A decreasing curve: British Government curve of January 2001.

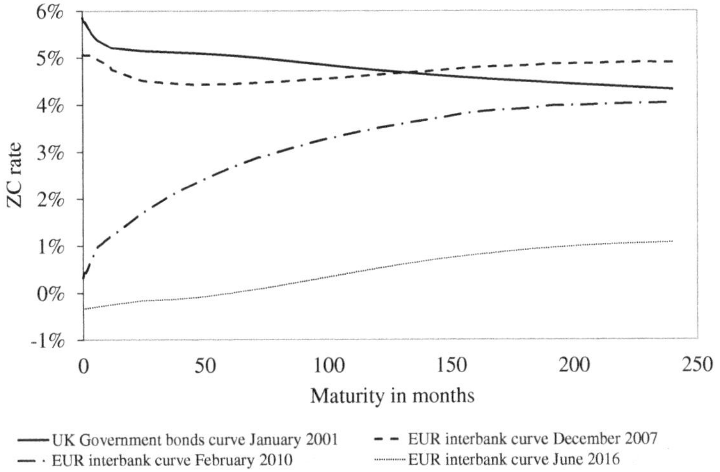

Figure 1.5: Various historical configurations of interest rates. The interest rates curve may exhibit many different shapes. The interest rates curve is different for each currency.

- A decreasing, and then rising curve: interbank euro curve of December 2007.
- A curve with negative interest rates: interbank euro curve of June 2016.

Figure 1.5 leads us to a first observation: short-term interest rates seem to be more volatile than long-term rates. This assumption is, by the way, confirmed by further historical statistics. That being said, those five configurations give only little information on the real dynamics of the interest rates curve. If each point on the curves evolved independently of the others, we would have to face an infinite number of sources of variability. Fortunately, history shows that the dynamics of the interest rates curve are governed by a few characteristic motions: this greatly simplifies and structures the risk analysis. In the present section, we show how to identify those main motions.

In order to do so, let us consider the theoretical case where the interest rates curve is restricted to two maturity points, for example, the 2-year and 7-year maturities. The set of possible joint variations

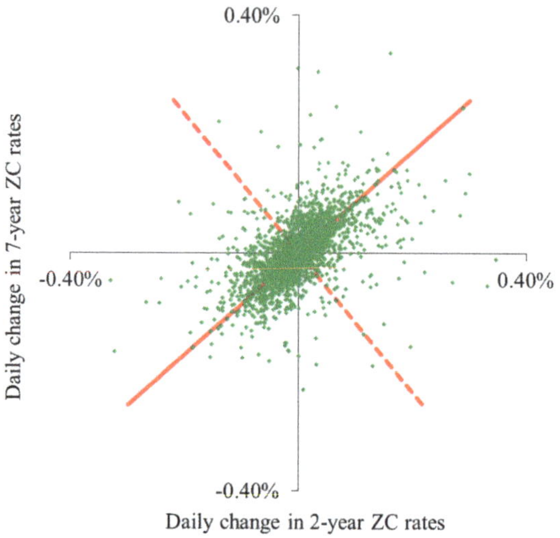

Figure 1.6: Joint representation of the variation of 2-year and 7-year ZC rates: each point represents a daily variation registered on the 2-year and 7-year ZC rates. The points pile up around the full red line close to the diagonal $y = x$, which indicates that the cases where the variations of the 2-year and 7-year ZC rates are roughly of equal proportion build up a privileged axis for the variations. On the contrary, the variations close to the dotted line perpendicular to the first axis (variations of the 2-year and 7-year ZC rates in opposite directions) seem less probable.

may then be represented in a two-dimensional plane where the variations of the 2-year ZC rate are given on the horizontal axis and the variations of the 7-year ZC rate are given on the vertical axis. This representation, applied to the daily variations of the British Treasury rates, between 2000 and 2014, is displayed on Figure 1.6.

The goal is to find a single motion of the two rates which accounts for most of the deformations observed on the figure. This motion can be, for example:

- An equal rise of the 2- and 7-year ZC rates.
- A rise of the 2-year ZC rate twice as large as that of the 7-year ZC rate.
- A fall of the 2-year ZC rate with a magnitude is equivalent to that of the rise of the 7-year ZC rate.

Each of these motions can be represented on the plane by a straight line. For example, a parallel rise of the ZC rates, that is an equal rise of all the ZC rates whatever their maturity, will be represented by the line $y = x$. It is obvious that a unique straight line will not be able to capture the whole plane, and thus the entire cloud of points. However, we are going to look for the straight line which is as close as possible to all the points. Intuitively, it is the line that goes through the cloud along its maximum width. Mathematically, this is the line that minimizes the sum of the squares of the distances between the points in the cloud and the line. By using Pythagoras' theorem, the interested reader will check that the criterion which is used comes down to maximizing the variance of the orthogonal projections of the points on the line. The red axis, represented as a full line in Figure 1.6, is the straight line corresponding to this definition, and it is approximately given by the equation $y = x$. Given the criterion used for the construction, the variance carried by this axis is as large as possible, and the residual variance will be carried by the orthogonal axis, as reflected by the dotted line in Figure 1.6. In our example, the first axis accounts for 79% of the total variance, versus 21% for the dotted axis. To sum up, we structured the variation of the 2-year and 7-year rates as follows: 79% of variations are parallel shifts with identical amplitudes, while the remaining 21% are explained by variations going in opposite directions.

The methodology which we briefly sketched in the preceding example is called the *principal component analysis*, or PCA. It is the traditional method used for identifying the principal axes of the deformations of the interest rates curve. In our example, we had two possible directions of deformation, 2 years and 7 years; we identified that parallel variations, that is equal variations of both rates, are the principal deformation axis and explain most of the rates variations. The secondary deformation axis, perpendicular to the first one, which is represented by variations of the two rates in opposite directions, explains the remainder of the variations. This construction can be extended to the entire set of maturity points, using a N-dimensional space if the curve is built with N maturity points. In this case, PCA

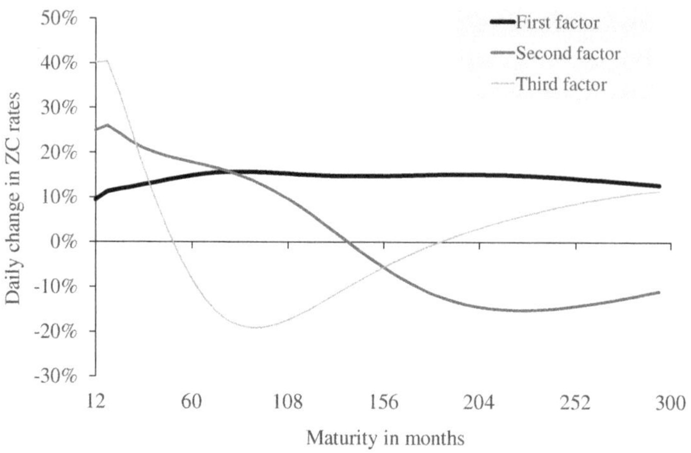

Figure 1.7: The three main deformation axes of the interest rates curve. Each of these axes is associated with a deformation of the interest rates curve which is displayed in Figure 1.8.

identifies N deformation axes which can be arranged from the most important to the most marginal. If we keep only the main axes, we may thus reduce the complexity of the analysis by focusing on the most important motions. Figure 1.7 shows the first three axes identified by the PCA methodology applied to the daily variations of the British Government rates curves.

Let us now interpret these results.

- The shape of the first axis may be assimilated to a horizontal straight line. This means that motions proportional to this axis are parallel shifts of the curve, upwards or downwards, as indicated in Figure 1.8.
- The shape of the second axis may be assimilated to a decreasing straight line intersecting the abscissa axis at the point of maturity 12 years (144 months). Deformations proportional to this axis are rotations of the curve centered on the point of maturity 12 years, as shown in Figure 1.8. One will then speak of steepening or flattening of the interest rates curve.
- The shape of the third axis may be assimilated to a parabola whose minimum is located at the point of maturity 7.5 years. This third

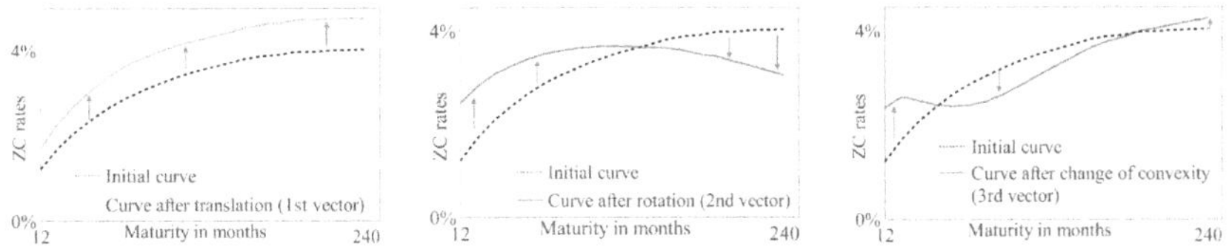

First axis: Parallel shift | Second axis: Flattening | Third axis: Increase of convexity

Figure 1.8: Illustration of the interest rates curve deformations induced by the three PCA principal axes. The graphs illustrate the impact on the interest rates curve of motions aligned along one of the three axes identified in Figure 1.7.

characteristic motion corresponds to an increase of the rates at both ends of the curve, and to a drop of the rates located in the vicinity of the 7.5-year maturity. One will then say that the curve is subject to an increase of its convexity. In the other direction, the motion will be that of a reduction of its convexity.

We have thus identified the three main types of deformations: parallel shifts, steepening (or flattening) and change of convexity. Those three factors can account, in our example, for 92% of the variance displayed by the cloud of points. The motions of the interest rates curve may hence be expressed using three axes, while it was necessary, before the implementation of PCA, to study the variation of every point on the curve. Nevertheless, we must now question these results.

First, this method is grounded on variance. Thus, the factors which are identified as being mainly responsible for the interest rates curve deformations will not necessarily be the most frequent ones, but only those which generated the most important variations in the history. Second, the question of the time stability of the results must be raised. The various studies of the interest rates curve dynamics through the PCA have been able to conclude that the decomposition over the first three factors (translation, twist and convexity) is very stable over time and space. Figure 1.9 illustrates these considerations by displaying comparable results over two distinct periods.

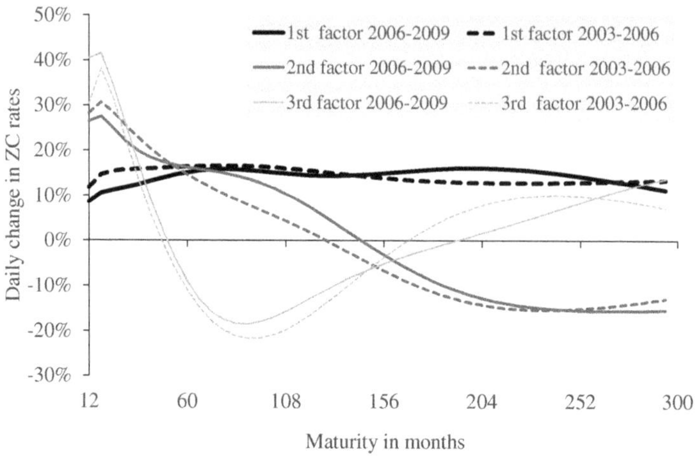

Figure 1.9: Stability of the first three main factors in the interest rates curve dynamics. The same three main deformation vectors are identified whatever the period under study: the analysis seems to be stable over time.

Most of the considerations which were discussed in the present chapter assumed we could manipulate pure interest rates. However, in practice, other considerations interfere with this concept, and in particular credit risk, which we shall introduce in the next chapter. It is impossible to distinguish in the bond prices the contribution of interest rates and that of other factors. The realization of this impossibility was recently reinforced by the sovereign debt crisis which contributed to undermine the assumption that a risk-free interest rate could exist. Nevertheless, this theoretical notion is essential for the modeling of financial products and for understanding their risks.

Chapter 2

Credit Risk Modeling

In the preceding chapter, we studied pure interest rates which compensate for the loss of an investment opportunity by the lender; the identity of the borrower does not matter much, as our reasonings assumed from the beginning that all future cash flows would be paid with certainty. In practice, as we already hinted at, this assumption is far from granted as the former creditors of Worldcom, Enron or Lehman Brothers experienced. Actually, every loan is subject to at least two risks:

- the risk of variations of interest rates, which we studied in the preceding chapter;
- the risk of non-payment of the cash flows which were planned in the contract, resulting from the bankruptcy or from the insolvency of a counterparty. This is what is called the credit risk.

To compensate for this additional risk, lenders ask for increased yields. Theories of credit risk try to model this risk, and to quantify it using the notion of *credit spread*, which we shall address in the first part. We illustrate in a second step, with the example of the *credit default swaps*, how the development of credit derivatives required the construction of new models consistent with market prices. The model of [Merton 1974], belonging to the family of structural models — which are models that attempt to describe the events leading to default — will then be briefly examined. The tricky modeling of the correlations between defaults will be addressed in the last part of this chapter.

2.1 Credit spread

It seems rather simple to draw intuitively a rough hierarchy of the credit risk depending on the borrower or the issuer of a bond. For example, a civil servant will seem to be a safer borrower than an unemployed person, as the US Government should be an issuer more reliable than a small Russian company. The justification and refining of this hierarchy is, by contrast, a much more tricky question. This is the job of credit ratings agencies such as Standards & Poors (S&P), Moody's or Fitch, which is based on a fundamental analysis of issuers. As an outcome, the agencies publish ratings supposed to quantify the credit quality of entities. During the so called *subprime* crisis, the limits of the rating agencies' methodologies were revealed. Nonetheless, they remain, as of today, the most independent and serious reference point, for the credit quality assessment of bond issuers. The formats of the ratings differ slightly between agencies, and we give below a simplified list based on that of S&P:

- AAA is the maximum rating, representative of the best credit quality. This rating applies to some governments, companies or quasi-public organizations, called agencies;
- from AA to BBB (AA, then A, then BBB according to a decreasing quality of credit), issuers are considered as being *Investment Grade*, that is, relatively safe;
- from BB to D (BB, then B then CCC and so forth, D meaning that the issuer defaults), issuers are considered as being *Non-Investment Grade*.

The impact of credit risk on the price of bonds cannot be immediately identified. Indeed, the price of bonds depends on different factors (value of the coupon, maturity and so on) and it is difficult to isolate the component which accounts for credit risk. It is thus necessary to use the bond yields. Figure 2.1(a) displays, as an example, some bonds whose prices are higher than those of other bonds which would seem less risky at first sight. The representation of their yields

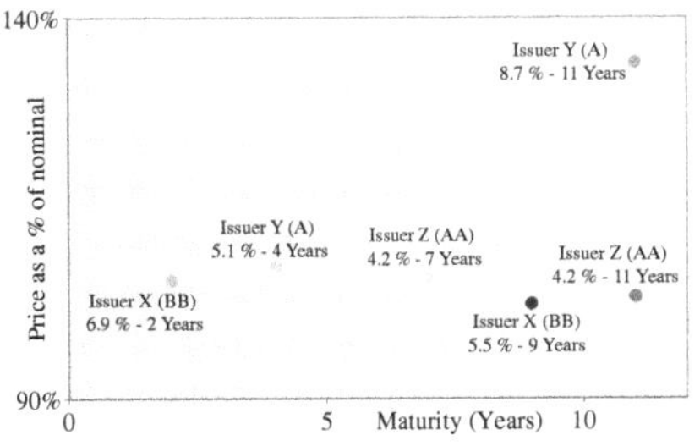

(a) Prices

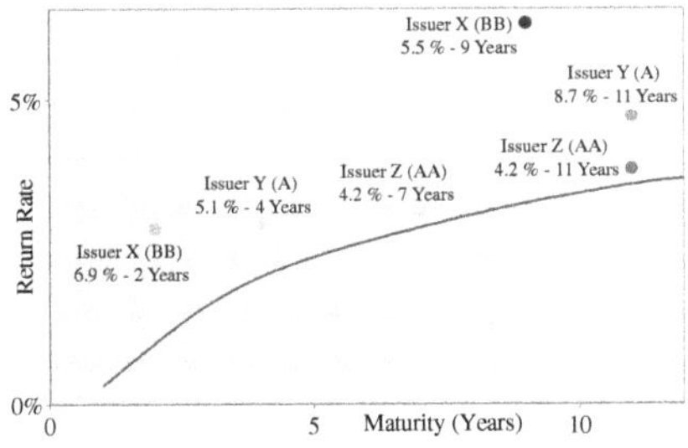

(b) Return rate (or yield)

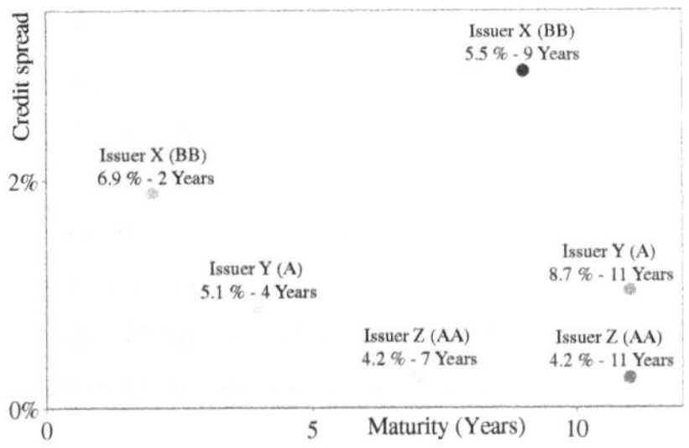

(c) Credit spread

Figure 2.1: The different steps in the building of credit spreads. The above diagrams represent six bonds, characterized by their issuer (issuer X which is rated BB, issuer Y which is rated A and issuer Z which is rated AA), their coupon (ranging from 4.2% to 8.7%) and their maturity (from 2 to 11 years). The representation of their prices on graph (a) does not account for the hierarchy of credit risk: prices are not arranged as a function of credit quality. Plotting yields on graph (b) reestablishes this hierarchy, provided we use the same maturity. Lastly, the computation of the credit spread, that is the gap between the risk-free rate (represented by the solid curve on graph (b)) and the yield, on graph (c) isolates the part of the yield associated with credit risk.

(Figure 2.1(b)), on the other hand, does account for the differences in the expected credit risk: the yields of the most risky bonds are higher, investors do require an additional yield as a compensation for the risk they have taken.

However, Figure 2.1(b) allows us to only compare two bonds of the same maturity. Indeed, the yield accounts for the loss of an investment opportunity (the pure interest rate) as well as for the credit risk. Now, the pure interest rates depend on the maturity; they usually rise with the maturity. This explains why, in Figure 2.1(b), the 11-year maturity bonds of Issuer Z, rated AA, provide a higher yield than the 2-year maturity bonds of Issuer X, rated BB.

For this reason, we must introduce the notion of *risk-free rate* which is the yield of bonds not subject to credit risk. This risk-free rate follows a term structure which can be deduced from non-risky bonds in the sense of the credit risk. Given the risk-free rates for each maturity, it is henceforth possible to determine for a risky bond the contribution of the credit risk to the bond's yield. This is precisely the difference between the yield of the risky bond and the risk-free rate corresponding to the same maturity. This difference is called the *credit spread*: if the yield is η and the risk-free rate is r, the credit spread is by definition $s = \eta - r$.

How do we build in practice the risk-free rates curve? Traditionally, market professionals considered that the big Western Governments (United States, Germany, France...) were very unlikely to default and therefore that the yields of their bonds could be assimilated to risk-free interest rates. But, without questioning the principle according to which governments like that of Germany or France are safer than most private companies, the recent crisis of sovereign debts showed the fragility of some governments such as those of Greece, Portugal or Italy; even the financial ratings of United States and France have been downgraded by rating agencies since 2011. Figure 2.2 which traces the history of government bonds yields gives a perfect illustration of these events.

Moreover, there exist collateralization mechanisms which consists in providing the lender with securities as a guarantee; those mechanisms strongly reduce the credit risk of some of the transactions performed on the interbank markets. The current interest rates observed on such markets may thus claim to represent more reliable risk-free rates. As of today, no absolute reference for the risk-free rate exists. Although from empirical studies it is possible to infer references for a privileged risk-free rate, it remains nevertheless important to understand that the risk-free rate is a theoretical notion which is hardly observable in practice.

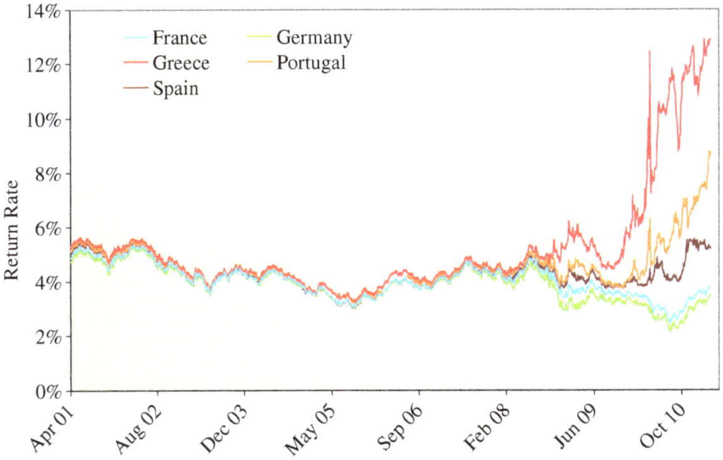

Figure 2.2: History of the yields of 10-year maturity bonds issued by various governments of the Eurozone. The results of the banking crisis which followed the default of Lehman Brothers clearly appear starting from year 2008. Gaps between yields are amplified during the sovereign crisis debt in year 2010.

2.2 Implied default probabilities

Up to now, we have presented the credit risk as an intuitive and relatively vague notion: the risk whose sums which are owed may not be paid. In practice, the uncertainty lies at two levels. First of all, the cash flow situation of a company may make it unable to meet some of the payments which are owed; one then says that the company defaults. This is the first level of risk, which may be evaluated by the probability that the company defaults.

However, this probability is not enough to quantify the risk of final loss. In practice, companies in default still own a remaining wealth sufficient to face, at least in part, the commitments they contracted. For the investor, the loss will thus be limited: eventually, the loss due to the default will be partially compensated by the liquidation of the company's assets. One then speaks of *loss given default (LGD)*. The LGD is generally expressed as a fraction of the face value of the bond; its complement, the *recovery rate*, is defined as $R = (1 - LGD)$. Figure 2.3 illustrates the two levels of uncertainty

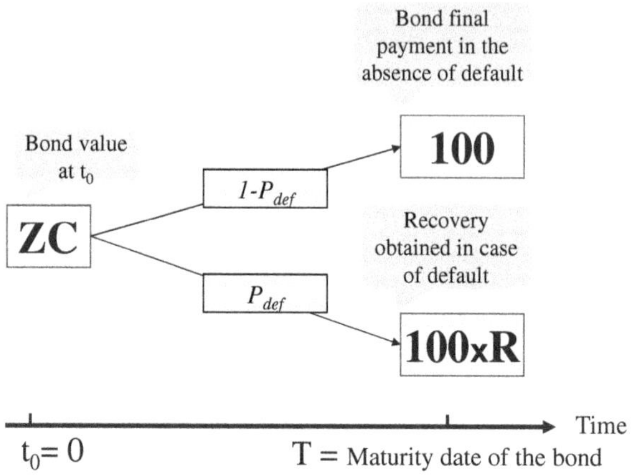

Figure 2.3: Representation of default risk in the framework of a zero coupon bond. The default occurs with a probability P_{def} and in this case the holder of the bond does not recover the face value, but $100 \times R$ which will likely be less than 100.

in the framework of a zero coupon bond, whose initial value is ZC, paying 100 at maturity if the issuer has not defaulted, or $100 \times R$, where R denotes the recovery rate, if it has defaulted. The default occurs with a probability which will be denoted P_{def}.

Assume that we are able to estimate the two parameters P_{def} and R: can we obtain the market price ZC of the bond? The intuitive answer is that we must compute the average present value of the cash flows, since receiving 100 with 50% probability seems at first glance similar to receiving 50 with certainty. If the experiment could be indefinitely repeated, this would be exact as, after a large number of trials, the cash flow which is paid would be very close to 50 on average. However, when purchasing a bond, the experiment cannot be repeated: the company defaults or it does not. An investor will then ask for a yield larger than the probabilistic average of the cash flows, otherwise he would not have any risk premium:

$$ZC > \frac{100}{(1+r)^T} \times [(1 - P_{\text{def}}) + P_{\text{def}} \times R] \tag{2.1}$$

In this equation, r is the risk-free rate associated with the maturity T. Mathematicians of the banking industry, called *quants*, do not in general compute a price based on economic parameters, but rather look for economic parameters which account for the market prices. In this framework, we shall not then work on the real default probabilities and recovery rates for which inequality (2.1) holds, but on data which are called *implied*: these are the parameters P_{def} and R which satisfy the equation:

$$ZC = \frac{100}{(1+r)^T} \times [(1 - P_{\text{def}}) + P_{\text{def}} \times R] \tag{2.2}$$

This way of looking at the world may surprise the reader. This is however an essential aspect of financial mathematics to which we shall repeatedly return. Our goal is not to compute market prices *ex nihilo*, but to deduce them from prices of similar products that can be observed on financial markets. This is exactly what we did in Chapter 1, when we interpolated the interest rates curves. In this respect, [Derman 2003] explains:

> "If you want to know the value of a security, use the price of another security that's as similar to it as possible. All the rest is modeling."

However, equation (2.2) raises an obvious problem: there are two unknowns for a single equation. In order to overcome this problem, the recovery rate R may be set at an arbitrary value; a default probability P_{def} is then deduced from the equation and is called the *implied default probability*. There will be as many implied default probabilities as there are ways of fixing the recovery rate.

We previously saw that the credit risk of a bond could be measured by its credit spread which we denote s. By the very definition of the spread, the yield of the bond is $r + s$, where we recall that r denotes the risk-free rate. We may thus compute the spread by substituting the appropriate expression for ZC in equation (2.2):

$$\frac{100}{(1+r+s)^T} = \frac{100}{(1+r)^T} \times [(1 - P_{\text{def}}) + P_{\text{def}} \times R] \tag{2.3}$$

To first order, and considering that P_{def} and r are much smaller than 1, we obtain the following expression for the spread:

$$s \simeq \frac{P_{\text{def}}}{T} \times (1 - R) = \frac{P_{\text{def}}}{T} \times \text{LGD} \tag{2.4}$$

Thus, there are two possible interpretations of the spread: it is by definition the excess yield with respect to the risk-free rate which pays for the default risk; it is also, to first order, the 1-year implied default probability, weighted by the loss given default. Another way of expressing the preceding statement is to consider that the spread is the average yearly loss that the investor may expect. In this sense, the spread should also represent, always to first order, the yearly premium that an investor is ready to pay to a third party to buy a protection in the case of default. This kind of protection does exist on the credit market in the form of *credit default swap*, or CDS, which we introduce below.

Box 2.1. Credit Default Swaps (CDS). A *credit default swap*, or CDS, is a contract signed between two parties, the buyer and the seller. The seller commits to pay the buyer the loss encountered in the case of default of a given issuer. As a compensation, the buyer pays a fixed premium. Thus, the CDS may be used as a protection against credit risk. However, the buyer is not necessarily exposed to the given issuer; he or she may simply speculate on the risk that the issuer defaults. CDSs are part of the family of credit derivatives.

Credit derivatives are financial products whose values depend on credit events such as the default of the issuer of a bond, for example. Credit Default Swaps are the most common credit derivatives. A CDS contract is a financial product which offers to its holder a protection against the credit risk of a given issuer, with, as a counterpart, the payment at regular intervals of premiums to the CDS seller. In the case of default, the CDS seller will compensate for the gap between the bond recovery and the face value. Thus, the CDS holder will not lose the invested amount: only the interests which have not yet been paid will be lost. Of course, the reasoning assumes that the CDS seller will not go bankrupt in turn. The recent crisis showed that the correlation between the risk of bankruptcy of the protection provider (the CDS seller) and the risk of bankruptcy of the entity on which the protection applies may be strong. In other words, the protection provided by the CDS is all the more illusory as the protection seller might go bankrupt if the reference entity itself goes bankrupt. This can happen for instance, if the CDS seller has sold more CDSs than he could meet. In this situation, financial market professionals speak of *wrong way risk*.

CDSs, which were initially designed to provide a protection to bond holders, soon became extremely liquid, that is, they became actively traded and not only among bondholders. In so doing, they even became the reference used by financial markets to quantify the credit risk of bond issuers. The development of the CDS market allowed traders to invest in credit risk, while being exempted from the constraints linked to the bonds market. As we showed with equation (2.4), the premium to be paid for the protection is, to first order, the credit spread of the reference issuer.

After this digression on credit derivatives, let us return to our initial example (Figure 2.3 and equation (2.3)). The market provides bonds and CDS prices corresponding to different maturities T_1, T_2 etc., which can be used to compute the implied default probabilities for these maturities. Credit models should lead to the computation of this implied default probability whatever the maturity T.

Consider the example presented in Table 2.1 below. Assume that we know the prices $ZC(T_i)$ of five zero coupon bonds issued by the same issuer whose maturities are spaced from 1 to 5 years. Let us also assume that we know the prices $ZC^*(T_i)$ of five zero coupon bonds reputed without risk. Making, as an example, the assumption that the recovery rate R is zero, we can deduce from these 10 bonds the implied default probabilities $P_{\text{def}}(T_i)$ associated to each maturity date (assuming a face value of 100 for all bonds):

In order to deduce from such data a structure for the implied default probabilities according to maturity, we shall introduce the

Table 2.1

Maturity (T_i)	Risk-free bond price ($ZC^*(T_i)$)	Implied risk free rate (r)	Risky bond price ($ZC(T_i)$)	Implied credit spread (s)	Implied default probability ($P_{\text{def}}(T_i)$)
1 year	97.1	3.0%	96.6	0.50%	0.48%
2 years	92.5	4.0%	90.7	1.00%	1.90%
3 years	87.6	4.5%	85.4	0.90%	2.54%
4 years	83.2	4.7%	80.5	0.87%	3.26%
5 years	78.4	5.0%	75.3	0.85%	3.95%

general principle of intensity models. These models introduced by [Jarrow and Turnbull 1995] are grounded on the fundamental assumption that the default probability of an issuer over a short time interval is proportional to the length dt of this interval: the longer one is exposed to credit risk, the higher the probability is that a credit event occurs. The proportionality coefficient, called the default intensity, and generally denoted $\lambda(t)$, may take many different forms:

- it may be constant: $\lambda(t) = \lambda$;
- it may be piecewise constant: $\lambda(t) = \lambda_i$ for $T_i \leq t \leq T_{i+1}$;
- it may be some other deterministic function of time;
- it may vary in a random way and be correlated to other economic factors.

The assumption that the probability is proportional to the time interval can be valid only over short time intervals. Moreover, one should bear in mind that the probability in question applies to future time intervals and can only have a meaning if the issuer has not defaulted before the beginning of the time interval. The modeled probability is hence conditioned by the fact that the issuer did not default before the beginning of the time interval. The rigorous transposition of this assumption in mathematical language, as well as the computations of the maturity dependent default probabilities, are explained in [Schönbucher 2003]. We shall simply observe that this assumption leads to the following result, plotted on Figure 2.4,

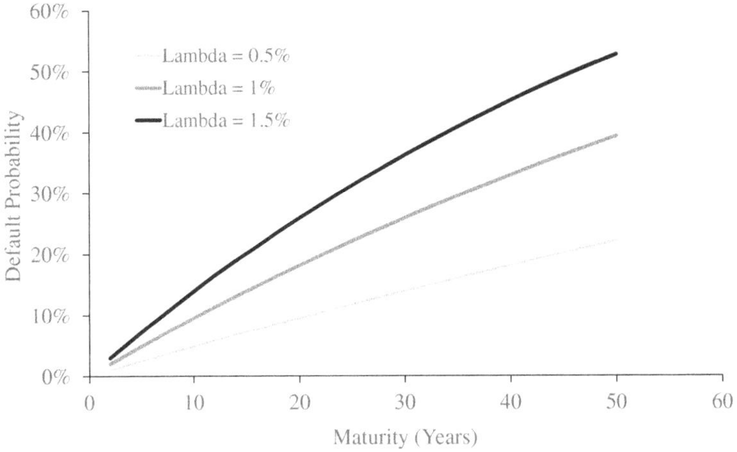

Figure 2.4: Implied default probabilities of an issuer between the calculation time and the future maturity in an intensity model. These probabilities are given by equation (2.5), and they are all the higher as the intensity λ is stronger.

in the case when λ is constant:

$$P_{\text{def}}(T) = 1 - e^{-\lambda T} \tag{2.5}$$

The interest of intensity models lies in that they provide a framework to deduce a consistent structure of default probabilities from the market prices of bonds or CDS, which allows us in turn to price almost all credit derivatives. Figure 2.5 shows that the model with constant intensity does not fit well the reality of market prices. Indeed, this model includes only one parameter and is too rigid to approximate the market prices. As for the model with piecewise constant intensities, it includes as many degrees of freedom as the number of available maturities. Therefore, it is perfectly adapted to fit the observed prices. All the issues which we encountered in the previous chapter regarding the interpolation of the interest rates curve also arise for the interpolation of default intensities.

Before closing this section, let us remind that:

➲ the credit risk is dual and depends on the default probability and on the recovery;

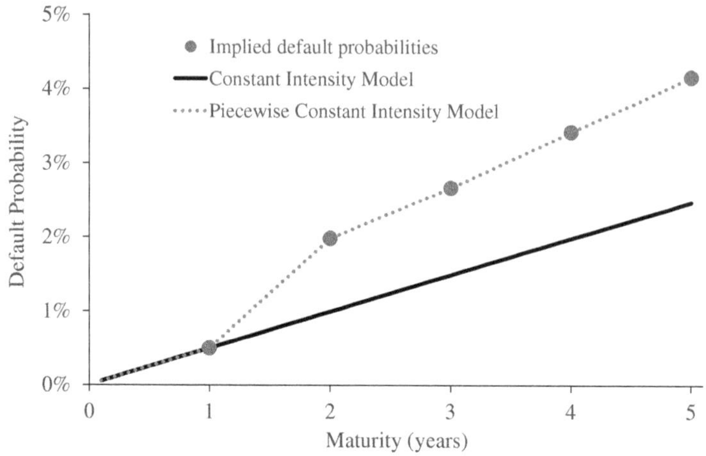

Figure 2.5: Implied default probabilities computed from risky bonds in the framework of two intensity models: a first model with constant intensity and a second one with piecewise constant intensities. The model with piecewise constant intensities can be used to fit the default probabilities implied from bonds prices (gray points on the graph) whereas the constant intensity model can only fit one of these points.

- the intensity models are used to compute implied default probabilities consistent with reference market prices and are hence useful to price other credit derivatives;
- the predictive character of the computed parameters must be considered with caution: they are implied parameters built to fit market prices but that have no reason to match real default probabilities nor recovery rates.

Intensity models display the peculiarity of not being interested in the real nature of the credit risk; their purpose is to imply, from prices of bonds, a representation of how risk is perceived by the market. Thus, their use as a tool to measure the credit risk or to interpret economically the financial structure of a given company is not relevant. The approach used by the so-called structural models is very different. Indeed, these models aim at replicating the balance sheet structure of issuers in order to obtain a measure of credit risk.

2.3 A structural model, the firm value model

How information issued from companies' books and records may be used to measure credit risk? [Black & Scholes 1973] and then [Merton 1974] answer this question by constructing the so-called *firm value model*, which relies on one of the fundamental characteristics of accounting: the balance sheet equilibrium. This notion may not be familiar to a number of readers, so a brief and simplifying foray into the domain of accounting is useful.

The balance sheet of a company is supposed to make an inventory of its wealth and commitments at a given instant. Among the wealth, that we shall call the assets in what follows, appear in particular the cash, and the value of its commodities, of its production means, of its real estate etc. As for the commitments, that we shall call the liabilities in what follows, they are composed of the amount of debt contracted by the company (bank overdraft or bonds, for example), the capital and the profit to be distributed to the shareholders etc. Liabilities can thus be divided into two sub-categories: the debts and the commitments of the company towards its shareholders. In theory, in the case of an instantaneous liquidation of the company, shareholders should divide the capital and the profit among themselves. Therefore, the value of the company, that is, the stock valuation, may be theoretically considered as being equal to the sum of the capital and the profit. We shall not go further into the description of the balance sheet which will thus be modeled by the following three values:

- the value of the company's assets (A_t);
- the value of the debt (D_t);
- the value of the commitments of the company towards its shareholders, which is assimilated to the stock valuation S_t.

The balance sheet of a company must be balanced, that is, the value of the assets must be equal to that of the liabilities. This accounting principle stems from the fact that the revenues must absorb the variations of the value of the debt and of the assets.

Therefore, there exists a link, valid at each instant, between the value of the assets and the stock valuation S_t:

$$A_t = S_t + D_t \tag{2.6}$$

This equation means that all of what a company owns, its assets, is due either to its creditors, which are the debts owners such as bondholders, or to its shareholders, which are the owners of the stocks. The firm value model is also grounded on the principle that there exists, in the case of a company's default, a reimbursement priority dependent on the creditors' nature. As an example, in France, the government and the employees will be paid first and foremost, then suppliers and then bond holders will be served in turn while shareholders will divide between themselves from the remaining assets. For simplicity, we shall assume in what follows that the whole debt may be represented by bonds. In our modeling, this means that if the company defaults, assets will be sold to first repay the bond holders, and then possibly the shareholders. More generally, whether the company has defaulted or not, if we assume that the face value N of the issued bonds must be reimbursed at time T, the same principle will apply: the amount of the assets, A_T, will be allocated in priority to the reimbursement of the bonds, and what is left, if any, will be the shareholders' property. Mathematically, this is translated into the following formulae[1]:

$$\begin{aligned} D_T &= \min(N; A_T) \\ S_T &= \max(0; A_T - N) \end{aligned} \tag{2.7}$$

Equation (2.7) illustrates that the stock S_T may be assimilated to a financial product which at time T would pay 0 if the value of the asset lies below some threshold N, and the difference $(A_T - N)$ otherwise. This category of products is widely spread and they are named "call options". We shall come back to these options and to the way their prices are computed in Chapters 4 and 5. For the

[1] The function $\max(x; y)$ is equal to the larger argument x or y, and the function $\min(x; y)$ to the smaller. For example, $\max(0; -1) = 0$ and $\min(2; 1) = 1$.

time being, it is enough to understand that modeling the balance sheet of a company allows us to link the value of its debts to the values of its shares and assets. Given assumptions on the evolution of the company assets — we shall study such models from Chapter 5 onwards — this balance sheet modeling can be used, for instance:

- ➲ to identify inconsistencies between the prices of the company bonds and the prices of its shares;
- ➲ to estimate the company's default probability, as we shall see hereafter.

Merton's model then assumes that the value of the company assets follows a well-defined evolution law. This does not mean that all the future values are deterministic and known, but only that we know the probability that the assets reach a given value at each instant in the future. If we know these probabilities, we may link the occurrence of the default to the value of the company assets, and deduce a default probability. Indeed, equation (2.7) induces a first definition of default: shareholders will file for bankruptcy if the company asset A_T is not sufficient to reimburse the bonds face value N. In this case, creditors receive the result of the liquidation of the asset A_T (which is less than N). Starting from this principle, it is possible to use more sophisticated modelings where the default may occur at instants other than T:

- ➲ Default may only occur at dates corresponding to the reimbursement of loans when the assets value is lower than the bond face value.
- ➲ Default may occur at any instant as soon as the assets value is lower than some threshold, which may be time independent or time dependent. Such a modeling of the default leads to an intensity model, whose default intensity is a maturity-dependent variable (see Figure 2.6).

The firm value model is appealing because it is able to account for the real financial structure of companies and of its impact on their

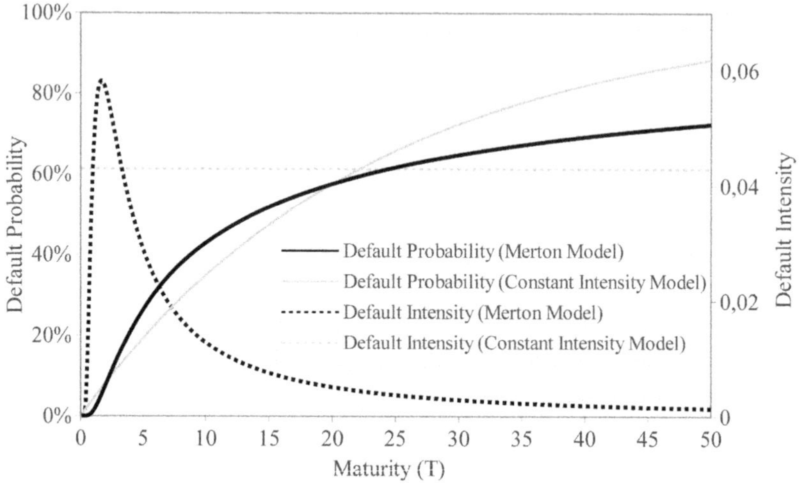

Figure 2.6: Default intensity and default probability in a Merton-type model, where the default occurs when the assets go below some reference threshold. Merton's structural model leads to an intensity model, where the intensity is a function of the maturity. Compared to a constant intensity model, defaults in Merton's model are less probable in the very short and long terms and more probable in the medium term.

credit quality. By contrast, the assumptions and approximations necessary in order to achieve the estimation of default probabilities are numerous: modeling of the company balance sheet, hypotheses on the evolution of the assets, modeling of the occurrence of a default etc. Indeed, to the first crude approximations briefly described in the present chapter, one may substitute more refined modelings, taking more faithfully into account the way the company functions in real life. Unfortunately, this additional complexity increases the number of parameters to be estimated as these parameters are not easily observable. Indeed, no explicit data is available on most of the required parameters. As a consequence of this piling up of hypotheses, information deduced from this kind of models is not supposed to be predictive, and not even to be compatible with market prices. Nonetheless, it seems accepted that these models lead to a rather reliable and robust classification of the quality of credit and can be used to build credit ratings models.

2.4 Correlations between defaults

Up to now, we have been interested in credit risk according to an individual risk criterion. Our aim was to measure the risk of losing a given debt, whatever the state of the economy or of any other criterion exogenous to the issuer. Now, it is commonly assumed and extensively proven in practice that company defaults occur in clusters as time goes by, as is shown in Figure 2.7. This means that there exists a *dependency* relation linking the occurrence of defaults. Simplifying to the extreme, if many companies defaulted in a recent past, it is likely that we shall observe other defaults in a near future.

This phenomenon of default dependency imposes to pay a particular attention to the analysis of the credit risk attached to a portfolio containing several debts. Indeed, the knowledge of individual default probabilities is not sufficient to measure the risk that issuers will default simultaneously. Moreover, the risk of default concentration is precisely the main risk which many financial institutions

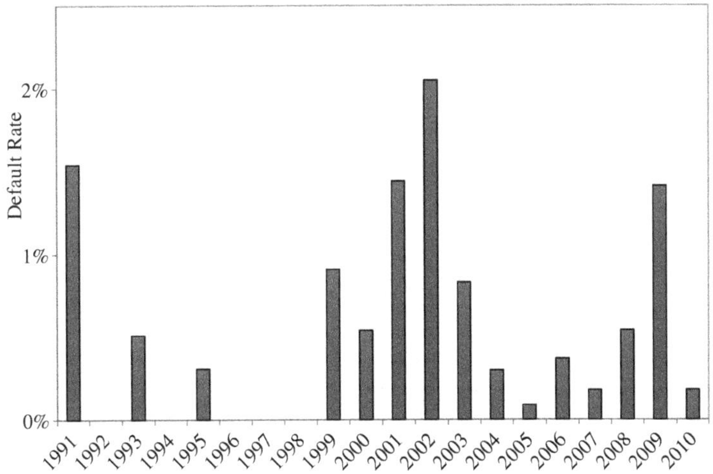

Figure 2.7: History of the default rate of issuers in the Eurozone. Defaults generally occur in clusters and as function of the cycles of the economy; peaks are observed around 1991, 2002 and 2009.

have to face. Taking this risk into account is thus a crucial issue for banks.

Let us imagine for an instant that we are the risk manager of a bank with 1,000 customers, each of the customers holding a \$1,000,000 loan. The maximum risk taken by the bank is thus that all its customers defaults, which would amount to a loss of \$1 billion. We need to estimate the risk that the bank goes bankrupt in a year, knowing that it will not be able to sustain losses larger than \$500 M. This phenomenon will happen if at least 50% of the customers default: how can we compute the probability that this event occurs? How can we quantify the probabilities of a simultaneous default of many borrowers, while we have seen how tricky the estimate of simple individual default probability could be? This problem gives a perfect illustration of the necessity to avoid having multiple parameters, to be estimated or fixed, especially regarding parameters used to model the default dependency. A simple solution, traditional and consistent with the observation drawn from Figure 2.7, is to link the occurrence of defaults with a unique state variable: the economic conditions.

The idea underlying such a model is to consider that the economy is represented by a random number X. By convention, the larger X, the more favorable the economic conditions are. Conversely, if X is deeply negative, economy is considered as being in recession. Of course, all the values of X do not occur with the same probability; although witnessing economic crises occurring one after another is bound to shake these certainties, euphoria periods or crisis periods are less frequent than intermediate situations. This is why the accepted modeling must take this characteristic into account. Accordingly, values of X close to zero must be more probable than extreme values, positive or negative. The probability associated with each possible value of X is traditionally modeled by a *normal law*, also called a Gaussian law, whose density function is drawn in Figure 2.8(a). This choice of modeling the economic conditions by a normal law is convenient, as statisticians have a good knowledge of its properties, but it remains arbitrary.

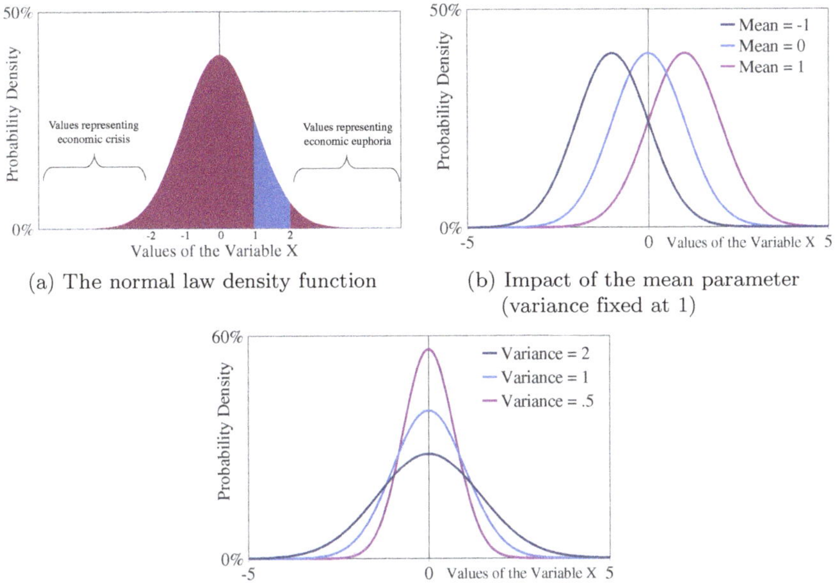

(a) The normal law density function

(b) Impact of the mean parameter (variance fixed at 1)

(c) Impact of the variance parameter (mean fixed at 0)

Figure 2.8: Modeling the economic conditions by a normal law. In graph (a), the blue area below the curve may be interpreted as the probability that the value of X lies between 1 and 2. The mean is a parameter which defines the abscissa around which the curve is centered, as graph (b) shows. The variance controls how the curve spreads around its mean, as illustrated in graph (c). The normal law is fully defined by these two parameters: mean and variance.

Our goal is to link the risk of default of a set of borrowers with the economic environment, that is, the value of the variable X: this is our instruction number 1. We also wish the model to be consistent with the individual default probabilities P^i_{def} which are supposed to have been already estimated: instruction number 2. The reasoning presented in the preceding section devoted to the firm value model is going to help us. In order to comply with instruction 2, we are going to build for each of our borrowers a random variable Y_i, representative of the economic health of the ith borrower. These variables will be used in a way similar to the value of the company assets which we modeled in the preceding section: if Y_i is less than some threshold K_i, then borrower i defaults. In order to comply with instruction 2, the threshold K_i must be carefully chosen: the probability that $Y_i \leq K_i$

must exactly be P^i_{def}. The next step is to link these variables Y_i to the variable X in order to comply with instruction 1. Properties of the normal law allow us to solve this ultimate step: it is possible to define a random variable N_i which follows a normal law independent[2] of X, such that:

$$Y_i = \sqrt{1-\rho^2}\, N_i + \rho X$$

Box 2.2. Random variables, expectation, and variance. A random variable may take different values according to some probability law. For example, the result of an unbiased dice roll is a random variable which is equal to one with a 1/6 probability, two with also a 1/6 probability and so forth up to six. The expectation of a random variable is nothing other than its mean value, 3.5 for our dice roll. The variance of a probability distribution measures the spread around the mean value: the larger the variance, the more scattered the values of the random variable. Among the laws which random variables may follow, the normal law, also called the Gaussian law, plays a particularly important role in the mathematical world. As illustrated in Figure 2.8, Gaussian laws are fully defined by two parameters, their mean value and their variance.

The parameter ρ, which must lie between -1 and $+1$, is called the *correlation* between X and Y_i. This parameter controls the intensity of the dependence between the economic conditions and the default of borrower i, as illustrated in Figure 2.9:

- if ρ is close to -1 or $+1$, then the probability that borrower i defaults will be strongly influenced by the level of X;
- if ρ is close to 0, then the occurence of the defaults will be insensitive to the value of X.

To sum up, the financial health of a borrower i is represented by a random variable Y_i. If this health is lower than a threshold K_i, then the borrower defaults. This individual financial health is decomposed into the weighted sum of two random variables, X, which represents

[2]This means that the values of N_i are in no way related to the realizations of X.

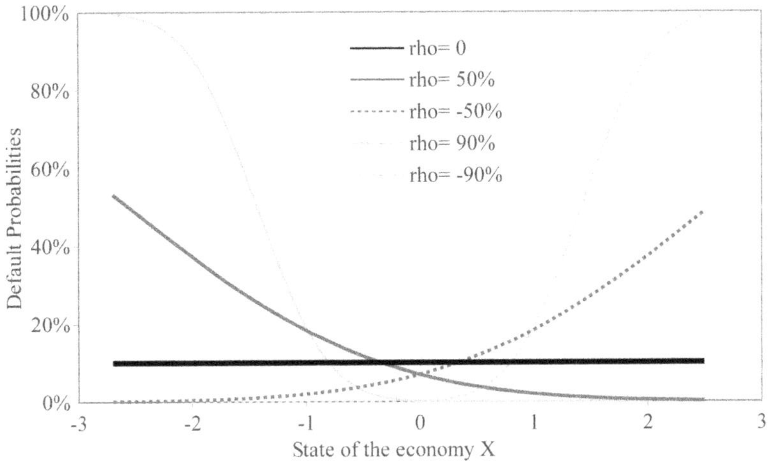

Figure 2.9: Default probability of a borrower as a function of the state of the economy, given different values of the correlation parameter ρ. If ρ is close to 1, the default probability of borrowers is strongly influenced by the value of X: for realizations of X which give low values, for example close to -3, this probability is close to 1; for realizations of X with high values, the default probability is close to 0. If $\rho = 0$ (straight line), the default probability is insensitive to the value of X and it is constant and equals to 10% in our example.

the global health of the economy and N_i, which represents the specific status of the borrower, independent of the rest of the economy. The weighting of the sum is parametrized by a variable ρ, the correlation, which measures to what extent the state of health of the borrower is influenced by the general economic conditions.

The ρ parameter has been chosen here identical for all the borrowers (i) but it would have been possible to fix different correlation parameters specific to each borrower. Indeed, nothing tells us that all the borrowers have the same sensitivity to the global economy. In practice, the choice of a unique correlation for all the borrowers is often used. It is indeed very difficult to estimate statistically correlations from historical data. The effects of a unique correlation are better mastered than when each borrower is assigned a particular correlation fixed more or less arbitrarily. It is quite clear that this choice generates in return a simplistic view lacking flexibility, which already proved to be detrimental during the crises which the credit markets witnessed since 2007.

We now have at our disposal a model, admittedly imperfect, but which brings an answer to our initial mandate: what is the probability that the bank goes bankrupt by facing losses greater than \$500 M? For the sake of simplicity, we shall suppose that the individual default probabilities of each customer are identical and equal to 10%. The graph presented in Figure 2.10 illustrates the answer to the above question, for different values of the correlation. One can read on the vertical axis the probability that a given number of defaults occurs in the portfolio. This model is the basis for the capital requirements that banks should respect as specified by the international norms Basel 2 and Basel 3.

In Figure 2.10, when the correlation vanishes, the loss is concentrated around 10%. As each individual has a default

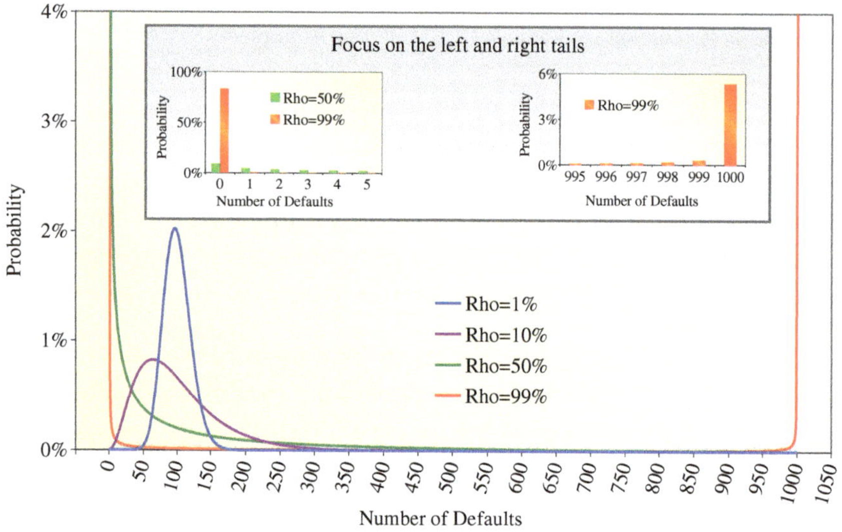

Figure 2.10: Probability of N defaults within a portfolio containing 1,000 loans, for various values of the correlation. The increase in the correlation does not make the portfolio more risky on average, but it changes the shape of the probability density of the default, by making the extreme cases more probable and the intermediate cases less probable.

probability of 10%, and as each individual is independent from the others, it is natural that, on average, one individual out of 10 defaults. When the correlation gets close to 100%, there are two possible modes only:

- Either all the customers default, and in this case the loss is \$1 billion (100% of the loans). The probability of this event is 10%.
- Or no customer defaults, and in this case the loss is zero. The probability of this event is 90%.

In all cases, the average loss is \$100 million, that is 10% of the total portfolio size. An increase in correlation leads to an increase of the probability of massive simultaneous defaults in the portfolio and hence of the bank's bankruptcy.

Modeling credit risk remains a crucial issue for banking and financial sectors, whether the question is to model the behavior of a debtor portfolio for the purpose of measuring its risks, or whether it is to provide consistent valuation tools for credit derivatives. The financial crisis which took place from 2007 to 2009 has, rightly or wrongly, discredited one category of models which were used as market standard tools up to then. In particular, modeling the dependency between defaults has focussed most of the criticisms. These criticisms singled out flaws among which some were mentioned in this chapter:

- the assumption that parameters extracted from market prices (implied default probabilities, implied correlations) are in line with the real parameters;
- lack of flexibility due to the reduced number of degrees of freedom used for the correlation modeling;
- the widely spread assumption of constant correlation while phenomena of correlation increase are observed in crisis periods.

However, some of these weaknesses are intrinsic to credit risk, because they are linked to the unobservable character of the behaviors one attempts to model. The major challenge of practitioners will not be so much to refine the existing models but rather to carefully ensure their appropriate use and to warn and to inform about their limits.

Chapter 3

Portfolio Management Theories

In this chapter, we take up the point of view of an investor who must select investment among the various possibilities provided by the market. This investor may be an individual, the manager of a regulated fund (pension funds or mutual funds for instance), or of a hedge fund; his goal is to build up a portfolio, that is, to buy various assets which may be stocks, bonds, real estate property, and so forth. This activity is called *asset management*. As examples, State Street or Blackrock are companies whose main activity is to manage money entrusted by retail or institutional investors.

Various theories have been developed to guide asset managers. Among them, that of Markowitz, called the modern portfolio theory, plays a major role. Developed in the 1950s — see [Markowitz 1952], [Tobin 1958] and [Markowitz 1959] — the theory defines a notion of investment optimality: *efficiency*. We shall explain this basic notion in the first section and the underlying details of the theory in the second one. In the 1960s, [Sharpe 1964], [Lintner 1965] and [Mossin 1966] have independently used Markowitz's theory in order to build a model of economic equilibrium, called the Capital Asset Pricing Model (CAPM), which is the subject of our third section. This model has then been widely studied, refined and extended. Next, in the fourth section, we shall turn our attention to a more recent development: the notion of co-integration introduced by [Engle and Granger 1987], which lies at the basis of trading strategies such as *pair trading*.

3.1 The risk-reward approach

Before delving into the heart of the subject, it is first necessary to look into the fundamental principle of any investment strategy: the equilibrium between return and risk. Let us consider the theoretical case where investment opportunities are restricted to four assets, A, B, C and D. Each of those four assets possesses:

- a level of risk;
- an expected return.

Furthermore, assume that the assets are fully described by those two characteristics as in Figure 3.1. According to any logical reasoning, every investor looking at this graph must acknowledge two facts:

- A should be preferred to D as, for the same level of expected risk, the return of A is larger than that of D.
- B should be preferred to C as, for an identical expected return, the risk level of B is less than that of C.

The principle which underlies this observation is that the investor seeks to maximize his portfolio's return at a given risk level or, conversely, to minimize his risk level under the constraint of a targeted return. Assets C and D are not interesting in the configuration of Figure 3.1, one says that they are *inefficient*. Now, what about the

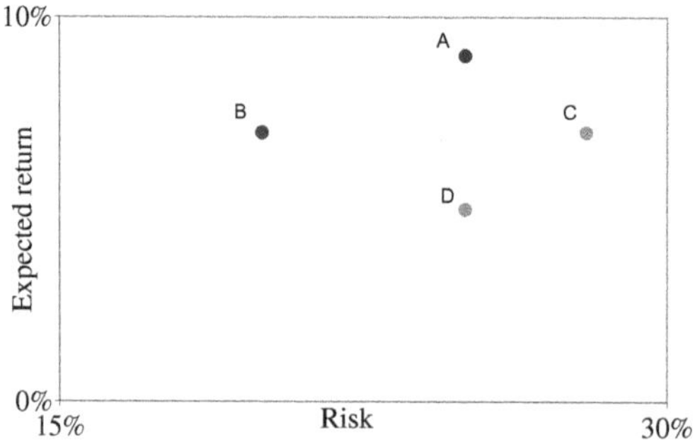

Figure 3.1: Two-dimensional theoretical representation of the risk (horizontal axis) versus expected return (vertical axis). In this configuration, assets A and B are efficient while assets C and D are not.

choice between A and B? Given information at our disposal, we cannot decide. In order to do so, we would have to know the individual preference of the investor, that is his risk aversion profile. The two assets A and B are called *efficient*.

Let us now come back to the notions of expected return and risk. In practice, which data may we choose to represent them? The return is measured as the growth rate of the price of an asset. This point meets a relative consensus. As for the risk, it may be apprehended in multiple ways. It must represent the uncertainty spread around the expected rate of return. The measure of risk which is mostly used in portfolio theories is the *volatility*. It represents the variability of the return rates around their mean value. The reader familiar with statistics will note that this volatility is nothing else than the standard deviation, or else the square root of the variance. However, other measures are often used, let us quote in particular:

- The *Value at Risk*, which we shall present in Chapter 8; it is the maximum loss at a given confidence level.
- The average loss, which is simply the average of the negative returns.

Rigorously speaking, anticipated returns and risks should be used. However, these data are difficult to predict, and practitioners are forced, in general, to use the hypothesis according to which past measurements are predictive of future ones. For example, Figure 3.2 places some U.S. stocks on the plane built with returns[1] and volatilities computed on the period spanning from 2000 to 2014.

On this figure, an efficient diagonal seems to appear with the stocks of Procter and Gamble, Mac Donald, Chevron and Boeing. This diagonal is representative of optimal choices according to the risk-return criterion with the measures defined above. In spite of this, is it true that General Electrics and JP Morgan stocks lack any

[1] For simplicity, the returns do not take into account dividends and other corporate actions (capital increase etc.). Taking this into account would modify the asset distribution in the plane.

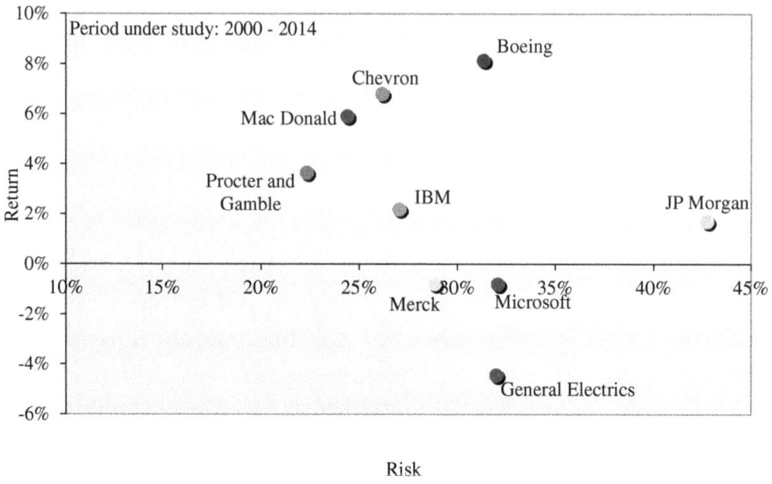

Figure 3.2: Two-dimensional representation of historical risk (horizontal axis), measured as the stock's volatility, versus return (vertical axis) for some stocks.

interest for an investor? Three arguments answer this question which is of purely illustrative purpose.

The first argument, the estimate of return rates and volatilities, as used in Figure 3.2, is quite tricky. Estimation periods must be very long so that the measured averages are as reliable as possible. However, over a long period of estimation, results are polluted by the so-called survivor bias: companies with a long lifetime are likely the most robust, which leads to a biased estimation sample. Furthermore, the longer the observation period, the more economic parameters are bound to change. On this account, Figure 3.3 shows that the analysis is very sensitive to the choice of the observation period: Boeing's stock is efficient during the period 2010–2014 and not efficient over the period 2005–2009. It is then necessary to constantly keep in mind that defining the right historical window is a difficult, if not unsolvable, problem.

In our opinion, assessing the average return is Achilles' heel of all models based on a risk-reward approach. Indeed, the average error on the return rate estimate is given by the formula $\sigma/\sqrt{N}$, where σ is the volatility of the return rates and N the number of observation

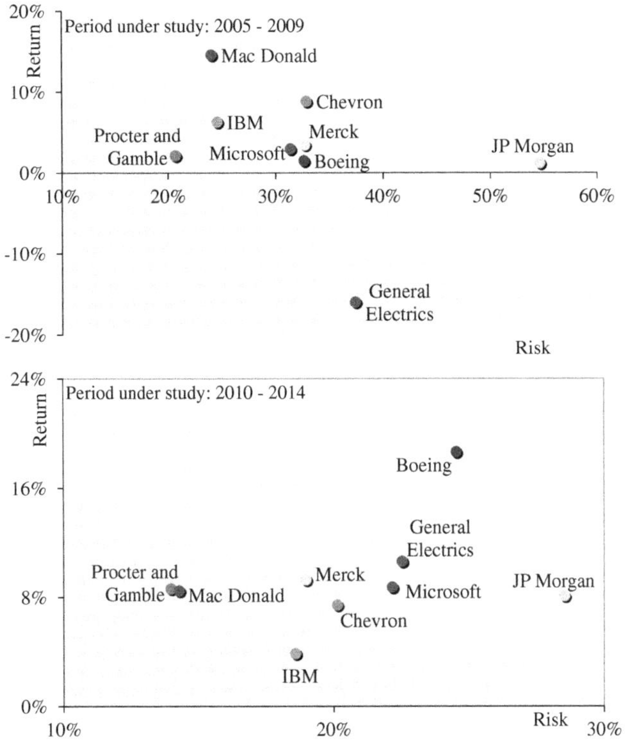

Figure 3.3: Two-dimensional representation of risk (horizontal axis), measured as the stock's volatility, versus return (vertical axis) for some stocks over different periods. The hierarchical organization of risk-return couples is very sensitive to the period studied; even the ranges of the return rates and the observed volatilities differ in the two periods.

periods. The lesson to be drawn is then the following: if we wish to know the return rates with a 1% accuracy, knowing that the yearly volatility of a stock is often close to 25%, as an order of magnitude, the number of necessary years of observation is computed as follows:

$$1\% = \frac{25\%}{\sqrt{N}} \Rightarrow N = 625\,\text{years!} \tag{3.1}$$

The second argument, the measure of the risk we have chosen, that is, the volatility, is not necessarily adapted. The use of the Value at Risk could, for example, modify the perception of risk associated to stocks and thus their degree of efficiency.

Finally, for last argument, up to now only the individual characteristics of the assets have been used. We did not consider the possibility of combining them in order to take advantage, for example, of the effects of diversification. Markowitz precisely built a model where one may explicitly compute the portfolios which make the best use of the diversification possibilities.

3.2 Markowitz's theory

Diversification is a fundamental concept in portfolio management. Theory and experiment contribute to demonstrating its interest in the construction of an investment portfolio. In order to tackle the theory, we shall model the returns of the assets by a Gaussian probability structure and Gaussian correlations; in this framework, the dependency between two assets is described by a single parameter, the correlation ρ. The risk-return profile, according to this model, of a two asset portfolio is shown in Figure 3.4: the curves describe the risk-return profile when one varies the proportion of wealth invested in asset S_1 or S_2, under different correlation configurations.

Box 3.1. Gaussian modeling of returns. Several mathematical models are based on the hypothesis that return rates of assets follow a normal (or Gaussian) law. Although there exist justifications of this hypothesis, which we shall see subsequently, it is most often used as a convenient assumption to simplify computations. In this modeling, returns are characterized by only two parameters: their mean value and their volatility.

There are also multiple ways for linking random variables together in order to take their dependencies into account. Once more, for simplicity, traditional modelings assume that dependencies between random variables follow a Gaussian correlation structure. We shall address this problem in more detail in Chapter 8. Let us remember, for the time being, that this dependency structure is a model among others, and that it has the advantage of being characterized by a single quantity, lying between -1 and $+1$: correlation.

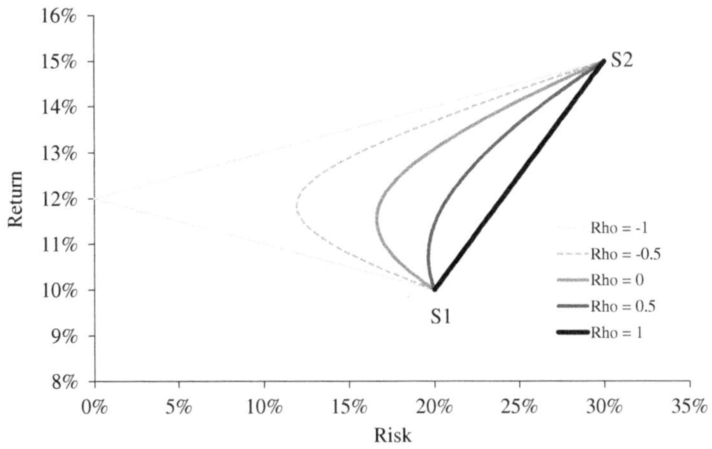

Figure 3.4: Variation of the risk-return profile of portfolios composed of two assets, S_1 and S_2, given various values of correlation between the assets. For example, each point on the dotted curve represents a possible risk-return profile of a portfolio, in the case where the correlation between $S1$ and $S2$ is -0.5. The reduction of the risk brought by diversification is all the more pronounced as the correlations between assets are weak. In the limiting case where $\rho = -1$, which means that the stocks' risks are exactly opposite, it is even possible to build a risk-free portfolio by buying the two stocks: the variability is neutralized thanks to the anticorrelation and the portfolio's return is constant.

In the case $\rho = 1$, the risk and the return rate of the portfolio will evolve on the straight line bounded by assets $S1$ and $S2$. When the correlation decreases, the curve is twisted towards the left, which witnesses a reduction of the risk: it is the result of diversification. The limiting case of a correlation $\rho = -1$ is interesting: when the assets' returns evolve in opposite ways, it is possible to hedge the risk and to build a risk-free portfolio, with zero volatility.

Markowitz's theory uses this result, by systematizing and generalizing it to a universe composed of any number of risky assets. The aim of this theory is to solve the following optimization problem: determine the set of portfolios whose volatility is minimal given an expected return. One then speaks of efficient portfolios. The theory leads to explicit equations for these portfolios, but we shall not dwell on these details. It is sufficient to admit that the method determines a curve called the *efficient frontier*. Each point on this curve represents a portfolio, that is a bucket of different stocks, whose volatility can be read on the horizontal axis and whose expected return can be read on the vertical axis. The portfolios of this curve have the best possible risk-return profile; in other words, they have the smallest volatility which may be obtained for a given expected return rate.

Figure 3.5(a) presents the results of applying the theory to a universe of U.S. stocks. The contribution of the model is blatant: the curve of efficient portfolios — the efficient frontier — outperforms by a wide margin the individual stocks. We succeeded in exploiting at full capacity the effects of diversification.

Introducing into the investment universe a risk-free asset, that is, an asset with zero volatility, brings a new feature. We ask the reader to admit that the optimization calculation mentioned above results in a new efficient frontier. As illustrated in Figure 3.5(b), the new efficient frontier is the straight line which starts from the risk-free asset and which is tangent to the efficient frontier of risky assets. The contact point between the line and the parabola defines a portfolio called the *tangency portfolio*. In practice, the risk-free asset may be assimilated to an investment made at the risk-free interest rate defined in the preceding chapter.

The tangency portfolio is the only portfolio of the efficient frontier built with only risky assets that remains efficient when a risk-free asset is introduced. All the efficient portfolios built with the risk-free asset are in fact a combination of the risk-free asset and of the tangency portfolio. This last result, which we ask the reader to admit, is important for the next section of this chapter.

Results brought by this theory are enticing. However, they remain very theoretical. First of all, we saw that the parameters used, in particular the return rates, are quite unstable, if not unobservable. Moreover, Markowitz assumes that assets may be modeled using a Gaussian distribution of probability and correlations. We shall have the opportunity to come back to this hypothesis which is fundamental in Capital Market activities, but largely at odds with observation.

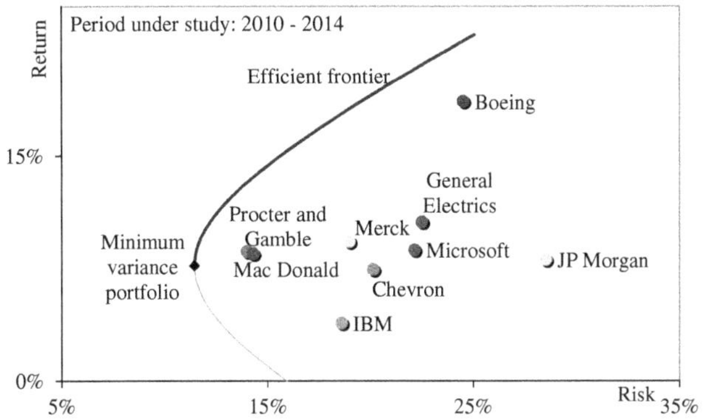

(a) Efficient frontier of a universe of risky assets

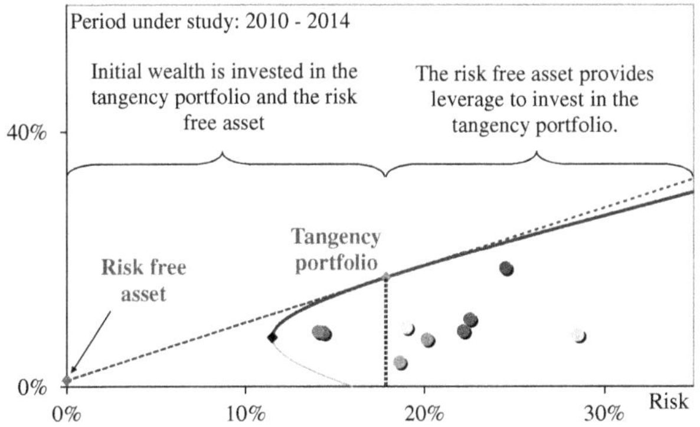

(b) Efficient frontier when a risk-free asset is added

Figure 3.5: Graph (a) shows the efficient frontier of a universe of risky assets. It represents the best risk-reward pairs which can be obtained using a linear combination of the various risky assets. The point to the extreme left of the frontier represents the portfolio with minimum variance which may be obtained given the existing assets. When a risk-free asset is added to the universe, in graph (b), the efficient frontier becomes a straight line, represented on the graph by a dotted line. The only point of this new efficient frontier common with the former one represents the unique efficient risk-reward profile which may be obtained combining risky assets only. The portfolio of risky assets which possesses this efficient profile is called the *tangency portfolio*.

Another hypothesis was implicit above, namely, there is no restriction to the exchange of assets: there are no transaction costs, nor taxes, and it is possible to hold whatever proportion of an asset, even negative (see Box 3.2 for a definition). At first sight, this hypothesis seems to be a fair approximation to reality without serious consequences. However, impacts of taxes and regulations may be very structuring. For example, one of the levers used by regulators to avoid or to control market runaways is to impose limitations on market efficiency.

Box 3.2. Short selling. Short selling amounts to selling an asset that one does not yet own, in the same way as borrowing money amounts to committing oneself to reimburse a sum of money one does not yet own. A short selling of securities is thus equivalent to a debt, which is translated mathematically into holding a negative amount of securities. For example, one can short sell a stock by:

- borrowing a stock from a counterparty A which owns the security;
- selling the stock to another counterparty B and receiving some amount of money in exchange of this sale.

It will be necessary to buy again the stock in order to give it back to counterparty A. If the stock price has risen by \$1, we shall lose \$1. This is equivalent to holding -1 stock.

Thus, making the theory reliable and more adapted to market realities is of the foremost interest. Hence, compliance with constraints on investments forces market practitioners to better take reality into account. For example, short selling may be difficult to implement in practice, and may even be forbidden for some assets. Figure 3.6 shows how forbidding short selling modifies the equilibria of the theory. Solving this kind of optimization problems under constraints is often tricky and requires the use of advanced numerical optimization algorithms. Using other risk measures, such as *Value at Risk*, as well as using other structures of correlations and the desensitization of efficient portfolios to errors on expected returns estimations, feature among the new avenues which are explored around Markowitz's theory.

3.3 The capital asset pricing model

We just learnt that efficient portfolios may be all structured with two investments, one being the risk-free asset and the other one being the

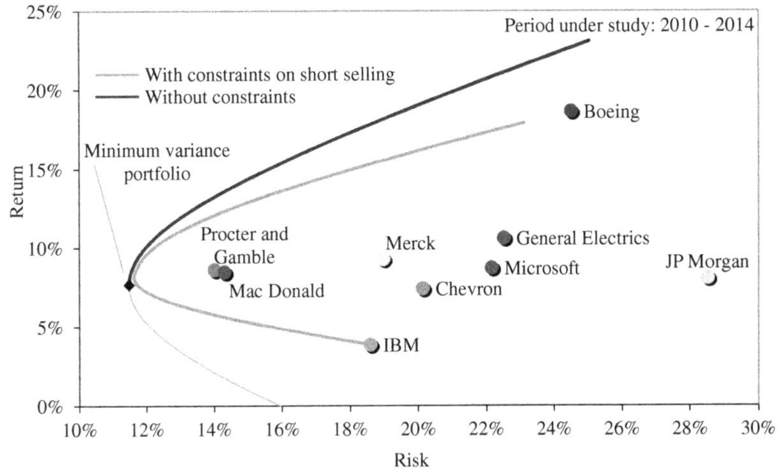

Figure 3.6: Impact of the constraint that forbids short selling on the efficient frontier. Forbidding short selling reduces the spectrum of portfolios which may be built; the portfolios which may be built without short selling provide a less interesting risk-reward profile.

tangency portfolio. The only characteristic which differentiates the various efficient portfolios is the proportion invested in each of these two assets. The *Capital Asset Pricing Model* (CAPM) makes the best use of this observation. Schematically, our reasoning will be as follows:

1. All efficient portfolios may be represented as a linear combination of two funds: the risk-free asset and the tangency portfolio.
2. With investors being rational, all the market players must own an efficient portfolio.
3. The prices of assets reach an equilibrium due to the law of supply and demand.
4. The equilibrium between supply and demand may be deduced from (1) and (2).
5. Thanks to this equilibrium, it must be possible to evaluate prices and returns of assets.

The assumptions which are necessary to successfully implement the preceding reasoning are particularly restrictive. First of all, the

CAPM model is framed in Markowitz's theory. It then uses the assumptions which we reviewed in the preceding section: Gaussian structure of returns and lack of restrictions on investment. The additional hypothesis, essential to CAPM, is that all investors carry out the same analysis of the risk-reward efficiency. This hypothesis is on the one hand the big strength of the model, as it allows one to push Markowitz's reasoning to its ultimate end, and on the other hand, its big weakness, because it is very restrictive. In particular, investors may have:

- various anticipations of return and volatility;
- various models for assessing the risks;
- various investment horizons;
- various investment restrictions, for example, the possibility of short selling, or not.

Therefore, the results which we are going to describe are only valid in a very idealized theoretical framework. We may already foresee that these results will not be directly usable in order to define investment strategies, but they are nevertheless able to provide structuring keys for understanding financial markets.

Let us come back to the model. For each stock A, we denote by w_A its percentage in the tangency portfolio. Let us recall that, in accordance with the preceding hypotheses, all investors have the same risk-return analysis and hence invest only in portfolios of the efficient frontier. This efficient frontier is a combination of the risk-free asset and the tangency portfolio. Hence, leaving aside the risk-free asset, all market investments are proportional to the tangency portfolio. Therefore, as the portfolio of every investor contains w_A of stock A, the total proportion of stock A held, across every investor, can only be w_A. In other words, the market capitalization of stock A, that is, the value of the sum of all the stocks A available on the market, represents w_A of the total market capitalization (the sum of all the market capitalizations). Naming the *market portfolio* the aggregated portfolio of all market participants, we just proved that the tangency portfolio can only be the market portfolio.

The first lesson of CAPM is that the tangency portfolio is built by holding all the stocks in proportion to their respective market capitalization. This market capitalization, which is the number of shares of a company multiplied by the share's price, is a financial information easy to get. In this way, CAPM bypasses the Markowitz calculations necessary to build the tangency portfolio. The definition of the market portfolio as a linear combination of all the stocks weighted by their market capitalization is simpler, more intuitive and less prone to parameter instabilities than the Markowitz calculation. On the other hand, this equivalence between the two approaches remains quite theoretical, as the CAPM assumes that constraints and objectives are universally shared by investors.

Before moving on to a second result, we must define the sensitivity of stocks to the market portfolio. We note β_A this sensitivity, and its definition is as follows[2]: for a 1% variation of the market, stock A varies on average of β_A%. Using this definition of β_A and using the assumption of a Gaussian structure of the returns, the return of stock A (which we note also A) is a random variable which can be decomposed as follows:

$$A = \beta_A \Pi_M + \tilde{\varepsilon}_A \tag{3.2}$$

where Π_M is a random variable representing the return of the market portfolio and $\tilde{\varepsilon}_A$ a random variable independent of the market portfolio. With this equation, we recover the definition of β_A: if $\beta_A = 50\%$, then the return of stock A will be 50% of the market return plus an independent random number; if $\beta_A = 150\%$, the return of the stock will be 150% of the market return plus an independent random number.

What is then the expectation for the return of the stock? Explicit computations lead to the following result: if R_A is the expected rate

[2]Formally, β_A is the ratio of the covariance between the stock and the market portfolio to the variance of the market portfolio:

$$\beta_A = \mathrm{Cov}(A, \Pi_M)/\mathrm{Cov}(\Pi_M, \Pi_M).$$

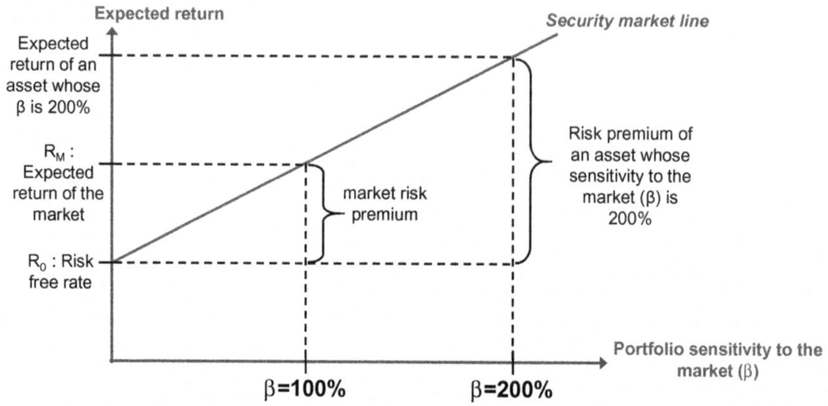

Figure 3.7: The security market line. The CAPM predicts that for every stock, its expected return over the risk-free rate is proportional to its β. Let us assume that a given stock has a β of 200%, which means that the stocks' variations are twice the market variations plus a random value, uncorrelated with the market. Under the CAPM hypotheses, the stock will necessarily have an excess return over the risk-free rate of $200\% * (R_M - R_0)$ (where R_M is the market average return and R_0 the risk-free rate). The part of the stock's return uncorrelated with the market cannot bring any additional return on average. The line that links a stock's β to its expected return is called the security market line.

of return of the stock (R_A is the expectation of A), R_M that of the market (R_M is the expectation of Π_M) and R_0 the risk-free rate, then

$$R_A - R_0 = \beta_A(R_M - R_0) \tag{3.3}$$

This equation draws, as in Figure 3.7, the so-called *Security Market Line*. This graph displays the quantities $R_A - R_0$ and $R_M - R_0$ which are called risk premiums: they represent the return surplus expected over the risk free interest rate, as a reward for the risk which has been taken. The main result of CAPM which we just presented in equation (3.3) asserts that the risk premium of the stock is equal to the market risk premium, weighted by the stock sensitivity to the market risk. Thus, the expected return of an asset only depends on its β, that is, its dependency on the systemic risk. The risk specific to the asset, which is traditionally called the idiosyncratic risk, does not bring any additional return.

What do we actually observe? We saw that it is very unlikely, given the necessary assumptions, that the results presented above are in fact observed in real life. The model predicts that the specific risk of a stock must not bring any additional return, on average. To check this, it is enough to measure the idiosyncratic return of a stock which we shall note α. With the preceding notations, the additional return of A over its theoretical return under the CPAM assumptions is $\alpha = R_A - R_0 - \beta_A(R_M - R_0)$. Within the theoretical framework of CAPM, α is zero for any asset.

In practical asset management, the quantity α plays a very important role. It is a theoretical measure of the profitability surplus brought by an asset, a strategy or an asset manager with respect to the market return. The ability for a manager to generate α, that is, to manage a fund providing an $\alpha > 0$, is often considered as a proof that the manager is able to outperform the market and bring an excess of profitability with respect to the market. This is in contradiction with CAPM, in which it is assumed that all players only invest in the market portfolio and in the risk-free asset.

The results of these computations on some U.S. stocks are presented in Figure 3.8. The model predictions are disastrous when compared to the actual numbers obtained from the numerical computations: α is far from being zero — it is negligible neither with respect to interest rates, nor with respect to returns or risk premiums — and β is not proportional to the risk premium.

Verifying thoroughly CAPM is a tricky exercise, which has been the subject of many analyses from the 1960s. Let us hinge on a famous study of [Fama and French 1992]. This study goes deeper into links between β, returns, market capitalization and other financial ratios over the period 1963–1990. The conclusion is indisputable: β does not in the least explains the returns which were observed over this period (even though a relation between β and returns may be identified before 1969). β is essentially correlated to market capitalization, while the latter is, in turn, correlated to returns. By contrast,

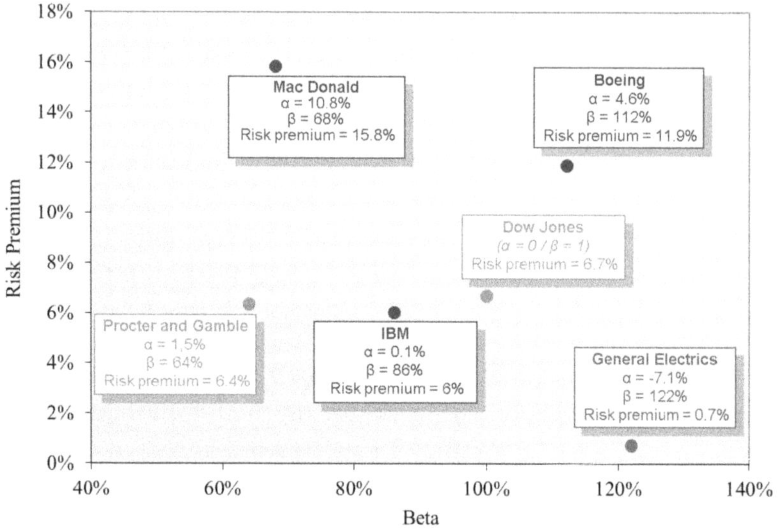

Figure 3.8: Security market line (returns expressed as a function of β) computed on historical data. Numerical calculations contradict CAPM predictions: α is not zero, the risk premium is not proportional to β. The theoretical straight line of Figure 3.7 is not actually reproduced.

β is not directly linked to returns. Indeed, we can see in Figure 3.9, drawn from data published by Fama and French, that

- Figure 3.9(a): if we divide companies according to market capitalization class, (portfolio 1A corresponding to the smallest capitalizations and 10B to the highest ones), we observe that the most important companies own a weaker β and a smaller return, thus exhibiting a quasi-linear link between β and return;
- Figure 3.9(b): if we divide companies according to classes of β (portfolio 1A corresponding to the smallest βs and portfolio 10B to the highest ones), then the link between β and return vanishes.

Although they cannot be used in practice, the CAPM principles are quite attractive and we may nonetheless remember the following lesson: the risk premium of an asset is decomposed into (i) a risk premium linked to the market and (ii) a specific risk premium. This analysis is generally developed in what is called the "1-factor model" described in Chapter 2 when we studied correlations between

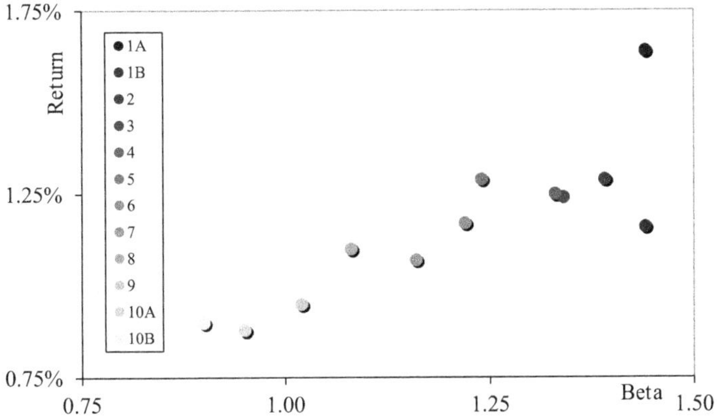

(a) Companies ordered by size

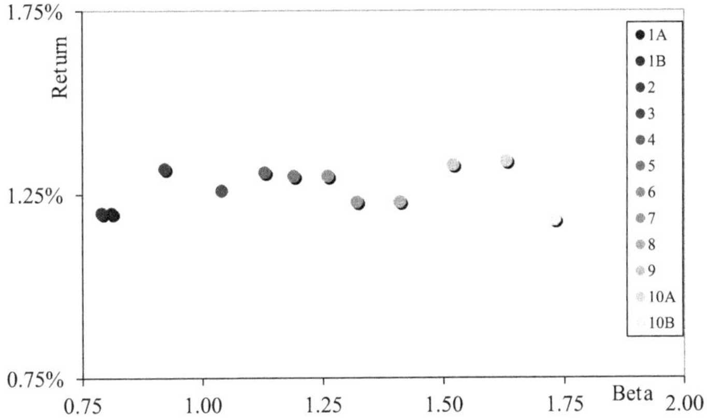

(b) Companies ordered by β

Figure 3.9: Representation of the return (vertical axis) as a function of β (horizontal axis) over 12 portfolios of companies classified by size or by β (data taken from [Fama & French 1992]). On Figure (a), we can see that the smallest companies have higher expected returns and higher β, which seems in line with the CAPM prediction according to which β and expected returns are linked. However, if the companies are grouped by β, as on Figure (b), there is no more link between the β and the expected return.

defaults. This model is based on equation (3.2):

$$A = \beta_A \Pi_M + \tilde{\varepsilon}_A$$

where:

- we do not make any hypothesis on the return of $\tilde{\varepsilon}_A$, by contrast with the CAPM which predicts that the returns of the specific risk are zero on average;
- we suppose, as in the CAPM case, that $\tilde{\varepsilon}_A$ is independent of Π_M;
- we assume in addition (this assumption is not necessary for CAPM) that the specific risks $\tilde{\varepsilon}_A$ of two different stocks are independent.

This model may then be extended to take into account many risk factors: the return of a stock may, for example, be decomposed into a general market return, a sectorial return and a geographical return, without forgetting the specific return $\tilde{\varepsilon}_a$, thus leading to a multi-factorial model. All this lies at the basis of *Asset Pricing Theory* (APT) introduced in [Ross 1976]. The reader who wishes to go deeper into the subject may, for example, refer to [Sharpe *et al.* 1998].

3.4 Correlation vs cointegration*

Models of portfolio management which we just developed rely heavily upon the notion of correlation between the stocks returns of companies. Now, as is shown in Figure 3.10(a), correlation between indices is a very unstable measure. From another point of view, Figure 3.10(b) is nevertheless indisputable: there does exist a link between the Dow Jones and the DAX index and there is little doubt that the curves follow each other. One of the big issues of portfolio management is to account for this link between assets thanks to a robust method; this is the exercise we shall undertake in the present section.

What do we mean by a robust method? Our aim is to exhibit a measure which is stable over time. This time stability is essential, because it ensures that properties observed in the past will hold true in the future. Figure 3.10(a) is an excellent counter-example of time

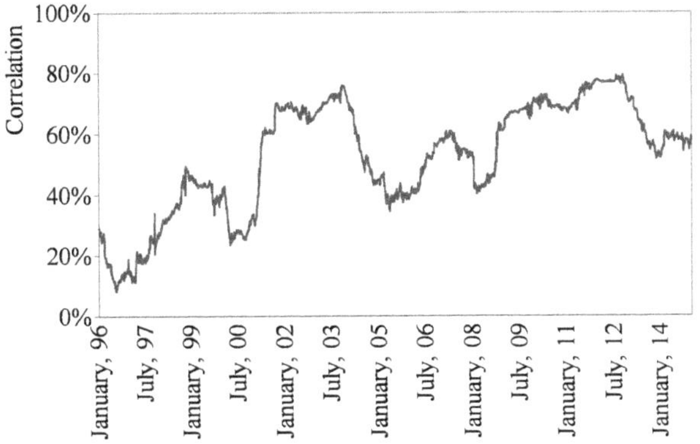

(a) Correlation between the DAX and the Dow Jones

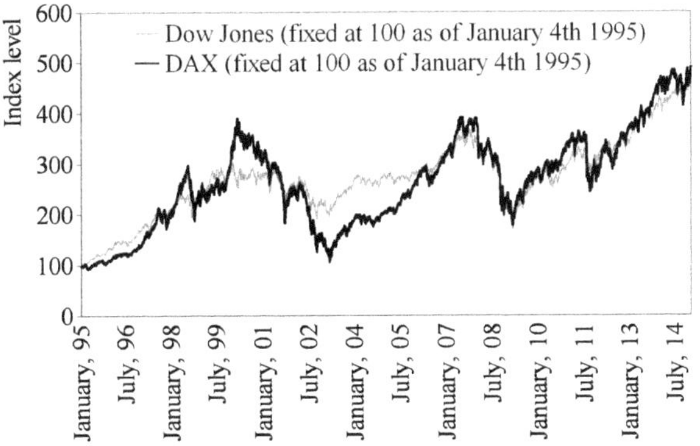

(b) Historical values of the indices

Figure 3.10: History of the German index DAX and of the US index Dow Jones between January 1995 and January 2015 and of their correlation.

stability: it exhibits correlations which go from 10% to 80%. Within this framework, it is clear that the past correlations do not predict future correlations. Mathematically, the time stability of random processes is expressed by the concept of *stationarity*. A series of random variables X_t labeled by the time t, is called stationary if:

- all the X_ts follow the same law: the law is independent of the time t;
- the links between X_t and X_{t-s} only depend on s: the links between the two variables only depend on the time lag s, but not on the time t when this link is observed.

In other words, the probability laws of the series are homogeneous over time: they do not change as time passes. An example of a stationary series is the results X_t of independent coin flipping, assuming an unbiased coin:

- X_t takes the value "heads" with a 50% probability and "tails" with a 50% probability, independent of draw t;
- $X_t = X_{t-s}$ if $s = 0$ and they are independent for $s \neq 0$: the correlation structure of the random variables is time-independent.

A natural counter-example of stationarity is the daily temperature: the weather is often colder in winter, the temperature series exhibits a season dependence; moreover, we are in a period of global warming, and the series exhibits a long-term tendency. Figure 3.10(a) showed that the correlations are not stationary either. By contrast, Figure 3.11 shows the time evolution of a series which is perfectly stationary. One observes, in particular, that the values of a stationary series do not drift from the mean value (3 in Figure 3.11), and that the variability around this mean value is quite stable.

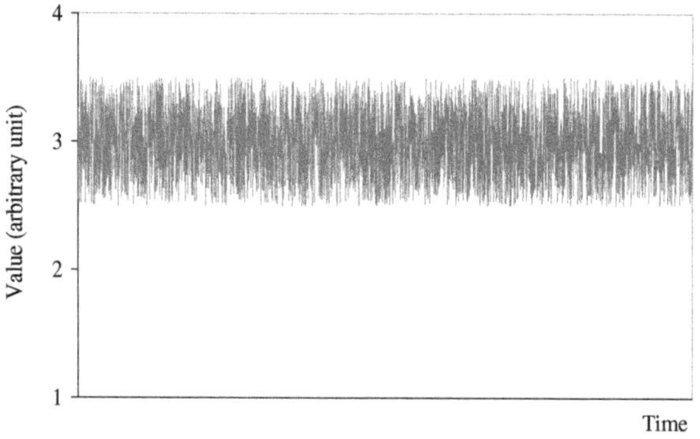

Figure 3.11: Example of a stationary series. The average and the variability of the series are constant with time.

If one could find a stationary portfolio of financial assets, this would allow one to own a portfolio whose price is confined around some average value, and it could only diverge from this average by following a known and always identical law. This would be an ideal trading tool. This is exactly the property which defines *cointegration.* A set of series A_t, B_t, $C_t, \ldots$, is cointegrated if it is possible to create a stationary linear combination of the series. In other words, the series A_t, B_t and C_t are cointegrated if there exist numbers a, b, c such that the series $X_t = aA_t + bB_t + cC_t$ be stationary.

There is little chance to find a set of stationary assets. Actually, the assets display a structure which is more multiplicative than additive. We are more interested in the return of a stock (a 10% gain for example) than by the absolute value of the gain (a gain of $10 for example). This is reasonable enough, given that the price of a stock is rather arbitrary: it is equivalent to issue ten times $50 stocks and five times $100 stocks. In the same way, knowing that stock A increased by $5 between two dates, and that stock B increased by $0.10 over the same period does not enable to compare the performances of the stocks: the absolute value of the gain must be weighted by stock prices.

In order to transform a multiplicative structure into an additive one, it is useful to work with logarithms: we do not consider the price S_t of an asset but rather its logarithm $l_t = \ln(S_t)$. The return of asset S_t may then be approximated by the increment[3] of the logarithms l_t:

$$l_t - l_{t-1} = \ln(S_t) - \ln(S_{t-1}) \simeq \frac{S_t - S_{t-1}}{S_{t-1}} \tag{3.4}$$

Thanks to the logarithm, a multiplicative structure can be transformed into an additive one. It is now more reasonable to hope that, given a set of assets $S_t^1, S_t^2, \ldots, S_t^n$, we are able to build a series $\alpha_1 \ln(S_t^1) + \alpha_2 \ln(S_t^2) + \cdots + \alpha_n \ln(S_t^n)$ which is stationary. In other words, we wish that the series $\ln(S_t^1), \ldots, \ln(S_t^n)$ be cointegrated.

From now on, we have two separate measures of the dependence between assets, correlation and cointegration. Note that the correlation is measured with the stock returns $\frac{S_t - S_{t-1}}{S_{t-1}} \simeq \ln(S_t) - \ln(S_{t-1})$

[3]We shall always use the following convention: the return is the increase rate $(x_t - x_{t-1})/(x_{t-1})$ and the increment is the linear increase $x_t - x_{t-1}$.

whereas the cointegration is directly evaluated from the logarithms of asset prices.

Correlation between returns appears when the motions of the assets are synchronous. For two assets to be correlated, the days when a falls and those when b falls should overlap. As for cointegration, it accounts for an effect of mean reversion. For two stocks a and b to be cointegrated, variations of a should be corrected by those of b, but not necessarily on the same day. In other words, when two stocks a and b are cointegrated, the motions of one stock statistically predict those of the other one: it may be that the motions of a explain those of b, or that the motions of b explain those of a, and even that the two motions are entangled. For example, if stock a falls on day D and does not rise any more, it will be necessary that further motions of b bring back the stationary linear combination of a and b towards its initial value. This property is what is called Granger's causality; this causality is necessary in order that the two series be cointegrated.

Correlation and cointegration are two closely related notions, which both measure a form of dependency between two assets, but which are clearly distinct. It is possible to observe cointegrated series whose motions are not correlated. Figure 3.12(a) shows cointegrated series with parallel evolutions, but with a time lag: the series plotted with a black line moves with a delay of five days with respect to series plotted in gray. Daily motions thus are independent, but the global tendencies are linked. As for Figure 3.12(b), it shows series whose motions are correlated, but which are not cointegrated. More precisely, the motions of the two series have the same random component, but they progressively diverge from each other through a phenomenon of deterministic drift.

Cointegration has the reputation of being more robust than correlation, in the sense that cointegration phenomena are more stable over time. One of the problems with correlation is that its measurement is easily biased by imperfections in the data (for example, a time lag between the instant where measurements are performed),

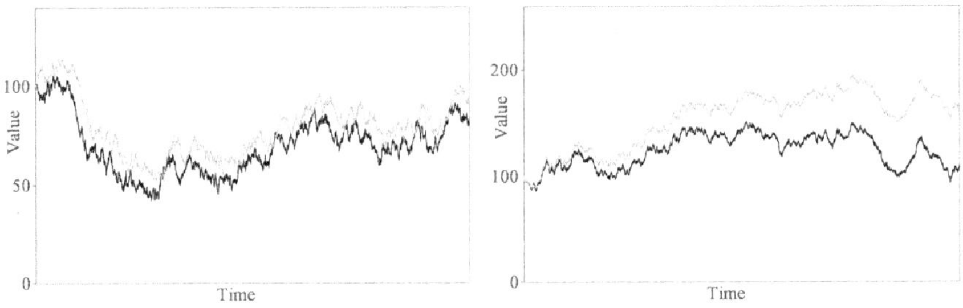

(a) Series cointegrated but showing no correlation

(b) Series correlated but showing no cointegration

Figure 3.12: Contrast between correlation and cointegration.

Table 3.1

Example of a pair trading strategy	
Assets	A_t and B_t are two stocks
Hypothesis	$2\ln(A_t) - \ln(B_t)$ is a stationary process of mean μ
Investment trigger event	At time t_0, as soon as $2\ln(A_{t_0}) - \ln(B_{t_0}) < \mu - \Delta$
Investment	\$2 of stock A and $-\$1$ of stock B
Investment initial value	$2 - 1 = \$1$
Investment selling trigger event	At time $T > t_0$, as soon as $2\ln(A_T) - \ln(B_T)$ returns to its mean μ. Mean reversion is guaranteed by the stationarity hypothesis.
Investment value at selling time	$2\frac{A_T}{A_{t_0}} - \frac{B_T}{B_{t_0}} \approx (1 + \Delta)$
Profit of the strategy	Δ

and by extreme motions; this point is dealt with in depth in [Alexander 2001]. This text also presents practical methods to identify cointegration phenomena.

It is important to note that cointegration contradicts the hypothesis of market efficiency. Indeed, Granger's causality implies that one may, at least on average, anticipate motions of a stock cointegrated to another one. This prediction capability is at the origin of trading strategies, such as those of *pair trading*, which is illustrated by an example in Table 3.1. Thanks to the cointegration of the two stocks A and B, we could generate a sure profit.

As for the *market efficiency* hypothesis — not to be confused with portfolio efficiency — it assumes that investors are well-informed and that all the available information is reflected in prices. Price variations can only arise from new information, which is random by nature. In the example of the above table, the market efficiency theory leads to the following result: if cointegration property were true, it would not be possible that $2\ln(A_t) - \ln(B_t)$ diverges from its average, since the smallest of gaps would instantly be corrected by investors. In other words, everyone would implement this pair trading strategy, which would make it unusable in practice.

This discussion is that of two economists who hang about in a street, when one of them notices a $10 bill lying in the gutter. When he stoops in order to pick the bill up, his colleague tells him "Silly, if the bill were real, it would already have been picked up" [Joshi 2008]. Globally, it is on this skeptical position that most of financial mathematics relies. The heart of financial mathematics theory relies indeed on the non-arbitrage theory, which we shall address in the following chapter.

Chapter 4

No-arbitrage Theory

The traditional saying *there is no free lunch*, often used by economists to recall that any favor has its counterpart, has been integrated in the vocabulary of financial markets to convey the following idea: one does not make money on financial markets without taking risks. *Quants* speak of *arbitrage* to describe a sure profit made, without risk, thanks to a counterparty that purchased too high or sold too cheaply. In fact, the mathematical models used in finance can be divided into two categories:

- Those which aim at identifying arbitrage opportunities. The models looking for cointegration which we examined in the preceding chapter belong to this category. In practice however, these models do not guarantee a risk-free profit — one can never be sure, for example, that a cointegration phenomenon observed in the past will continue in the future.
- Those which aim at modeling risks and asset evolution in an environment without any arbitrage possibility. It is indeed crucial that computed prices are arbitrage free. No counterparty should be able to take advantage of an overevaluation or underevaluation of asset prices. This is the category of models we shall, from now on, be interested in and whose framework will be defined in the present chapter.

We open this chapter with binomial trees, which represent a simple and rich model to address the problematics of no-arbitrage.

They confront us with different concepts which we shall explicit in the second section; we shall then be able to state the famous no-arbitrage theorem, formalized by Harrison, Kreps and Pliska between 1979 and 1981. Unfortunately, this theorem does not ensure the existence of a unique arbitrage-free price. Sometimes, a whole range of prices is possible: this is the problem of completeness, which we shall study in the third section. The original theorem was formulated in a simplified framework, and its adaptation to the general case was the subject of technical work by [Delbaen and Schachermayer 1994] and [Delbaen and Schachermayer 1998]. We shall attempt to explain in the last section some problems raised by this generalization.The reader with a good background in advanced mathematics and who wishes to study the subject in depth is referred to [Delbaen and Schachermayer 2005].

Box 4.1. Quants. The name *quant* refers to people in charge of mathematical modeling in banks and more generally in the financial industry, with the exception of insurance where mathematicians are rather called actuaries. The expression stems from the adjective "quantitative", often used because financial mathematics are termed *quantitative finance* and people in charge of modeling are *quantitative analysts.*

4.1 Binomial trees

Binomial trees are models of asset prices evolution which are particularly simple, useful and highly instructive. In these models, at each time t, assets have only two possibilities of evolution. For example, an asset which is worth 100 at $T = 0$ in Figure 4.1 can only be worth 95 or 110 at time $T = 1$. If the asset was worth 110 at $T = 1$, at $T = 2$ it can only evolve towards 115 or 100, and so forth.

The number of nodes of the tree grows exponentially in this configuration: at the beginning, the asset can only have one value, which is observed today on markets. After the first time step, tomorrow, two values are possible, four after the second time step, and then eight, 16, 32 ... and 2^n at $T = n$. Bearing in mind that 2^{365} is larger than the number of atoms in the Universe, we are at a clear

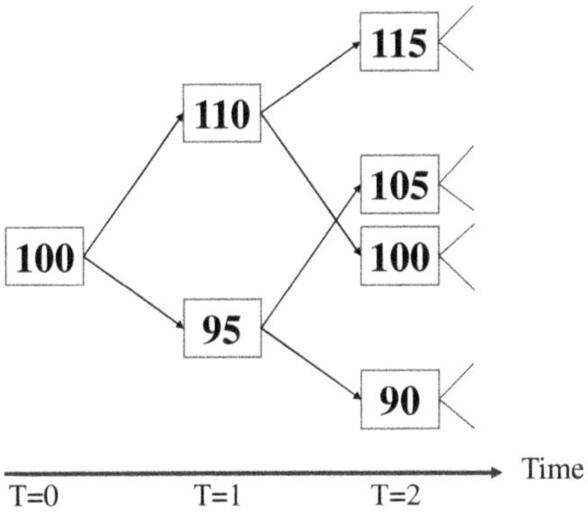

Figure 4.1: Example of a binomial tree. At each node, the asset has two possibilities of evolution.

risk of encountering a technical problem. This issue is bypassed by using recombining trees: in these trees, it is equivalent to go up and then down, or to go down and then up. Nodes are said to recombine. In this new configuration, illustrated in Figure 4.2(a), the number of final nodes evolves linearly with the number of time steps: there exist two possible values of the asset price at the first time step, three at the second one, four at the third one ... and 101 after 100 iterations. This looks much more reasonable.

We thus described binomial trees: the asset starts at time $t = 0$ from a known value and evolves at each instant following a tree such as drawn in Figure 4.2(a). The different trees will be distinguished by:

- the value of the asset at each node;
- the probability for the asset to access the lower or the upper node.

Let us first examine a degenerate tree, that of Figure 4.3. In this tree, the value of the asset can only increase. By investing in such an asset, we can make a sure profit, that is, an *arbitrage*. Such a situation is very unlikely to occur in markets: were it the case, everyone would invest in this asset, which would automatically increase its price until its evolution does not any longer guarantee a sure profit. We can also see the problem in the following way: no counterparty will sell 100 an asset whose value will evolve with certainty either towards 105

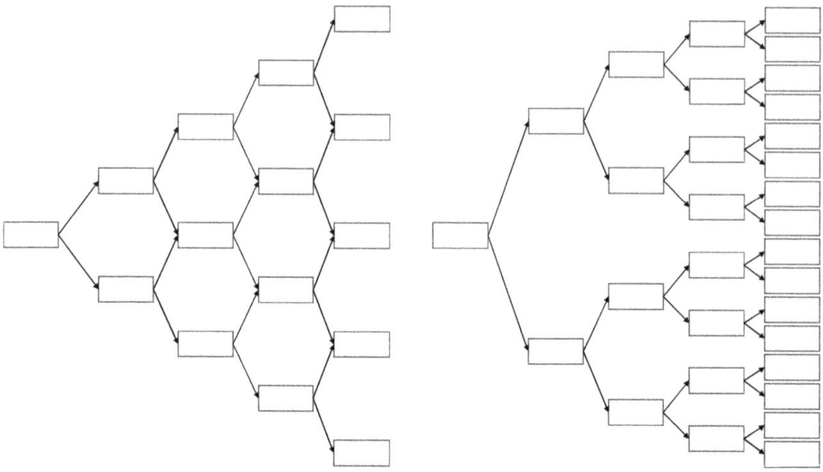

(a) Recombining tree (b) Non-recombining tree

Figure 4.2: Recombining tree (a) and non-recombining one (b) after four time steps. The left-hand tree possesses five final nodes, and the right-hand one 16 final nodes.

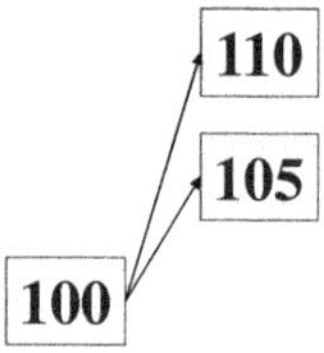

Figure 4.3: Example of a degenerate tree where the asset value can only grow.

or towards 110. The counterparty will necessarily ask for a fair price lying between 105 and 110.

We need to somewhat refine the preceding considerations as the present valuation phenomena studied in the first chapter were not yet taken into account. As studied in the preceding chapter, actual profits are measured by the excess of return over the risk-free rate. Thus, if the interest rates in one time step are 7%, Figure 4.3 does not present arbitrage opportunity any longer: the asset may bring either a profit (if it rises to 110) or a loss (if it only rises to 105), compared to the risk-free rate. In order to make the reasoning of the preceding paragraph completely valid, one has to study at each node of the tree the present value of the asset rather than the projected future values. This present value effectively accounts for today's value (at $T = 0$) of a product which is financed at the risk-free rate. For the benefit of clarity, we shall neglect in what follows interest rates and present valuation phenomena. In other words, we shall assume that interest rates are zero.

Box 4.2. Arbitrage. Arbitrage consists in taking advantage of an imperfection of financial markets, for example a counterparty which sells financial products too cheaply, to make a profit without any risk of loss. In other words, an arbitrage strategy generates a profit with a non-zero probability, but never entails losses. The no-arbitrage theory aims at exploring the mathematical consequences of the assumption according to which there are no arbitrage opportunities. This hypothesis is motivated by the idea that any opportunity of this kind is immediately grabbed by traders, which leads to a new market equilibrium. It is postulated by quants, not because they are sure that there are no arbitrage opportunities, but in order to ensure that their models do not lead to prices exhibiting arbitrage opportunities. However, it may happen that a model leads to arbitrage opportunities in theory, but not in practice, given the costs and margins in transactions, the impossibility of a continuous intervention on markets, the difficulty in implementing some short sellings, etc.

The no-arbitrage constraint thus prevents a situation like that of Figure 4.3, and the asset price necessarily lies between its future minimum and maximum values. Let us keep in mind this first property and study a second property, which deals with the price of derivatives. Let us imagine that we wish to market the following financial product: let us note S_1 the price of an asset at $T = 1$, and let us offer to our customers the value S_1 if $S_1 > 98$ and 98 otherwise. This is a simple and legible derivative product: we allow our customers to benefit from a possible rise of the asset while ensuring that the final payment will be in all cases at least 98.

$$\text{payment at } T = 1 : \begin{cases} S_1 \text{ if } S_1 > 98 \\ 98 \text{ otherwise} \end{cases} \tag{4.1}$$

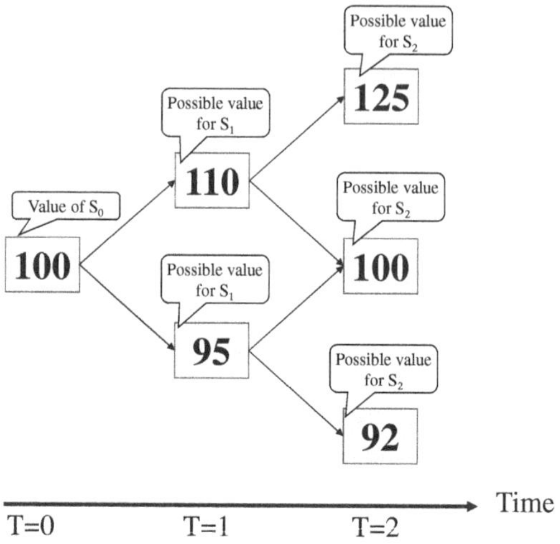

Figure 4.4: Example of an evolution model of a stock in a recombining binomial tree.

Our question is then the following one: at which price should we sell our financial product? With binomial tree models, under the no-arbitrage hypothesis, there is only one right answer to this question. Indeed, suppose that our asset evolves in conformity with the binomial tree of Figure 4.4 and let us build the following portfolio:

- purchase of \$22 of cash, that is, a deposit of \$22 on our bank account;
- purchase of 4/5 of the stock, that is \$80 of stock (since the stock is exchanged at \$100 at $T = 0$).

The price of this portfolio is \$102, without any ambiguity. It is the price which was paid for purchasing it ($22 + 80$). At time $T = 1$, it exactly duplicates the financial product:

- **Case 1:** $S_1 = 110$. The portfolio is worth at $T = 1$: $22 + 80\% \times 110 = \$110$.
- **Case 2.** $S_1 = 95$. The portfolio is worth at $T = 1$: $22 + 80\% \times 95 = \$98$.

We have just duplicated the financial product which we wished to market, and which is described by equation (4.1), from a portfolio composed of cash and of the underlying stock. The duplication of a financial product with a portfolio of other very simple financial products (cash and stocks) is named *replication*. This possibility of replicating the financial product is not due to chance, and we will come back to it. It ensures that the sole possible price of the financial product is \$102. Indeed, Table 4.1 below shows how one might implement an arbitrage, a sure profit, if someone tried to sell the product at another price.

Table 4.1

	Arbitrage strategy if the given price is lower than \$102	Arbitrage strategy if the given price is greater than \$102
Given price for the financial product	100	104
Arbitrage strategy	Buy the financial product, for \$100 Sell 4/5 of a stock, for −\$80 Borrow \$20, for −\$20	Sell the financial product, for −\$104 Buy 4/5 of the stock, for \$80 Keep \$24 in cash, for \$24
Initial cost of the strategy	\$0	\$0
Strategy value at time $T = 1$ if $S = 110$	$110 - 80\% \times 110 - 20 = \$2$	$-110 + 80\% \times 110 + 24 = \$2$
Strategy value at time $T = 1$ if $S = 95$	$98 - 80\% \times 95 - 20 = \$2$	$-98 + 80\% \times 95 + 24 = \$2$
Riskless profit	\$2	\$2

This capacity of replicating financial products from cash and underlying stocks may be extended to every product if one assumes a binomial tree dynamics. Figure 4.5 displays the replication of a product similar to that we just examined, but whose time of application of the formula is $T = 2$ and not $T = 1$. The fundamental reason for this result is a mere consequence of elementary algebra: replicating a derivative product amounts to solving for each node a system of two equations with two unknowns. In a binomial tree, the asset can, at each node, only rise or fall; there is only one degree of freedom

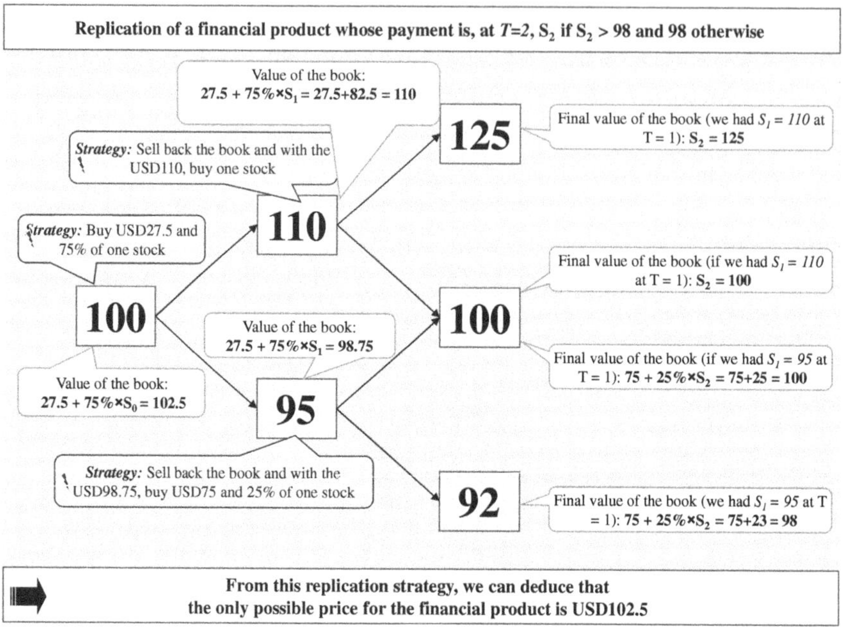

Figure 4.5: Replication of a derivative product within the framework of a binomial tree.

for the evolution. When we replicate a product, we choose at each node the proportion of cash and the proportion of the underlying stock which we may hold, and we also have a single degree of freedom. There are thus as many possibilities of replication as of asset evolution. Of course, in a more complex model of asset evolution, the result is no longer necessarily valid.

Thanks to the possibility provided by binomial trees to replicate financial products, we have been able to compute a product price which is the sole arbitrage-free one. The reader may have been surprised to notice that, up to now, we did not make any assumption on the probabilities of the asset evolution. Whatever the probabilities of rise and fall of the asset, the reasoning we followed is always valid and the price of the derivative can only be 102! Yet, it seems obvious that an investor, who thinks that the asset has practically no chance of rising, will be reluctant to purchase 102 such a product (the latter having, according to the expectations of the investor, hardly any chance to differ from the stock which is bought at a price $100 < 102$). Let us remind the reader that our goal here is not to predict market evolutions, but to deduce from the market structure the properties of assets. If it is really true that the stock has practically no chance to rise, then the market is wrong when assigning the value 100 to the stock. But, given today's value of 100 and the possible tomorrow's values of 95 and 110, the derivative product can only be worth \$102.

Everything goes on as if the asset's probability of rise was 1/3 and if today's prices were the average of the possible future prices. Indeed, in that case, the average value of the future asset price is $110/3 + 95 \times 2/3 = 100$; the average value of the future price of the derivative product defined by equation (4.1) is $110/3 + 98 \times 2/3 = 102$. This evolution probability is a fictitious one, nothing indicates that the asset actually has a 33% probability of rise. This means that there exists a fictitious probability under which we can compute today's prices as the average of future prices. This result is illustrated in Figure 4.6. This probability is called the risk neutral probability, because, under this probability measure, risk is not rewarded. In reality, a quite opposite opinion prevails, since if one invests in a stock, it is not with the idea that its future average value will be equal to today's. In fact, taking a risk must be rewarded, and the future average value must be larger than the present one.

The existence of this risk neutral probability leads to a drastic simplification of the computations. Suppose, for example, that the possible future values of the asset are no longer 95 and 110, but 90 and 115. The risk neutral probability of this new tree is easily computed; it corresponds to a 40% probability of rise and a 60% probability of fall. These are the only probabilities $\text{Prob}_{\text{rise}}$ and $\text{Prob}_{\text{fall}}$ which obey:

$$\text{Prob}_{\text{rise}} \times 115 + \text{Prob}_{\text{fall}} \times 90 = 100$$

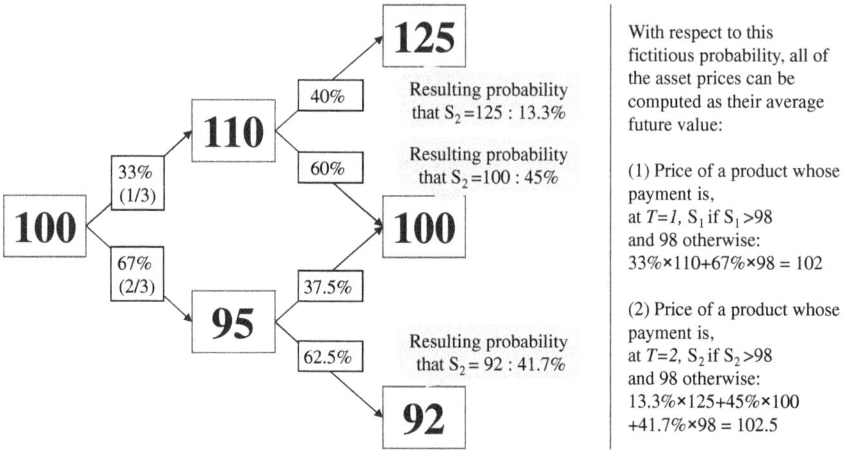

Figure 4.6: Risk neutral probability in the binomial tree under study.

Knowing these risk neutral probabilities, we can compute the value of the derivative product thanks to the formula:

$$40\% \times 115 + 60\% \times 98 = 104.8$$

We did not have to detail the entire replication strategy in order to compute the price.

Does this fictitious risk neutral probability always exist? The answer is positive, thanks to the no-arbitrage property. Let us recall the first consequence of no-arbitrage which we have exhibited, namely the one that states that the tree of Figure 4.3 cannot exist: the present asset price must lie between its maximum and minimum future values. In this configuration, it is always possible to correctly assign a probability to events in such a way that the current value of the asset is the weighted average of its future values. Thus, no-arbitrage ensures the existence of a fictitious risk-neutral probability measure.

Is this probability always unique? This answer is positive for binomial trees. The uniqueness of this probability stems from the algebra of the degrees of freedom: there is one degree of freedom for the probability, since $\text{Prob}_{\text{rise}} = 1 - \text{Prob}_{\text{fall}}$, and one equation of constraint: the weighted future prices is equal to today's.

The binomial tree model is highly instructive. We learned that, in this particular model:

- It is possible to replicate all derivative products.
- Prices of derivative products do not depend on the actual rise or fall probabilities of the asset.
- One can define a unique probability under which prices of all assets are their future average values.
- This allows us to compute the unique arbitrage-free price of derivative products.
- The price depends, however, on the tree structure, that is, on the value listed at each node of the tree.

In the next section, we shall leave the specific framework of binomial trees and study these properties in the general case.

4.2 The no-arbitrage theorem (discrete case)

We are by now familiar with the modeling of the prices of financial products by a random process S_t: S_0 is today's value of the asset and S_t, which represents the asset price at time t, is for $t > 0$ a random variable — that is, a variable which can take different values according to some probability laws. For example, in the case of the binomial tree of Figure 4.4, we have $S_0 = 100$, $S_1 = 110$ with some probability and $S_1 = 95$ otherwise.

A trading strategy is simply to hold at time t some quantity of asset and some amount of liquidity, called cash. These quantities are also random variables, which may depend on the asset past values, but not on its future values. A strategy will be termed self-funded if it is not necessary to bring cash during the strategy to implement it. For example, the strategy displayed in Figure 4.5 is self-funded: when one modifies the proportion of stock and cash, this is done without cash inflow nor outflow. The self-funded strategy is materialized by a simple equation; the interested reader may look for it as an exercise (define the amount of cash c_t and of stock α_t, and link $c_t, c_{t+1}, \alpha_t, \alpha_{t+1}, S_t$ and S_{t+1}).

Thanks to this formalization, we can rigorously define what is an *arbitrage opportunity*: it is a self-funded strategy which may generate profit but never generates losses. In other words, we make money with a non-zero probability, while being sure of never losing any. *The no-arbitrage hypothesis precisely states that this kind of strategy does not exist.* We shall now address the consequences of this hypothesis.

Let us go on with our generalization: we saw that, under some probability, the future average value of the asset is equal to its current value. This property bears a name in mathematics: *martingales.* A random process S_t is a martingale if at every instant T and knowing that $S_T = s$ (mathematicians say conditionally to $S_T = s$), the average value of S_{T+1} can only be s. This is exactly the property observed on the binomial tree of Figure 4.6: the value at each node is equal to the weighted average values of the asset at the following nodes. In other words, a martingale is a stochastic process in which the expectation of the next value knowing the current value is the current value.

Mathematical martingales are endowed with numerous properties which we shall not review here. Nevertheless, one of them is useful to better understand martingales, the "optional stopping theorem". Let us consider a martingale M_t and assume it represents the value of a trading porfolio. We recall that the average value of the martingale at every instant t is its initial value M_0. Let us imagine that we define a strategy which requires to stop trading at time τ. This time τ may itself be a random variable which depends on previous values of M_t, but not on future values. Once more, we forbid any predictability. The crucial point is that τ be bounded, that is, there exists a predetermined time $T_{\max}$ such that $\tau \leq T_{\max}$ (for example, $T_{\max} = 100$ years, with the idea that any strategy which ends up in more than a century is useless). For example, the strategy may be to stop at time τ as soon as $M_\tau = \$10{,}000$, or after 100 years if M_τ never reaches \$10,000 during the century. The optional stopping time theorem states that the average value of M_τ, when applying the halting strategy, is M_0; in other words a strategy which unwinds in a bounded time cannot bring any profit on average. It is precisely for this reason that casino gamblers cannot win: since the evolution of a balanced game follows a martingale (in a mathematical sense), any strategy which stops within a finite time interval brings zero profit on average. If the game is biased against the gambler, as in a casino, the strategy will be a losing one on average. However, we may try to adopt the following classical double or quit strategy: at each move, if the global profit is positive, we stop the game, otherwise, we double down. This strategy does bring a sure profit, as it only stops when a profit is observed. True enough, but the optional stopping theorem then proves that this strategy may last indefinitely. Thus, using mathematical martingales and the optional stopping theorem, mathematicians demonstrate that we cannot bias a fair game in our favor.

Before concluding, one needs to introduce the last pillar of the theory: the equivalent probability measure. Mathematicians consider financial assets as random variables subjected to some probability laws. They give themselves the possibility to build an imaginary world in which probabilities can be modified. The difficulty is then to make the link between their fictitious world and the actual one. We saw in the framework of the binomial tree that we could sit in a fictitious "risk neutral" world in which actual asset prices were future average values weighted by fictitious probabilities, named risk neutral probabilities. This is exactly what we are going to do in a general case, however with the following constraint: the probability measures, actual and fictitious, must be "equivalent", that is, events with non-zero probabilities must be the same in the two probability measures. In the case of a binomial tree, it means that the fictitious measure must exactly have the same nodes, it can neither add nor subtract a node which does not exist in the actual measure. We now have at our disposal the three key notions (arbitrage strategy, martingale, equivalent probability measure) necessary to state the no-arbitrage theorem.

Theorem. If there are no arbitrage opportunities (that is, no risk-free profit), there exists a fictitious probability measure, equivalent to the actual probability measure, under which the real prices of all assets are martingales.

In practice, this theorem leads to three consequences in modeling product prices:

- The random process S_t cannot be any process: it must admit a probability measure, equivalent to the actual one, under which it is a martingale. This implies that model builders are not at liberty to do whatever they like when designing their models, and, for example, situations such that of Figure 4.3 must be avoided.
- We can take the point of view of the imaginary world, of the fictitious risk-neutral probability, to simplify computations. Today's prices are the same under the actual and fictitious measures, otherwise the measures would not be equivalent. Actual current prices may thus be computed as the average of future values weighted by the probabilities of the fictitious measure. Examples of this computation technique will be given in the next chapter.
- In some models, such as the binomial tree, there exists only one equivalent measure under which the process S_t is a martingale: thus, the theorem allows us to compute without ambiguity the price of any financial product, regardless of actual probabilities.

We shall address in detail the last two points in the following chapters, as all our models will be considered within the framework of the equivalent risk-neutral measure. Let us come back to the first point. Suppose that someone suggests that you invest money in a product whose value is at each instant the square of the Dow Jones index (DJ) level. You can be sure that this person is incompetent, as the offer looks like a free lunch: his product contradicts no-arbitrage. Indeed, there exists no probability measure such that S_t and S_t^2 are martingales (except if S_t is a constant, which is not the case for the DJ). Building the associated arbitrage strategy is an interesting exercise which is left to the reader. By contrast, a dealer may propose an investment whose value at given time T will be given by the square of the value of the DJ at T. Between t and T, the value of the investment will necessarily be different from the square of the DJ level.

4.3 Completeness

The no-arbitrage theorem is very powerful, but it does not solve all problems: the case of the binomial tree, where the equivalent risk-neutral measure is unique, is a fortunate accident, but it cannot be generalized. Indeed, in the general case, nothing ensures that there exists only one single risk-neutral probability measure. Let us, for example, look at trinomial trees such as those represented in Figure 4.7.

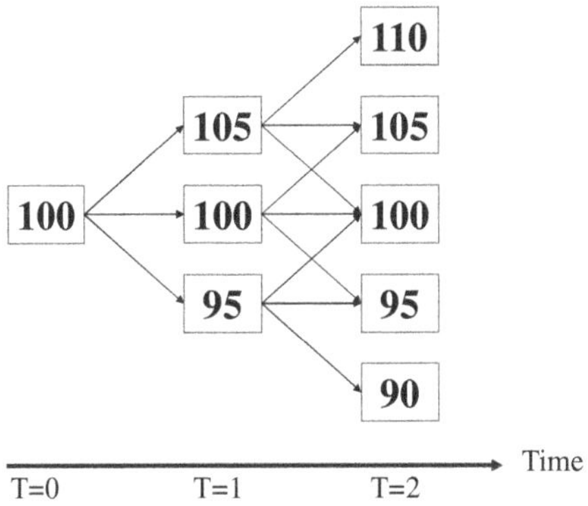

Figure 4.7: Example of a trinomial tree.

It is clear that there exist many probability measures under which the asset evolving along the tree of Figure 4.7 is a martingale. This is illustrated in Figure 4.8. Contrary to the framework of the binomial tree, we have one additional degree of freedom which makes possible the existence of many risk-neutral measures.

In the section dealing with binomial trees, we considered two financial products: the first one paid at $T = 1$, S_1 if $S_1 > 98$, and 98 otherwise; the second one paid at $T = 2$, S_2 if $S_2 > 98$, and 98 otherwise. We are dealing with financial assets, and thus their prices must be a martingale under the risk-neutral measure. Now, using the measures A and B from Figure 4.8, we land on different prices as shown in Table 4.2.

Table 4.2

	Financial product 1	Financial product 2
Description	Payoff at $T = 1$: S_1 if $S_1 > 98$ and 98 otherwise	Payoff at $T = 2$: S_2 if $S_2 > 98$ and 98 otherwise
Price under risk neutral measure A	$40\% \times 105 + 20\% \times 100 + 40\% \times 98 = 101.2$	$16\% \times 110 + 16\% \times 105 + 36\% \times 100 + 16\% \times 98 + 16\% \times 98 = 101.76$
Price under risk neutral measure B	$30\% \times 105 + 40\% \times 100 + 30\% \times 98 = 100.9$	$3\% \times 110 + 42\% \times 105 + 13\% \times 100 + 36\% \times 98 + 6\% \times 98 = 101.56$

What is the right price for our financial products? To the best of our knowledge, the two prices are correct: it is not possible to select a price which would be better than the other. Indeed, there is no arbitrage strategy which would allow us to take advantage of prices computed either from measure A, or from measure B. All prices computable from equivalent risk-neutral measures are correct in the sense that they do not generate arbitrage opportunities. Thus, in the case of a trinomial tree, no-arbitrage does not guarantee a unique price, but a whole range of arbitrage-free prices.

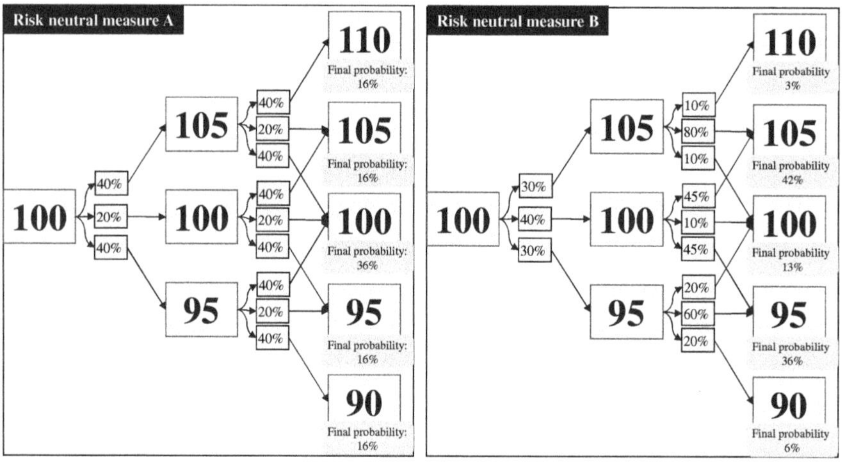

Figure 4.8: Two equivalent risk neutral measures on the same trinomial tree.

It is even possible to precisely compute this set. Let us concentrate on the financial product 1 which stops at $T = 1$. If we note Prob_{95}, Prob_{100} and Prob_{105} the risk neutral probabilities for the asset evolution, we can show[1] that $\text{Prob}_{95} = \text{Prob}_{105}$, with, of course, $\text{Prob}_{100} = 1 - \text{Prob}_{95} - \text{Prob}_{105}$. With respect to the binomial tree, we have one additional degree of freedom, to which is associated the arbitrary choice of Prob_{95}. In order that all probabilities lie between 0 and 1, it is necessary and sufficient that $0 < \text{Prob}_{95} < 0.5$. The arbitrage-free prices of the financial product 1 will be all the prices which may be computed from the formula:

$$\begin{aligned} 105 \times \text{Prob}_{95} + 100 \times (1 - 2 \times \text{Prob}_{95}) + 98 \times \text{Prob}_{95} \\ = 100 + 3 \times \text{Prob}_{95} \\ \in]100; 101.5[\end{aligned} \tag{4.2}$$

Thus, thanks to the no-arbitrage theorem, we could state that the price of the financial product must lie between 100 and 101.5. This is already a piece of information, but it is not enough to define a price.

Mathematical models for the evolution of financial products are clearly divided into two categories. Complete models (binomial tree, Black-Scholes model which we shall study in the next chapter) are those which admit a unique equivalent risk-neutral measure. These models are simple, and not realistic. By contrast, the advantage of the uniqueness of the arbitrage-free price is tremendous. In these models, financial products may be replicated by simple strategies. There is no need to make assumptions on the actual probabilities of asset evolutions. This point is crucial, as modeling probabilities of future events is by definition the kind of guesswork which mathematicians generally hate.

Incomplete models, such as trinomial trees, are those for which there is no uniqueness of risk-neutral measure. Unfortunately, these models represent a large part of more refined models (models with stochastic volatility, models with jumps etc.), some of which will be examined in Chapters 6 and 9. In these models, the sole assumption of no-arbitrage is not sufficient, and additional choices are necessary to determine prices of financial products.

---

[1]Use the equations $\text{Prob}_{95} \times 95 + \text{Prob}_{100} \times 100 + \text{Prob}_{105} \times 105 = 100$ and $\text{Prob}_{95} + \text{Prob}_{100} + \text{Prob}_{105} = 1$.

4.4 The continuum case*

In Sections 4.1 and 4.2, we implicitly assumed a discrete universe, that is, a universe where time $T = 1, 2, 3\ldots$ and asset values, $S_T = 95, 100, 105\ldots$ take discrete values. In a general framework, we rather work with a time T and price possibilities S_T that are continuous variables which may take any positive value. Adapting the no-arbitrage theory to the continuum framework is a very important issue, as most models of asset evolution use, in fact, continuous variables.

We saw in the discrete case that it is crucial that process S_t displays, in any situation, an opportunity of profit and an opportunity of loss. This characteristic is actually equivalent to either one of the two properties (i) there is no possibility of arbitrage and (ii) there exists an equivalent martingale measure. The equivalence between (i) and (ii) is indeed enunciated by the no-arbitrage theorem. In the continuum framework, one must take into account an additional component: the process variability. This variability represents how erratic the process can be, or, in other words, the extent to which its variations during an infinitesimal time interval may be large. This introduces an additional dimension into the analysis, which makes it more complex.

Considering a random process S_t, we may be interested in the possible different values of S_T at a given time T. We may also be interested in the different paths S_t which the process may follow for $0<t<T$ to go from its initial value S_0 to its final one S_T. It is clear that many different paths may start from the same initial point, then part and arrive at the same final point. In a continuum framework, these paths may be more or less erratic, they may be smooth and continuous (in a mathematical sense), continuous but with many sharp fluctuations, completely discontinuous, etc.

The variability issue does not arise in the discrete case, as time itself is discrete and variations from one instant to another can only proceed by jumps. It is interesting to notice that a risky asset cannot be governed by a random process for which all paths are smooth: this

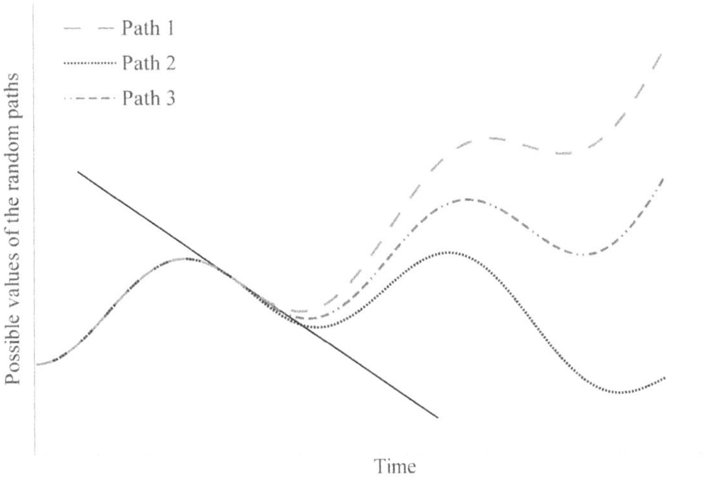

Figure 4.9: An example of a random process whose trajectories (three trajectories in this case) are smooth. The trajectories part only slowly from their tangent.

would create arbitrage opportunities. Indeed, smooth enough curves possess a tangent, and they evolve close to this tangent at least during a short period of time. During this period of time, evolution is predictable (at least to first order) since it follows the tangent: if, for example, the slope is negative, one is sure that, at least for a short period of time, the asset will fall whatever path is followed. This is illustrated in Figure 4.9. If evolution is predictable, there is an arbitrage opportunity. Thus, in the absence of arbitrage opportunity, risky assets cannot be modeled by processes that are too regular.

The first idea is thus that processes must be variable enough so that they cannot be predictable. Conversely, if the processes are completely erratic, we face other problems. We shall see, later on, that martingales have a well-defined variability and that a process where the variations are too erratic cannot be a martingale. Let us take the example of a random process where each value of S_t is independent from the other values $S_{t'}$, $(t' \neq t)$; one says that the process has no memory of its past values. Such a process is completely erratic as S_t is completely disconnected from $S_{t+\varepsilon}$, however small ε is. This situation also leads to an arbitrage opportunity, since it is enough to invest as soon as S_t lies below its average value and to sell the investment off as soon as S_t goes above it. As the S_t values are entirely independent, the strategy certainly works in an infinitely short time interval since between T and $T + \varepsilon$, the asset takes an infinity of independent values: it is certain that at least one of them, say the value of S_τ, will be larger than the average. And since S_T was smaller than the average, one makes a profit by buying S_T and selling S_τ.

The variability of the process paths is thus an essential issue which must be quantified. The first indication is the path length. Assume that a stock is worth 100 at $T = 0$ and 110 at $T = 10$. The shortest path from one point to another is a straight line, so the least variable path is given by a linear interpolation: in this case, for $0 < t < 10$, the value of the stock would be $100 + t$ (curve 1 of Figure 4.10); the length of the path traveled by the stock is then 14.14. However, a stock does not generally follow a straight line. If it followed curve 2 of Figure 4.10, the traveled distance would be larger; it is easy to visualize this, and the computation shows that the exact length is then 24.12. However, we just saw that a stock cannot follow a smooth curve, and paths rather look like curve 3. The length of this curve is actually infinite. Thus, we just defined a first qualitative notion of

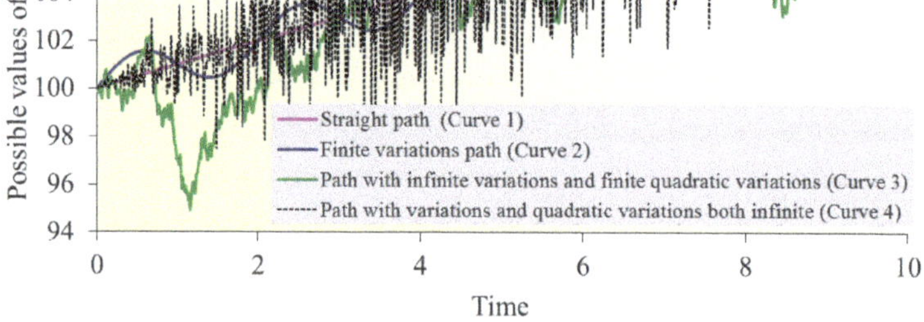

Figure 4.10: Illustration of the path variability: to go from 100 to 110, there are many, more or less regular, or more or less erratic, trajectories.

variability, which is the length of the path. A first question arises: should the path length of a random process that represents a risky asset be finite or not?

If the length of all the paths of a random process is finite, one says that the process has a finite variations. If all the paths are of infinite length, the process is said to have infinite variations. There may also exist degenerate processes such that some of its trajectories have a finite length and some other trajectories an infinite one. For a given process, whose all trajectories have a finite length, this property is still valid when one uses equivalent fictitious probability measures. Indeed, we may reformulate this property as follows: the probability that this process has a path of infinite length is zero. Since, by the very definition of the equivalent probability measure,[2] we are not allowed to modify events with zero probabilities, the property will hold true for all the equivalent fictitious probabilities. Thus, the fact that a random process has a finite variation does not depend upon the probability measure that is used.

Among the paths of infinite length, it is possible to single out those which are more regular than others. We shall not enter the mathematical details, but it is important to be aware that one may compute a second-order variation, which is a refinement of the first-order one, namely the path length. This second-order variation is termed the quadratic variations. Processes of finite variations will generally have zero quadratic variations; processes with non-zero quadratic variations will generally have infinite first-order variations. The quadratic variations is a higher order measure of path variability. For example, curve 3 of Figure 4.10 exhibits infinite variations, but finite quadratic variations; it is more regular than curve 4 whose variations and quadratic variations are infinite. We could pursue with the elaboration of other variability measures in order to single out processes with infinite quadratic variations, but we shall stop here for a simple reason: martingales, which model products' prices in

[2]Recall that probability measures are said to be equivalent if the events with non-zero probabilities are the same in the two probability measures.

risk-neutral worlds as they guarantee the absence of risk-free profit, are random processes with finite quadratic variations. It means that all their paths are of finite quadratic variations.

The analysis of variability can also be used to decompose processes into two components: drift and randomness. The drift represents the evolution of the average which should evolve smoothly, it is a finite variations process. In usual models, randomness has finite quadratic variations and has no drift: it is a martingale. Indeed, processes that model financial assets are the sum of two components:

- a component representing pure randomness, which must be a martingale;
- a component representing the drift, the predictable evolution, which must be a finite variations process.

The processes just defined above are termed *semi-martingales.* In order to characterize these semi-martingales, quants write

$$\mathrm{d}S_t = u \times \mathrm{d}t + \mathrm{d}M_t \tag{4.3}$$

This equation conveys the decomposition defined above.

- The term $\mathrm{d}S_t$ represents the variation over a very short time interval of the process S_t, that is, its increase $S_{t+\mathrm{d}t} - S_t$.
- The term $u \times \mathrm{d}t$ is the drift. Indeed, $\mathrm{d}t$ is the time variation and u the drift per unit of time. On average, the process grows with time for positive u, and decreases when u is negative. The drift u may be time dependent, for example to predict that the growth of the process is going to slow down with time. It can even be a function of S_t, for example to account for the fact that if S_t is too large, the drift will become negative to bring the process back to its average, and conversely.
- The term $\mathrm{d}M_t$ is nothing else than the evolution $M_{t+\mathrm{d}t} - M_t$ of a martingale over the time interval $\mathrm{d}t$.

Within our present state of knowledge, the continuum version of the no-arbitrage theorem uniquely applies to the framework of semi-martingales, and not to all random processes. Before stating the theorem, it is necessary to refine the notion of the absence of arbitrage opportunity. We must introduce the notion of *no free lunch with vanishing risk*, that is, the absence of any arbitrage strategy whose risk tends towards zero. In the discrete framework, we forbade the possibility of making money while being sure of not losing any. *Stricto sensu*, the arbitrage strategy is risk free: the probability that this strategy loses money is zero. In the continuum case, we forbid making money with a risk of losing that is arbitrarily small. The lower the risk that is taken, and the lower the profit must be. If it is possible to achieve a given profit with an arbitrarily small level of risk, there is an arbitrage opportunity in the sense of a free lunch with vanishing risk. These considerations allow us to state the continuous version of the no-arbitrage theorem, in the form proven by [Delbaen and Schachermayer 1998].

Theorem. If assets are represented by semi-martingales, and if there are no arbitrage opportunities with an arbitrarily small risk, then there exists an equivalent probability measure under which asset prices are martingales.

It is important to notice that we have entered a completely abstract world; that of continuous processes. In reality, stock prices are discrete. In reality, our clocks and our reaction times do not have a perfect accuracy: continuous time remains an abstraction. We thus built an imaginary world, and for this imaginary world to be consistent, we had to impose restrictions, among which one is very important: stock prices must not be too erratic, and their evolution is necessarily represented by a curve with finite quadratic variations. But this idea of variability is somewhat an abstraction, since it only exists in the imaginary world of continuous processes. Whether or not modeling actual processes by continuous processes with finite quadratic variations is a fair approximation of reality, remains an open question.

Chapter 5

The Black-Scholes Model

In 1997, Robert Merton and Myron Scholes won the Nobel prize in economy for their work carried out with Fisher Black (deceased in 1995) on the pricing of derivatives. They devised the Black-Scholes model, also called the Black-Scholes-Merton model, which we shall study in the present chapter. This model underlies the framework of most of the financial mathematics.

The mathematical basis of the model is the Brownian motion which we shall address in the first section. The founding father of the use of Brownian motion in finance is Louis Bachelier, who introduced it in his thesis [Bachelier 1900]. However, the structure of Brownian motion is not directly applicable to financial products: for example, Brownian motions may take negative values, while stocks' values can only be positive. We shall see in Section 5.2 in what sense the exponential of Brownian motions, called lognormal motion, properly characterizes financial assets. In 1973, [Black and Scholes 1973] and [Merton 1973] introduced and structured the use of this lognormal motion in finance. They built a risk-neutral environment designed for the valuation and study of financial products. This led to the Black-Scholes model, which is the subject of the third section. We shall conclude the chapter with the notion of implied volatility, which is a way of taking into account the fact that the stocks dynamics are not lognormal in reality.

5.1 Brownian motion

The preceding chapter has led us towards a mathematical object fundamental in finance: continuous stochastic processes. Continuous stochastic processes are described mathematically by random variables X_t labeled by a continuous time t. As future stocks prices are not predictable, it is common to assume that their value are modeled by a random variable X. This random variable depends on time horizon t : the probability distribution is different between tomorrow's prices, at $t = 1$ day, and next year's one ($t = 1$ year). Intuitively, the more the time passes, the more the prices are uncertain and hence, the more volatile is the random variable X_t. By convention, the current time is $t = 0$ and the current stock value is X_0 (X_0 is a real number, not a random variable).

In the present section, we study the most famous continuous stochastic process: Brownian motion. Intuitively, one should be able to build a continuous stochastic process as the limit of a discrete time process, in the same way as a continuous function may be

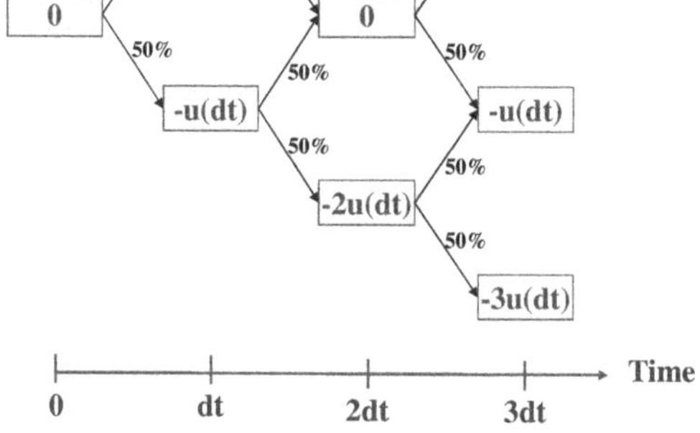

Figure 5.1: Regular binomial tree whose time step is dt and whose variation at each step is $u(dt)$. In this representation, one should imagine trees whose time step dt is infinitesimal.

approximated by a piecewise constant one when the steps go to zero. In the framework of stochastic processes, our building block is the binomial tree. We are thus going to build Brownian motion as the limit of binomial trees with smaller and smaller time steps.

In order to do so, we start from the simplest trees: the time step of the tree is noted $\mathrm{d}t$ and, at each node of the tree, the process has a 50% probability of going upwards and a 50% probability of going downwards. The size of the variations is constant over time, but it depends on the time step $\mathrm{d}t$ — it is noted $u(\mathrm{d}t)$ and it is positive by convention. At each node, the process can thus rise or fall by $u(\mathrm{d}t)$ as in the tree represented in Figure 5.1. The value of the process at time T, that is after $T/\mathrm{d}t$ time steps, is a random variable noted B_T.

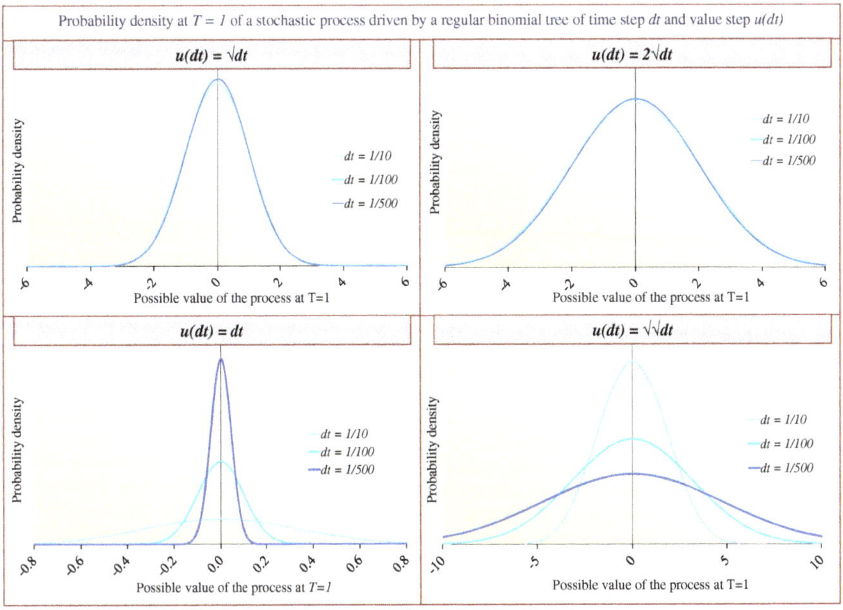

Figure 5.2: Probability distribution of B_T, at time $T = 1$, when the process evolves in a binomial tree such as represented in Figure 5.1 as a function of the time step $\mathrm{d}t$ and the values of $u(\mathrm{d}t)$. When $u(\mathrm{d}t)$ is proportional to $\sqrt{\mathrm{d}t}$, the distribution converges towards a bell shape curve. In the other cases, the distributions collapse towards the vertical axis (B_1 thus takes the single value $B_1 = 0$), or towards the horizontal axis (the very large values are then more and more probable, which prevents convergence).

In order to get closer to continuous processes, we consider the case where the time step $\mathrm{d}t$ is close to 0.

Let us study the possible values of the random variable B_T, for a given time T, according to the various values of $u(\mathrm{d}t)$. Figure 5.2 displays the following features which can be mathematically proven.

- If $u(\mathrm{d}t)$ is on the order of $\sqrt{\mathrm{d}t}$ (in the two upper graphs of Figure 5.2), the distribution of the random variable B_T converges towards a bell shape function, which is nothing else than a normal law.
- If $u(\mathrm{d}t)$ is very small with respect to $\sqrt{\mathrm{d}t}$, for example if $u(\mathrm{d}t) = \mathrm{d}t$, the distribution of B_T is concentrated around the value 0 (the distribution shrinks towards the vertical axis). The smaller the time step, the larger is the probability that $B_T = 0$. In other words, the tree converges towards a constant process, with zero value in our example.
- If $u(\mathrm{d}t)$ is very large with respect to $\sqrt{\mathrm{d}t}$, for example if $u(\mathrm{d}t) = (\mathrm{d}t)^{1/4}$, the distribution of B_T spreads more and more, it becomes close to the horizontal axis. The extreme values are more and more probable and the tree diverges.

There exists a unique situation where the binomial tree converges towards a non-degenerate stochastic process: the case where the size of the variations is proportional to $\sqrt{\mathrm{d}t}$. If variations are larger, then the tree diverges; if they are smaller, then the tree collapses onto zero. We face the same general problems as those evoked in the preceding chapter, that is the question of the variability of continuous stochastic processes. The standard mathematical framework in which these stochastic processes evolve is that of stochastic processes with infinite variations, but with finite quadratic variation. If, on a short time step $\mathrm{d}t$, the characteristic variations of the process are of magnitude $\sqrt{\mathrm{d}t}$, then, it can be proven that the quadratic variation is of magnitude $(\sqrt{\mathrm{d}t})^2/dt = 1$, which means that it is finite.

The knowledge of the characteristic size of the variation is very important to correctly understand the motion. The quantity $\sqrt{\mathrm{d}t}$

is large with respect to dt, which means that a stochastic process varies wildly over very short-time intervals. However, the property that all these variations take randomly positive or negative values ensures that the process remains in general finite and does not diverge at infinity. For variations larger that $\sqrt{dt}$, compensations between positive and negative values do not suffice to contain the tree which finally diverges towards infinity.

When $u(dt)$ is proportional to $\sqrt{dt}$, regular binomial trees converge towards a stochastic process which is nothing else than the famous Brownian motion. In our example (Figure 5.2), this motion will be centered, because we limited ourselves to balanced probabilities: a 50% probability to go upwards, and a 50% probability to go downwards. Within this framework, the motion does not drift, its mean value remains equal to zero. In the general case, the probability distribution of the process at t follows a normal law with a mean value $m \times t$ and a variance $v \times t$, where m and $v > 0$ are parameters which depend on the probabilities of rise and fall of the binomial trees and on the size of their variations $u(dt)$. For example, the binomial trees described in Figure 5.3 are regular, but with unbalanced probabilities, and they converge towards a Brownian motion with an average parameter $m \neq 0$ and a variance parameter $v = \sigma^2$. The m factor thus serves to bias the rise and fall probabilities: if $m = 0$,

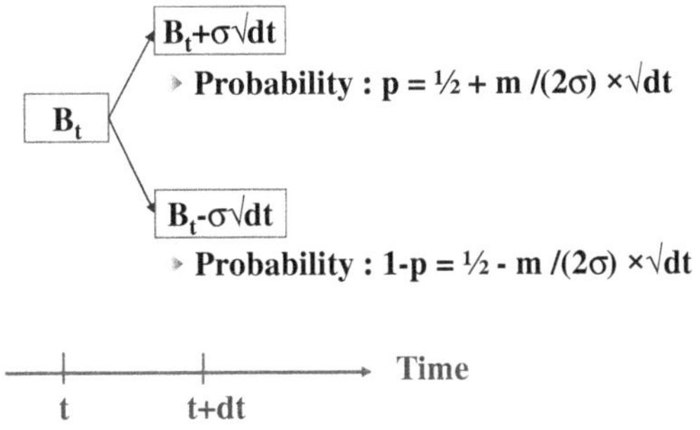

Figure 5.3: Node of a binomial tree with a time step dt, a variation step $\sigma \times \sqrt{dt}$, and whose probabilities of rise and fall move off center by a factor of m. When dt tends to zero, this tree converges towards a Brownian motion of drift m and volatility σ.

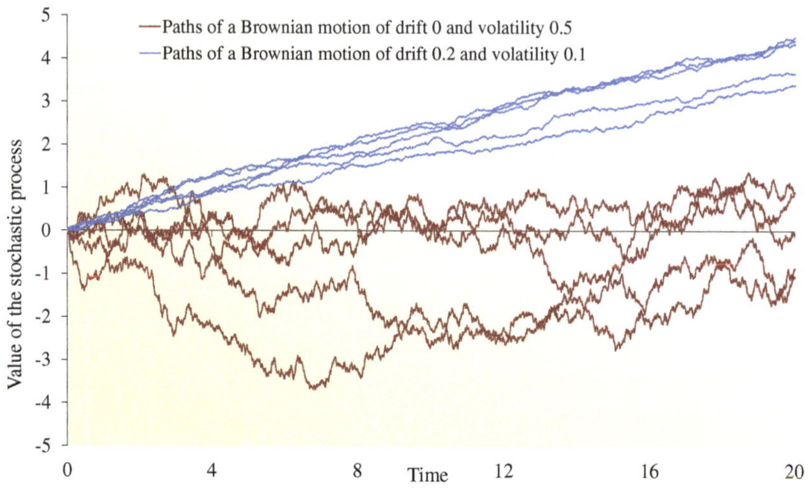

Figure 5.4: Example of random draws representing Brownian motions. Draws are centered around their drifts (0 for the red curves and 0.2 per year for the blue ones) and they diverge all the more as the volatility is larger.

the tree is balanced; if $m > 0$, the probability of a rise is larger than that of a fall, and conversely if $m < 0$. This explains that the tree corresponds to a motion which drifts towards a rise (if $m > 0$) or towards a fall (if $m < 0$).

The motion is thus characterized by two quantities (we systematically use one year as a unit of time):

- the yearly drift m of the process;
- the yearly volatility σ of the process, which is, as we must remember, the square root of the variance of the process: $\sigma = \sqrt{v}$.

We could have started from other discrete time processes in order to result in Brownian motion. For example, trinomial trees suitably parametrized converge as well towards a Brownian motion. However, binomial trees have not only the advantage of simplicity, but they also give a remarkably faithful vision of Brownian motions. In particular, transforming probability laws comes, in the binomial tree of Figure 5.3, to modifying the drift parameter m while leaving constant the tree structure. It implies that the characteristic variation size remains unchanged even when the probability law is modified. The very same phenomenon occurs for Brownian motion when we change the probability measure: it is possible to act on the drift m of the motion, but the resulting process will remain a Brownian motion of volatility σ. This property is specific to binomial trees, to Brownian motion and to some of its by-products; it can be shown that it ensures the uniqueness of the equivalent risk-neutral measure. The uniqueness of the equivalent risk-neutral measure ensures in turn the uniqueness of the arbitrage-free prices within the model.

Properties of Brownian motions are rich and numerous, and it is the reason why this motion is frequently encountered in many domains, for example in biology (the motion was named after the biologist Robert Brown) and most particularly in physics. We will not review all the characteristics of Brownian motion, but we shall quote some of its properties which are most useful in finance.[1]

Property 1. We already discussed this property, but it is useful to come back to it: Brownian motion is characterized by two quantities, its drift, which evolves linearly with time, and its volatility, which evolves proportionally to the square root of time. It is customary to define a *standard Brownian motion* as a motion with a zero drift and whose yearly volatility is 1. Noting W_t this standard Brownian motion, a motion B_t with drift m and with volatility σ is defined by the equation:

$$\mathrm{d}B_t = m \times \mathrm{d}t + \sigma \times \mathrm{d}W_t \tag{5.1}$$

In this equation, $\mathrm{d}t$ represents the time step, $\mathrm{d}B_t$ the variation of process B_t over this time step and $\mathrm{d}W_t$ the variation of the standard Brownian motion.

Property 2. The trajectories of a Brownian motion are continuous as they do not display jumps. This means that $B_{t+\mathrm{d}t}$ is close to B_t. It is

[1]The reader who had a look at the last section of Chapter 4 will also be able to observe that the quadratic variation (the sum of the squares of the variations of the trajectories) of tree 5.3 between t and $t + T$ is exactly $T \times \sigma^2$, whatever the trajectory which was followed. This remarkable phenomenon is characteristic of Brownian motion.

even possible to go further: $B_{t+\mathrm{d}t} - B_t$ has a characteristic size of $\sigma\sqrt{\mathrm{d}t}$ which does tend towards zero when $\mathrm{d}t$ tends to zero.[2]

Property 3. The motion is a martingale when the drift is zero. This means that if the value at t of a Brownian motion with zero drift is V, then the expectancy of future values at $T > t$ of the Brownian motion is V.

Property 4. Increments of the Brownian motion are independent. This means that the law for the variations $B_{t+s} - B_t$ of a Brownian motion is independent of the values of B_u for $u < t$. The process has no memory, all its variations are independent from each other.

Property 5. Increments of a Brownian motion are stationary, which implies that increments follow at every instant the same probability law. In other words, the variations $B_{t+s} - B_t$ of a Brownian motion depend only on s, not on t. For example, the evolution probability after six months, $B_{t+0.5} - B_t$, is the same whatever the time t under consideration.

Property 6. Increments of a Brownian motion follow a normal law. More precisely, the variations $B_{t+s} - B_t$ follow a normal law with mean value $m \times s$ and volatility $\sigma\sqrt{s}$, where m and σ are respectively the yearly drift and the yearly volatility of the process.

Properties 2, 4 and 5 taken together suffice to define a Brownian motion. Actually, rather than building our Brownian motion from binomial trees, we could have defined this motion from those preceding properties. Brownian motion is the unique stochastic process which obeys the following properties:

- its trajectories are continuous (no jumps);
- its increments are independent (no memory);
- its increments are stationary (unchangeable laws for the increments).

[2]This also proves that the trajectories of Brownian motion are not differentiable: $(B_{t+\mathrm{d}t} - B_t)/\mathrm{d}t \simeq \sigma/\sqrt{\mathrm{d}t}$ tends to infinity when $\mathrm{d}t \to 0$.

The fact that these sole three properties are by themselves sufficient to characterize Brownian motion is very important, since none of these conditions refers to arbitrary parametrizations nor assumptions. These are structural hypotheses on the motions, and we may already contemplate that they may be adapted to many modelings. The fact that increments of Brownian motions follow normal laws is a consequence of the three structural assumptions: continuity, independence, stationarity. Those three building blocks are well adapted to financial assets modeling, as we are going to see in the next section.

5.2 Lognormal processes

Lognormal processes are the theoretical ground on which the Black-Scholes model is built; we will study them before uncovering the famous Black-Scholes model in the next section.

The three conditions which characterize Brownian motion: continuity, independence and stationarity are at first sight reasonable assumptions to model the evolution of a financial asset, but for one detail — Brownian motion has an additive structure, it is based on a law for increments $(X_{t+s} - X_t)$, while financial assets have a multiplicative structure, based on returns $(X_{t+s} - X_t)/X_t$. As was mentioned in Chapter 3, increments are polluted by an arbitrary size factor, contrary to returns which are directly comparable within themselves, whatever the initial value of the asset. Our hypotheses for modeling a stock S_t can be adapted in the following way:

➲ Its market values are continuous.
➲ Its returns $(S_{t+s} - S_t)/S_t$ are stationary.
➲ Its returns are independent of the past values of the stock.

Let us emphasize once more that these requirements do not contain any arbitrary assumption. For example on the law of motion, they only include structural hypotheses on the characteristics of the motion. While any of these hypotheses may be questioned — we are going to do so in particular in Chapters 6 and 9 — none of them is unreasonable. Continuity of stock prices seems to be a mild approximation, as it is always possible to interpolate continuously a discrete set of points; for example, a continuous process which gives the correct value of the stock prices, every second within a cent, may be considered as an excellent model. The stationarity of returns means that laws that govern returns are stable with time, which looks natural, at least over a reduced time window. Returns are independent of past values, as it should not be possible to predict the future evolution by using past history of prices.

For these reasons, these hypotheses are widely accepted as the foundations of models for asset price evolution. We stated that the first set of conditions defining Brownian motion is not adapted to financial assets, as it is endowed with an additive structure. As for the second set of conditions listed above, it defines a *lognormal motion*, which is in fact the exponential of a Brownian motion. Starting from three hypotheses which seem to be natural and to cover a broad spectrum of possibilities, we have restricted the field of possible models to only one: the lognormal motion. Besides, this lognormal motion is very easy to use, which certainly contributes to its popularity.

Consider an asset S_t which follows a lognormal motion. Its logarithm $\ln(S_t)$ is by definition a Brownian motion. Its motion is then described by the stochastic differential equation, a consequence of (5.1):

$$\mathrm{d}(\ln(S_t)) = m\mathrm{d}t + \sigma\mathrm{d}W_t \tag{5.2}$$

where W_t is a standard Brownian motion (of variance 1 at $t = 1$ and of zero drift). This kind of equation is called stochastic because it contains a random function W_t. It is possible to show that this equation is strictly equivalent to:

$$\begin{cases} \mathrm{d}S_t = S_t \times (\mu\mathrm{d}t + \sigma\mathrm{d}W_t) \\ \mu = m + \dfrac{\sigma^2}{2} \end{cases} \tag{5.3}$$

Quants generally prefer the second writing, as it is more easily interpreted: $(\mu\mathrm{d}t + \sigma\mathrm{d}W_t)$ is actually the return of the modeled asset on a single time step $\mathrm{d}t$ (since the ratio $\mathrm{d}S_t/S_t$ represents the quantity

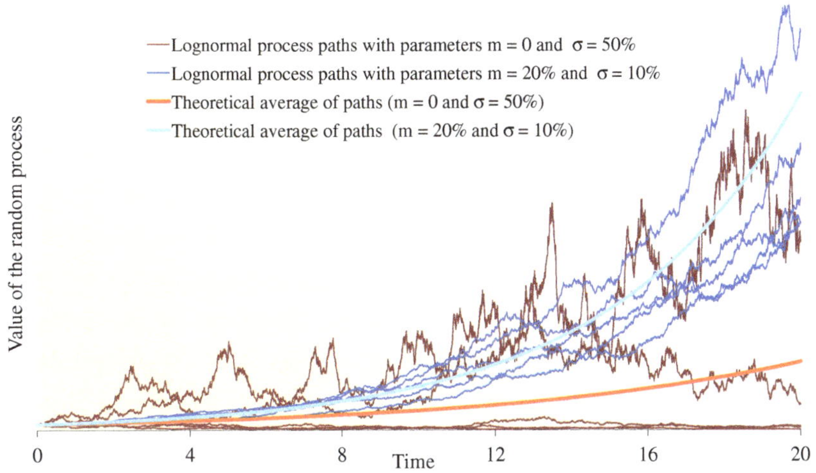

Figure 5.5: Example of lognormal processes: the graph represents two sets of five successive draws of lognormal processes (the parameters m and σ are defined in equation (5.2)). The processes progress on average in an exponential way.

$(S_{t+\mathrm{d}t} - S_t)/S_t$, which is exactly the return rate). This return rate contains two components:

- a predictable component associated with the drift $\mu \mathrm{d}t$, which is the instantaneous average return;
- a random component $\sigma \mathrm{d}W_t$, which is zero on average and accounts for volatility.

In the absence of volatility, when $\sigma = 0$, we have $S_t = \mathrm{e}^{\mu t}$: the motion progresses exponentially in a deterministic way, similar to a savings account which capitalizes at a compound interest rate[3] $\mathrm{e}^{\mu} - 1$.

The parameter μ, the instantaneous rate of return, is a *continuous rate*. In the following, we will work directly with these continuous rates. There is no conceptual difference between the interest rates we used until then, named "compounded" interest rate, and the continuous interest rates. Any continuous rate r has its equivalent compounded interest rate c, and conversely; the link is given by

[3] If $r = \mathrm{e}^{\mu} - 1$, then $(1 + r)^t = \mathrm{e}^{\mu t}$.

the equation:

$$e^r = 1 + c \qquad (5.4)$$

Recall that, in the first chapter, for the computation of present value, that is the current value of a future cash flow that will be paid in a time t, we multiplied the cash flow by the factor $(1+c)^{-t}$. The multiplication was called "discounting" and $(1+c)^{-t}$ was named the "discount factor". With continuous interest rates, the discount factor is simply e^{-rt}; this can be directly deduced from the previous equation.

5.3 The Black-Scholes model

The lognormal model for the evolution of asset prices which we just described is the famous Black-Scholes model. Going beyond the theoretical description of the process, we must now enter the crucial question of financial mathematics: how, starting from a model of asset price evolution, do we assign a price to various financial products? Two methods are regularly used in the framework of Black-Scholes model, and we shall study them in turn.

5.3.1 *The risk neutral measure*

In the Black-Scholes model, the log-return $\ln(S_t)$ is a Brownian motion of drift m and volatility σ, and it is thus the limit of a regular binomial tree of the kind displayed in Figure 5.1. Therefore, it is enough to apply the exponential function to the tree previously studied to get to the lognormal motion. Noting $S_t = \exp(B_t)$ and applying the exponential to the tree in Figure 5.3 leads to the tree of Figure 5.6.

In the preceding chapter, we showed that the valuation of financial assets is simple in the framework of binomial trees: the price is unique and may be computed as the average of future values under the risk-neutral measure. This risk-neutral measure is the fictitious probability under which asset prices are martingales.

Up to now, we neglected interest rates, and we are going to reintegrate them but without taking their maturity structure into account

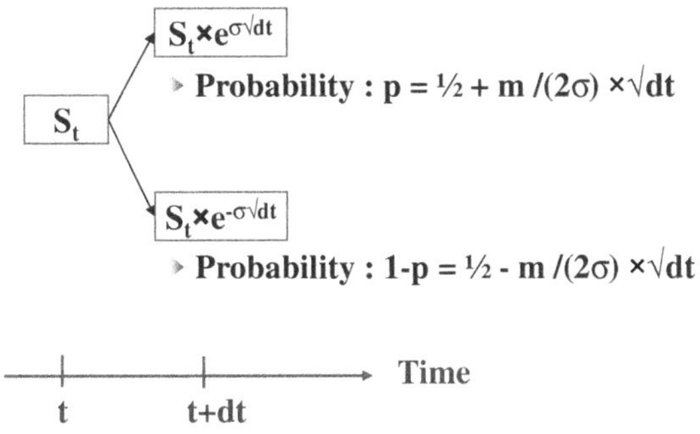

Figure 5.6: Node of a binomial tree converging towards a lognormal motion with parameters m and σ, when the time step $\mathrm{d}t \to 0$. This tree is a representation of a lognormal motion by a discrete process with an infinitesimal time step.

(*cf.* Chapter 1). Let us then note r the continuous interest rate. In order to compute the equivalent risk-neutral measure in tree 5.6, we must find the probability p^* for which the discounted future average price of the asset is equal to its initial value. We translate our sentence into an equation:

$$\left(p^* S_t e^{\sigma\sqrt{\mathrm{d}t}} + (1-p^*) S_t e^{-\sigma\sqrt{\mathrm{d}t}}\right) \times e^{-r\mathrm{d}t} = S_t \tag{5.5}$$

In this equation $(p^* S_t e^{\sigma\sqrt{\mathrm{d}t}} + (1-p^*) S_t e^{-\sigma\sqrt{\mathrm{d}t}})$ is the future average price (which is $S_t e^{\sigma\sqrt{\mathrm{d}t}}$ weighted with a probability p^* plus $S_t e^{-\sigma\sqrt{\mathrm{d}t}}$ with a probability $(1-p^*)$), and this price is divided by $e^{r\mathrm{d}t}$ in order to take present valuation into account given the interest rate r; this discounted average future price must be equal to the initial value, that is, S_t. This equation leads to:

$$p^* = \frac{1}{2} + \frac{r - \sigma^2/2}{2\sigma}\sqrt{\mathrm{d}t} \tag{5.6}$$

We discovered that the risk-neutral probability p^* has exactly the same form as the original probability p, where m is replaced by $r - \sigma^2/2$. This point is particularly interesting since, if we let the time step $\mathrm{d}t$ go to zero, the binomial tree will converge towards a lognormal motion of yearly drift $r - \sigma^2/2$ and of volatility σ.

Hence, under a risk-neutral measure, the asset price follows a lognormal motion of yearly drift $r - \sigma^2/2$ and of yearly volatility σ.

Moreover the risk-neutral measure is unique: the lognormal model is complete in the sense that there exists a unique risk-neutral measure. Under this measure, the average return rate (the parameter μ in equation (5.3)) of the asset is:

$$r - \frac{\sigma^2}{2} + \frac{\sigma^2}{2} = r$$

that is the risk-free interest rate. Therefore, there is no risk premium under the risk-neutral measure: the average return of an asset will always be r whatever its risk σ. Knowing the evolution of an asset price under the risk-neutral measure is very valuable: as shown in the preceding chapter, this allows us to compute the price of any derivative.

Let us take the example of a financial product, a purchase option, which is traditionally called a *call*. It is a financial product which, at time T, pays 0 if the stock is worth less than some threshold K, and otherwise the difference $S_T - K$. The time T is called the expiry date of the call and the threshold K its *strike*. We will attempt to price this call.

Box 5.1. Options, calls and puts. An option is a financial product providing its holder with the possibility, but not the obligation, to buy or to sell, at a given date and at a price K fixed in advance, another predetermined financial product. The threshold K is called the *strike*. Buy options are called *calls* and sale options *puts*. Therefore, a call of expiry date T and strike K will bestow on his holder the right to buy a stock at price K, even if the stock price is different from K. Noting S_T the stock price at expiry date T:

- if $S_T > K$, then the holder will exercise the call as this will provide him with a gain $S_T - K$;
- in the other case, the holder will not exercise the call, as it would be irrational to buy at price K what could be bought cheaper ($S_T < K$).

In the end, the call option brings at expiry date the cash flow $\max(S_T - K; 0)$.

Let us consider the framework of the Black-Scholes model and assume that the stock follows, under the real probability, a lognormal process of volatility σ, whatever its drift. Let us denote r the continuous interest rate. The option price is the expectation, under the risk-neutral probability, of its future cash flows. As the risk-neutral probability is unique in this model, it is possible to compute a unique price. Under this risk-neutral measure, the stock follows a lognormal process of instantaneous return r and of volatility σ:

$$\frac{\mathrm{d}S_t}{S_t} = r\mathrm{d}t + \sigma \mathrm{d}W_t$$

Within this framework, S_t is a lognormal process; we can prove that, at a time T, the random variable $\ln(S_T)$ follows a normal law of mean $ln(S_0) + (r - \sigma^2/2) \times T$ and volatility $\sigma\sqrt{T}$. Thus, the call price is the expectation:

$$E\left(\max\left[S_0 \mathrm{e}^X - K; 0\right]\right) \mathrm{e}^{-rT} \tag{5.7}$$

where X follows a normal law with the mean and volatility given above. We shall show in Chapter 7 how to numerically solve this kind of equation. In this particular case, it is possible to derive an explicit formula, which is rather long and will not be explicitly developed here; however, the numerical values of the price of a call in the Black-Scholes model are represented in Figure 5.7.

The price of the option does not depend on the anticipated return of the stock. It is an essential aspect of the Black-Scholes model, and of financial mathematics in general, which we already mentioned in the framework of the binomial tree, where prices of financial products did not depend on the real probabilities of rise or fall. Under the risk-neutral measure, all financial products progress on average following the risk-free interest rate, there is no risk premium.

To sum up, we have shown that:

➲ In the Black-Scholes model, it is possible to determine the unique risk-neutral measure; this is done simply by replacing the forecast return μ by the risk-free rate r.

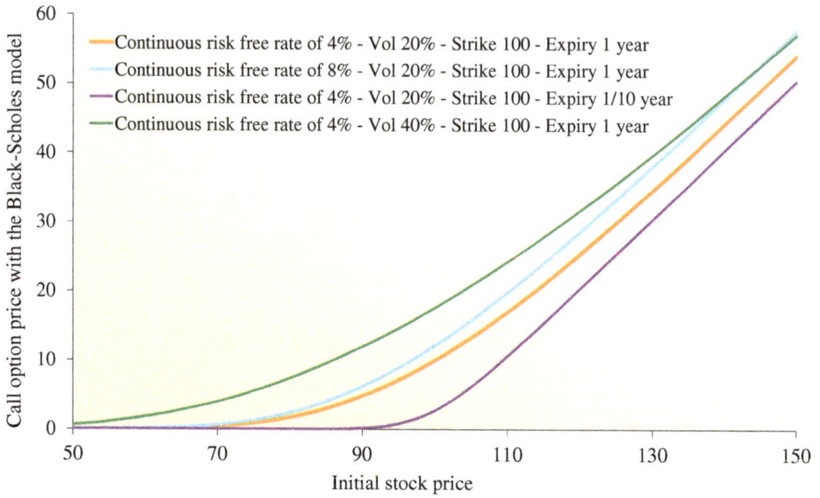

Figure 5.7: Price of a call in the Black-Scholes model as a function of the initial stock price (S_0) with various configurations of volatilities (σ) and expiry dates (T). When the time to expiry is very small, as for the purple curve, the future price S_T does not have time to leave S_0 and the discount factor is close to 1; hence the option price can be approximated by $max(S_0 - K; 0)$.

➲ Prices of all financial products can be computed using a mathematical expectation which we shall learn how to numerically solve in Chapter 7.

➲ For some simple products such as calls, there exists an explicit equation of pricing which we represented numerically in Figure 5.7.

5.3.2 *Delta hedge*

In this subsection, we shall introduce a second method for pricing financial products within the Black-Scholes model, the *delta hedge* method. Of course, the two techniques lead to the same price, as they result from the same model hypotheses, but each of them sheds a different light on the model.

The idea behind the delta hedge is to neutralize the risk by hedging the asset, that is, we attempt to buy a second asset, called the hedge, whose risk goes in the opposite direction. From this construction, the portfolio composed of the asset and its hedge evolves in a deterministic way, without variability. The price of such a portfolio will then easily be computed, and this will allow us to determine the price of the asset that we try to evaluate. We have thus explained the "hedge" part of the "delta hedge" expression.

What is then the meaning of "delta"? We shall understand it by referring, once more, to binomial trees. Consider a financial product Π to be priced; this financial product has a given payoff built from a reference stock S, like a call on stock S for instance. Prices of the product and the stock at an instant t are noted Π_t and S_t: we shall attempt to hedge the product Π_t by holding some proportion α_t of the stock. We wish to neutralize the risk, that is, we wish $\Pi_t + \alpha_t S_t$ to evolve in a deterministic manner.

Let us examine how to proceed in the case of the binomial tree of Figure 5.8. Our goal is that $\Pi_t + \alpha_t S_t$ be known without uncertainty (without any ambiguity on its future price), that is:

$$\Pi_t^+ + \alpha_t S_t^+ = \Pi_t^- + \alpha_t S_t^- \tag{5.8}$$

In other words, the proportion α_t is given by:

$$\alpha_t = \frac{\Pi_t^+ - \Pi_t^-}{S_t^+ - S_t^-} \tag{5.9}$$

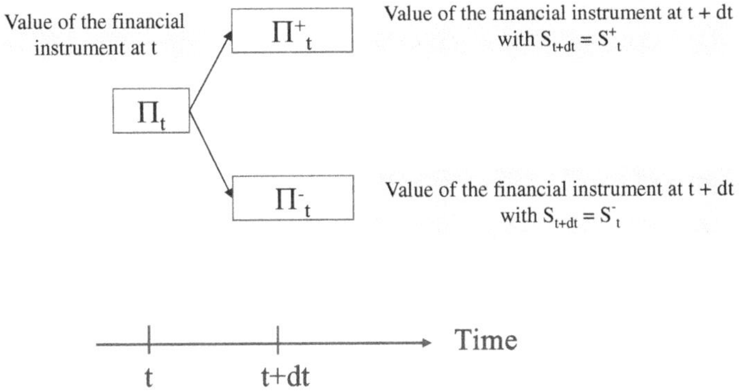

Figure 5.8: Evolution of a financial product Π_t in a binomial tree of time step $\mathrm{d}t$. As seen from time point t, the financial product has two possibilities of evolution at $t + \mathrm{d}t$, Π_t^+ or Π_t^-, according to the evolution of the reference stock S.

This equation has a precise mathematical meaning: it is the variation of the price of the product Π induced by the variation of the underlying stock S. In other words, it is precisely the derivative (in the mathematical sense of the word) of Π with respect to S. Differential expressions such as derivatives or variations are traditionally noted Δ, hence the origin of the term *delta*.

Formally, the price of a financial product depends on many parameters, among them the value of the underlying stock S, the time t, the interest rates, etc. We shall thus denote $\Pi_t(S, r, \ldots)$ this price which we seek to compute. At any instant t, it is possible to theoretically compute the derivative of $\Pi_t(S, r, \ldots)$ with respect to S, which is called the *delta* of the product, noted Δ_t. At this point, the values of the derivatives are unknown (since $\Pi_t(S, r, \ldots)$ itself is unknown), and we only acknowledged the theoretical existence of Δ_t:

$$\Delta_t = \frac{\partial \Pi_t(S, r, \ldots)}{\partial S} \tag{5.10}$$

It is however possible to demonstrate, as we have shown with binomial trees, that the portfolio composed of a financial product Π_t and of $-\Delta_t$ stocks evolves in a risk-free (thus deterministic) way in the Black-Scholes model. Let us temporarily denote η_t the return rate of this portfolio. This return rate is certain, there is no variability around this rate since the risk has been neutralized thanks to the delta hedge. The return η_t can only be the interest rate r, otherwise there would exist a possibility of arbitrage. Indeed, if $\eta_t > r$, it is possible to borrow money at an interest rate r to invest it at the return rate η_t: this is an arbitrage. Conversely, if $\eta_t < r$, there is also an arbitrage opportunity. In a world where arbitrage is excluded, we must have $\eta_t = r$. This reasoning is translated into the following equation:

$$\Pi_{t+\mathrm{d}t}(S_{t+\mathrm{d}t}, r) - \Delta_t S_{t+\mathrm{d}t} = \mathrm{e}^{r\mathrm{d}t}(\Pi_t(S_t, r) - \Delta_t S_t) \tag{5.11}$$

Actually, the left-hand side $\Pi_{t+\mathrm{d}t}(S_{t+\mathrm{d}t}, r) - \Delta_t S_{t+\mathrm{d}t}$ is the price of the portfolio at $t + \mathrm{d}t$; it is equal to the initial price $(\Pi_t(S_t, r) - \Delta_t S_t)$ of the portfolio capitalized at the continuous interest rate r

during the time step dt. We shall not dwell into the details of the calculations which, starting form equation (5.11), lead to a famous partial differential equation, the Black-Scholes equation:

$$\frac{\partial \Pi_t}{\partial t} + rS_t \frac{\partial \Pi_t}{\partial S} + \frac{1}{2}\sigma^2 S_t^2 \frac{\partial^2 \Pi_t}{\partial S^2} = r\Pi_t \tag{5.12}$$

It is neither necessary nor useful to master this equation in what follows. The important idea is that it can be solved numerically, and therefore used to compute the prices of financial products. We shall remember that:

- in the Black-Scholes model, it is possible to neutralize the risk carried by financial products;
- in order to do so, it is enough to protect the product with its delta hedge;
- this method can be used to compute the prices of financial products.

The possibility of neutralizing the risk in the Black-Scholes model is intimately linked with the possibility to replicate products in binomial trees (*cf.* Chapter 4). This is possible since the model is complete, that is, there exists as many sources of variability as there are possibilities of replication/hedge of the risk. It is also this property which guarantees the uniqueness of the risk-neutral measure and thus of the price.

The Black-Scholes model is rich and efficient. It is the consequence of a set of assumptions which is both natural and intuitive: continuity (no jumps), independence (no memory), and stationarity (laws stable with time). It can be approximated by binomial trees, which makes it very intuitive and of easy access. It is complete, which leads to non-ambiguous prices as well as hedging and replicating possibilities. It is built from normal laws, familiar to mathematicians and easy to manipulate. Prices of standard options, such as calls, are computed with a simple formula. For all these reasons, it is the basic model of financial mathematics.

5.4 The implied volatility

Unfortunately, the Black-Scholes model does not exactly reflect reality. The calls described above are products listed on markets, it is then possible to compare the market prices of the calls to the Black-Scholes model prices, for a given stock and for different levels of strikes and expiry dates. In all cases, this comparison leads to the following conclusion: there are no entry parameters (r, σ) of the Black-Scholes model which allow the model to reproduce the prices of all calls listed on the market for a given stock. There can only be one explanation: the stock evolution anticipated by the markets is not a lognormal motion, and the model assumptions are incorrect.

Figure 5.9 does show that the Black-Scholes model is untrue, but it nevertheless remains a good first approximation for the prices. Furthermore, having a model is very useful for risk management, because it gives tools for the interpretation of the motion (decomposition into a drift effect and a volatility effect), and it allows one to compute Δ and other risk indicators. This model exhibits the many advantages

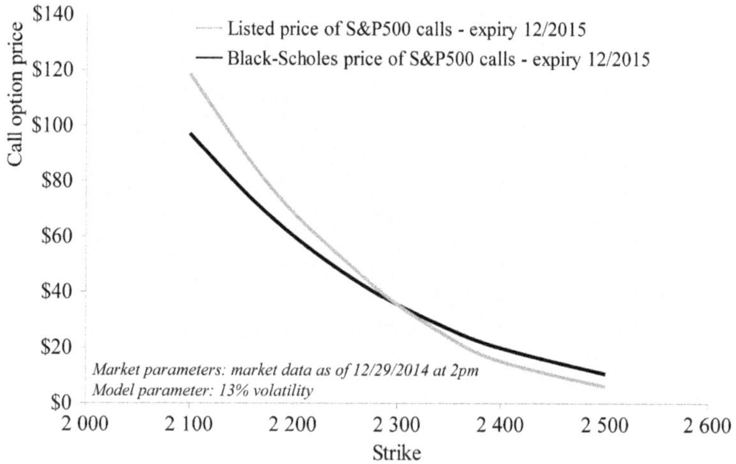

Figure 5.9: Prices of S&P500 calls as a function of the strike, as observed on the market (gray curve) and as computed with Black-Scholes model (black curve). Prices predicted by the model differ from prices observed on the market.

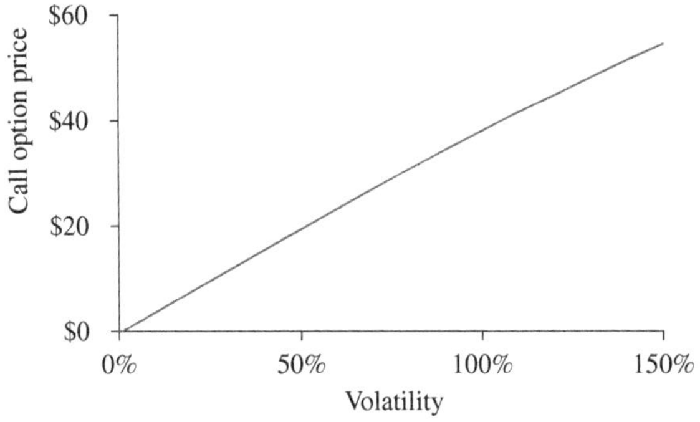

Figure 5.10: Price of a call in the Black-Scholes model as a function of the volatility: whatever the price π, it is possible to find a volatility σ_π associated with this price.

listed above. Its main drawback is to price incorrectly the options listed on financial markets.

In order to use the model, one must set its input parameters. The risk-free rate may be observed on the markets. The only unknown parameter remaining is then the volatility. Given an interest rate r, the formula for the call price under the Black-Scholes model may be seen as a one-to-one function of the volatility into the prices. The phenomenon is illustrated in Figure 5.10.

In other words, given a call whose market price is π, it is always possible to compute a volatility σ_π for which the Black-Scholes model price of the call is exactly π. This σ_π volatility is called the *implied volatility*. To quote [Joshi 2008], the implied volatility is the wrong entry parameter of the wrong model which gives the right price.

Each call listed on the market has its own implied volatility, which will thus depend on the expiry date and of the call strike. Were the Black-Scholes model valid, the volatility would only depend on the underlying stock: it is difficult to justify theoretically that a stock obeys a lognormal motion of 10% volatility when pricing a call of strike 95, and that the *same* stock obeys a lognormal motion of 15% volatility when pricing a call of strike 105. It is nevertheless what is done to adapt the model to market reality.

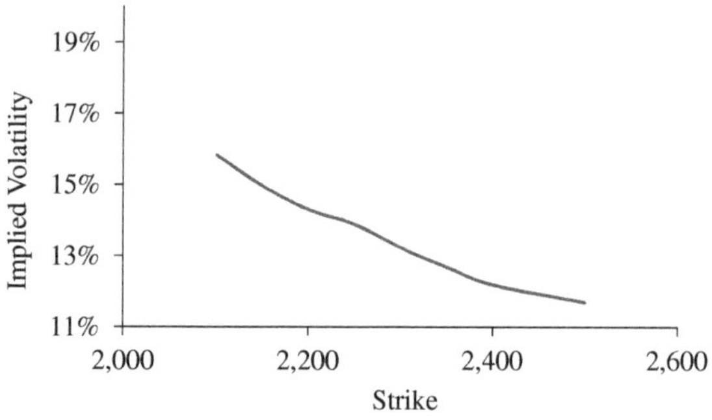

Figure 5.11: Implied volatility as a function of the strike (volatility skew), at a fixed expiry date. The graph represents for each level of strike the volatility parameter σ_π which allows the Black-Scholes model to reproduce the market price π of Figure 5.9.

Therefore, in practice, a given stock does not have a unique implied volatility σ, but a volatility surface $\sigma(K, T)$ which depends on the expiry date T and on the strike K of the studied call. At a given expiry date, the function $K \to \sigma(K, T)$ may exhibit a U-like shape, which looks like a smile, so that one speaks of a *volatility smile*, or it may exhibit a downwards slope, and one then speaks of a *volatility skew*. Figure 5.11 represents the volatility skew associated with the data of Figure 5.9.

The shape of the implied volatility curve, at a fixed expiry date T, gives information on the risk-neutral probability law of S_T which is anticipated by the markets. In its simplest form, the implied volatility is constant, which means that markets "think" that S_T follows a lognormal law (the exponential of a normal law). When this curve exhibits, as in Figure 5.11, a downwards slope, this means that markets consider that there is more variability in the case of a fall of the stock than in the case of a rise: the probability distribution of S_T anticipated by markets is asymmetrical; it overweights, with respect to the lognormal law, a likelihood of an important drop in prices. In the case of a volatility smile, the two sides of the distribution are overweighted: this means that markets anticipate that variations with a large amplitude are more likely than those predicted by the log-normal law; conversely, the low amplitude variations are considered

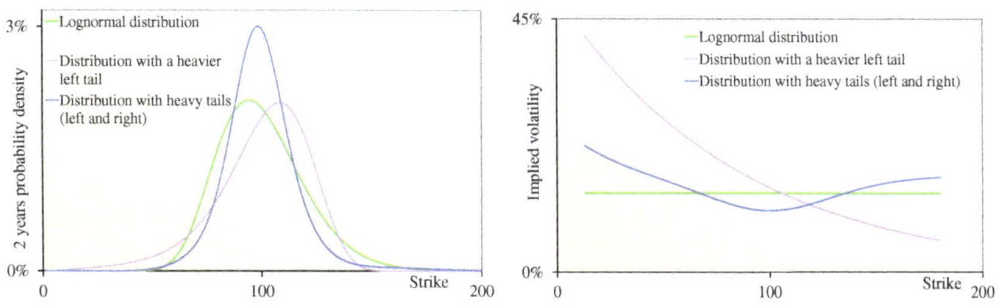

Figure 5.12: This graph presents on the left-hand side the probability densities of the underlying asset price at the expiry date of an option, and on the right-hand side the implied volatility curves which are deduced from them. Unsurprisingly, the implied volatility curve deduced from a lognormal density is a straight line, since the final distribution is supposed to be lognormal in the Black-Scholes model. A more broadly spread density on the left-hand side gives to the implied volatility curve the shape of a downward slope, which is called the volatility skew: in this configuration, negative variations with a large amplitude are more likely, while positive variations of prices remain of lower amplitude. Therefore, options with a smaller strike have a tendency to be more expensive, while options with a higher strike are cheaper. A density more broadly spread on the right and left sides, that is, presenting large variations which are more likely and small variations which are less likely, increases the convexity of the curve of implied volatilities: this is the volatility smile. As the extreme values of the underlying asset are more probable, prices of options with extreme strikes are higher.

less likely. This link between the curve of implied volatilities and the probability distribution of the price of the underlying asset is illustrated in Figure 5.12.

These three shapes of implied volatilities (constant, skew, smile) are regularly observed on markets. In order to be convinced, let us take a look at Figure 5.13, which represents the implied volatility of the DJ index, as observed on July 27th 2011, for different strikes and expiry dates. The result is a surface which is traditionally called the implied volatility surface. Let us note that the volatility smile, and then the skew, decreases for long-term expiry dates, which shows that traders consider that the hypotheses of the Black-Scholes model are more acceptable in the long run than in the short one.

The implied volatility is used to adapt the Black-Scholes model to market realities, while providing an intuitive interpretation of the

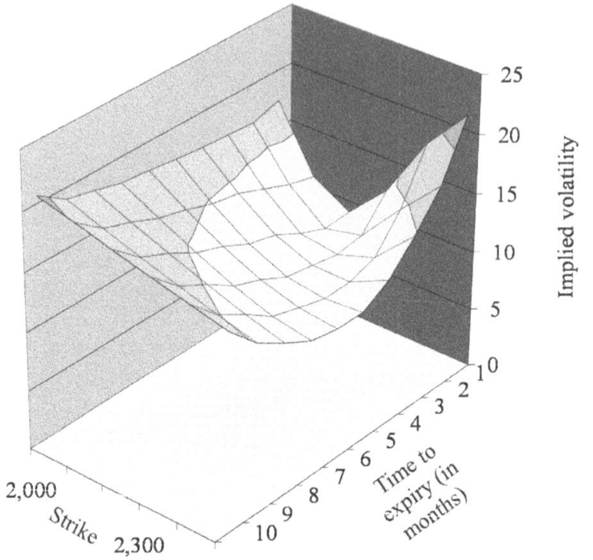

Figure 5.13: Implied volatility surface of DJ. For short expiry dates (approximately one month), curves reflect a volatility smile, that is a convex implied volatility curve. Then the surface is deformed into a simple slope which materializes a volatility skew. For longer expiry dates, the surface straightens up and the implied volatility associated with a given expiry date seems quasi constant.

various shapes of the volatility surface. However, let us recall that the implied volatility is a computational trick and does not constitute a consistent model, as it assumes that the same stock follows different laws depending on the characteristics (strike, expiry date) of the product to be priced. There are many refinements of the Black-Scholes model which attempt to solve this problem; these refinements will be the subject of the next chapter.

Chapter 6

Volatility Models

The preceding chapter taught us that the implied volatility is an artificial entry parameter of an imperfect model chosen to fit the observed market price. We could stop our reasoning with this observation and consider that any attempt to analyze the modeling of volatility would only be a matter for intellectual curiosity or a superfluous refinement. After all, it would be enough that traders are in a position to agree on option prices: the Black-Scholes model and the implied volatility are sufficient to reach this goal. Nevertheless, since the first appearance of a volatility smile (as defined in the previous chapter) on the stock market after the 1987 crash, market professionals and quants had no rest in their attempts to understand the behaviour of this volatility smile and to deduce a possible modeling.

The reasons are simple: traders, quants and other market practitionners are not satisfied with the simple one-to-one correspondence price$\Longleftrightarrow$implied volatility. They need to understand the mechanisms for the formation of implied volatility surfaces, in order to figure out what are the risks and profitability of trading strategies or to build new models aimed at valuing more complex derivatives. Indeed, on top of being a pricing parameter for derivatives, volatility also quantifies the variability of the prices' returns and hence determines the risk level associated to an asset.

The first section of this chapter is devoted to a deeper analysis of the implied volatility, in particular its inadequacy for the valuation of complex options. We then turn to the two main families of volatility models, whose strengths and weaknesses are examined:

➲ the local volatility models, popularized by the works of [Derman and Kani 1994] and [Dupire 1994], who attempt to model volatility as a deterministic function of time and of the underlying asset;

➲ the stochastic volatility models which describe volatility as resulting from a new random factor, to which belongs the model of [Heston 1993] that will be examined in some detail.

As we shall see, the performances of these various models are far from being universally acknowledged. As a consequence, modeling volatility is currently one of the most dynamic and controversial topic in financial mathematics.

6.1 Valuation with implied volatilities*

Let us sum up what we know about volatility and implied volatility.

➲ The implied volatility is the input volatility parameter, which, when injected into the Black-Scholes model, allows it to reproduce the prices of the calls as observed on the markets.

➲ In the Black-Scholes model, the volatility parameter is supposed to be the volatility to which the underlying asset is submitted before the expiry date of the option.

At this point, the implied volatility only allows us to value products whose prices we already know! Now, models are only useful if they can compute options prices which are not directly quoted on financial markets. We will now show that it is in fact possible to use implied volatilities in order to value other types of options.

Let us begin with the simple case of a sale option, called a put. We are going to demonstrate an important equation in finance known as the call-put parity. It links the price of a call and that of a put with the same strike K and the same expiry date T. Let us note r the risk free interest rate, S_t the value of the underlying stock at time t and let us build two portfolios A and B in the following way.

➲ Portfolio A is composed of a cash amount of $Ke^{(-rT)}$, invested at the risk-free interest rate r, and of a call of price Call Price.
➲ Portfolio B is composed of the underlying stock whose value is S_0 when the portfolio is initialized, and of a put of price Put Price.

At the expiry date T, the two portfolios will bring the same return, a fact that can easily be verified by the skeptical reader. Thus, in order to comply with the no-arbitrage principle, the two portfolios necessarily have the same value at every instant t. At the date $t = 0$, this statement is translated into the following formula:

$$\text{Call Price} + Ke^{-rT} = \text{Put Price} + S_0 \tag{6.1}$$

Equation (6.1) is called the call-put parity. It is independent of any modeling assumption, therefore it must be verified by any model prices, including Black Scholes prices, but also by real prices of options. This can be expressed by the following formulae:

$$\begin{cases} \text{Call Price}_{\text{real}} + Ke^{-rT} = \text{Put Price}_{\text{real}} + S_0 \\ \text{Call Price}_{\text{BS}} + Ke^{-rT} \ = \text{Put Price}_{\text{BS}} + S_0 \end{cases}$$

From this we infer:

$$\text{Call Price}_{\text{real}} - \text{Call Price}_{\text{BS}} = \text{Put Price}_{\text{real}} - \text{Put Price}_{\text{BS}}$$

This last relation confirms that the implied volatility of the call — it is the Black-Scholes volatility for which the left-hand side vanishes — is equal to the implied volatility of the put. This important result leads to the uniqueness of implied volatilities surface of puts and calls: the implied volatilities surface may therefore be indifferently built from the prices of calls or from those of puts.

Up to now, we have only defined the most simple options, called "vanilla" in the financial jargon, but the spectrum of options exchanged on financial markets is very broad, the most complex products being named "exotic". Let us give a brief overview of the most common financial options (*cf.* [Hull 2011] for a more complete and detailed review).

- **European options.** They are financial products whose value at the expiry date T is a function of S_T, the value of the stock at T; this function is called the payoff. Among them we may quote:

  — The call options — or calls — (purchase options) which appear frequently in this book for illustrative purposes, whose payoff is $\max(S_T - K; 0)$; they have been defined in Box 5.1 (Chapter 5).
  — The put options — or puts — (sale options) whose payoff is $\max(K - S_T; 0)$.
  — Binary options whose payoff is \$1 or \$0 depending on whether the asset is above or below the strike K. For example, the payoff of a binary call option is \$1 if $S_T > K$ and zero otherwise.

- **Asian options.** For these options, the payoff does not depend solely on S_T but on the average of the past values of the stock.
- **American options.** For an American option, in contrast to a European option only valid at the expiry date, the option holder may exercise his option at any instant. Thus, an American call gives his holder the right to receive $\max(S_t - K; 0)$ at any instant t over the lifetime of the option (but the holder can claim his right only once).
- **Barrier options.** Barriers are thresholds that activate or deactivate the option if the underlying stock price goes above or below the threshold. For example:

  — A European call with a deactivating barrier above the current level of the asset price (named *up and out*) pays the payoff of the call at the expiry date, except if the underlying stock went above the barrier during the lifetime of the option, in which case the option's payoff is zero.
  — An American put with an activating barrier above the current level of the asset price (named *up and in*) gives his holder the possibility to receive the payoff $\max(K - S_t; 0)$ at any instant over the option's lifetime, provided the market price of the underlying asset S_t has crossed the barrier beforehand.
  — The Asian case is less usual for barrier options, but is theoretically possible.

➲ **Forward start options.** For these options, the absolute value of the strike is not fixed in advance, but it is defined at some intermediate step, as a function of the underlying asset. For example, this may be a European call whose payoff at the expiry date T is $\max(S_T - S_\tau; 0)$, where τ is the date of the forward start ($\tau < T$).

We have studied the implied volatility of calls and puts. Let us pursue with binary options. As in the case of puts, prices of binary options may be deduced from those of the calls, independently of any assumption relative to the evolution of the underlying asset. Let us now consider a binary purchase option with strike K and expiry date T, and let us study a strategy consisting in buying a fraction $(1/\varepsilon)$ of a call with strike $(K - \varepsilon)$ and selling $(1/\varepsilon)$ of a call with strike K. At the expiry date T, the result of such a strategy is

$$\begin{cases} 0 \textit{ if } S_T < K - \varepsilon \\ \frac{S_T - K + \varepsilon}{\varepsilon} \textit{ if } K - \varepsilon < S_T < K, \\ \qquad \textit{knowing that in this case } 0 < \frac{S_T - K + \varepsilon}{\varepsilon} < 1 \\ 1 \textit{ if } S_T > K \end{cases}$$

This strategy leads to a result closely similar to the binary option as defined above, except for values of S_T lying between $(K - \varepsilon)$ and K. Therefore, for ε small enough, we may consider that the strategy does replicate the binary option; the price of the replicating portfolio must then be equal to the price of the binary option. Denoting $\text{Call Price}(x)$ the price of a call of strike x, the price of the binary purchase option of strike K is

$$\begin{aligned} \text{Binary Price}(K) &= \lim_{\varepsilon \to 0} \frac{\text{Call Price}(K - \varepsilon) - \text{Call Price}(K)}{\varepsilon} \\ &= -\frac{\partial \text{Call Price}(K)}{\partial K} \end{aligned} \tag{6.2}$$

The knowledge of the implied volatility surface, which is equivalent to that of all call options prices, allows us to value without ambiguity binary options, provided we bypass the pitfall presented in Figure 6.1. These binary options are particularly interesting, as they are directly

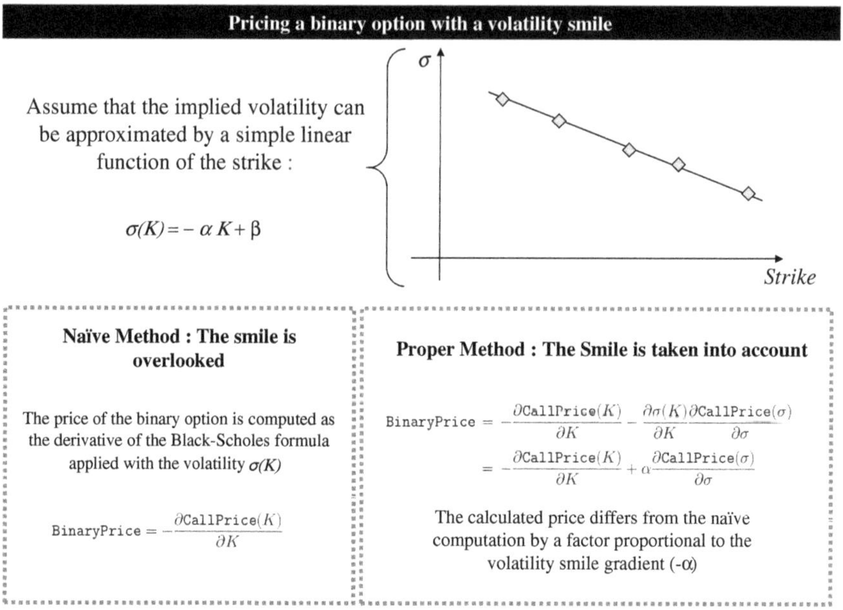

Figure 6.1: Valuation of a binary option given a volatility smile. The naïve use of the Black-Scholes valuation formula leads to a biased result, since the implied volatility depends on the level of the strike. For a correct valuation, one must smooth off or interpolate the existing points to a continuous volatility surface.

linked with the risk-neutral probability distribution of the underlying asset S_T. Indeed, as we have already seen, under the risk-neutral measure, the price of any asset is the expectation of its discounted future values. Now, the binary call option is worth 1 at the expiry date if $S_T > K$ and 0 otherwise: its value at the expiry date is by definition the probability that S_T be larger than K. Noting $P(\bullet)$ the probability under the risk-neutral measure, we just proved that:

$$\text{Binary Price}(K) = e^{-rT}\, P(S_T > K) \tag{6.3}$$

Equations (6.2) and (6.3) are central in our construction: they show how we can deduce the risk-neutral distribution of S_T at any instant T from the implied volatilities. Now, the knowledge of the risk-neutral measure of S_T at any instant T is naturally sufficient to value all European options, since the price is the discounted expectation of the payoffs. We can complete our reasoning by closing the loop: thanks to the risk-neutral distribution of S_T at any instant T we can value all the calls, and thus compute the implied volatilities surface $\sigma(K,T)$ for any expiry date T and for any strike K. In other words, we just observed the remarkable equivalence between the following information:

1. Knowing the implied volatility surface $\sigma(K,T)$ for any expiry date T and for any strike K.
2. Knowing prices of calls for any expiry date T and any strike K.
3. Knowing prices of all European options, for any expiry date and whichever the payoff.
4. Knowing at any instant T the risk-neutral distribution of S_T.

In practice, one can only observe a limited number of prices of calls and puts on financial markets. The exercise to be performed by a quant who wishes to deduce the prices of all other European options will be to build a continuous surface $\sigma(K,T)$ from the observed points. As in the construction of the interest rates curves studied in Chapter 1, modeling can be carried out via piecewise interpolation techniques or via the use of a parametrized surface. In all cases an uncertainty remains on the points where the volatility is not observed, this uncertainty being all the more important as computed implied volatilities lie further from the observed points. In practice, the theoretical equivalence demonstrated above will have to be adjusted; the facts are closer to the following reasoning:

- We know a discrete sub-set of implied volatilities points from the observation of quoted transactions on calls and puts.
- We can infer from those points a continuous surface of implied volatilities.
- The choices of implied volatilities for extreme strikes and long-term expiry dates are completely arbitrary.
- We can compute the prices of all the European options, but with an uncertainty which will be all the higher as the price will be more sensitive to extreme or long-term events.
- The prices of options with discontinuous payoffs for which the calculation of derivatives is mandatory, as in equation (6.2), are also very dependent on the chosen interpolation model.

We must note that binary options market has become widely traded. Hence, prices of these options can be easily observed. Therefore, it is possible to deduce the probability distributions of market prices directly from the observation of the binary options prices, rather than from the implied volatility surfaces of calls and puts.

We may already record two major handicaps of valuation methods using implied volatility surfaces. The first one was addressed in the preceding chapter: implied volatilities do not provide a consistent model of asset evolution; they rather are a computational trick. The second, which we just described, and which is shared by any modeling, is the uncertainty on the prices that one may be able to compute in practice. This uncertainty is intrinsic to what is generally called the model risk and leads to specific provisions in the banks books. The fair assessment of this model risk is a difficult exercise and subjective by its very nature. The assessment which is carried out in practice is thus always open to criticism, either by those who think banks are not prudent enough in the contingency reserves which they build to face risk and uncertainty, or by those who think that these mechanisms of provisions are over evaluated and are detrimental to banks competitivity and market efficiency.

We conclude this section by examining a third handicap. With the exception of the European options, none of the options listed above can be valued directly using implied volatility surfaces. In fact, European options give us information on the distribution of S_T at each instant T, but not on the path taken by the underlying asset to arrive there. In order to get convinced, let us assume that there only exist two expiry dates T_1 and T_2 and let us consider two random variables X and Y which follow the same probability law. Let us imagine two situations:

➲ Case 1: The stock is worth X at $T = T_1$ and again X at $T = T_2$.
➲ Case 2: The stock is worth X at $T = T_1$ and Y at $T = T_2$.

These two cases describe two different evolution models of a stock price; we will study how options' prices may differ or not between the two models. In both cases, the distributions of S_{T_1} and S_{T_2} are identical, since X and Y follow by construction the same probability law. These two models therefore lead to the same prices for all European options and thus to the same implied volatilities surface. Yet, the two models are very different: in the first model, the stock does not evolve between T_1 and T_2, while in the second model the price of the stock at time T_1 is independent of its price at T_2. All options whose final prices depend jointly of S_{T_1} and S_{T_2} will have different prices in the two models, barring accidental coincidence. It is thus impossible to deduce from the implied volatility surfaces the prices of non-European options, unless one assumes additional hypotheses. The valuation of these options thus demands the development of new models which are called volatility models, as they aim at establishing a framework describing the volatility surface dynamics and thus to value in a consistent way any kind of option.

6.2 Modeling volatility*

The model proposed by Black and Scholes does not correctly describe the behavior of the underlying assets anticipated by traders. If it did, neither volatility smile nor skew would be observed. Starting from this observation, there are two possibilities:

- calling fundamentally into question the Gaussian framework, which is what we shall do in the last chapter of this book;
- keeping the Gaussian framework intact while modifying the hypothesis according to which volatility is constant.

The volatility models which we present below follow from this second assumption. Let us start from the lognormal process that underlies the Black-Scholes model, now familiar to the reader:

$$\mathrm{d}S_t = S_t \times (r\mathrm{d}t + \sigma \mathrm{d}W_t) \tag{6.4}$$

In this equation, $\mathrm{d}S_t$ represents the infinitesimal quantity $S_{t+\mathrm{d}t} - S_t$, in other words the infinitesimal increase of the underlying asset price. This increase is governed by two components, the first one

$S_t r dt$ is the deterministic drift proportional to the risk-free interest rate, the second one

$$S_t \sigma \mathrm{d}W_t \simeq S_t \sigma (W_{t+\mathrm{d}t} - W_t)$$

is the random perturbation proportional to the volatility σ. The rigorous formulation of this equation necessitates the use of Itô's integral calculus, which the mathematically oriented reader may find presented in depth in [Le Gall 2011].

Calling into question the idea that σ is a constant can be addressed in various ways. At first, it is possible to consider that volatility is a deterministic function of time t, of the underlying asset price S_t, or of both. In this case, the resulting volatility function is called the *local volatility*. It is also possible to consider that the variation of the volatility contains a random component, specific to it. This assumption is the building block of *stochastic volatility* models.

Before presenting the two types of models, it is important to recall that volatility modeling may meet various aims: prediction of future volatilities, consistent valuation of all options types, help for hedging risks generated by options trading, economic analysis of the financial markets etc. Our assessment of the quality and limits of the presented models will be mainly based on their capability to value all types of options and to allow an efficient hedging of risks. In this respect, we recall that our models are essentially designed to compute arbitrage-free prices in line with market prices, and not to account for the historical or future market parameters. However, our point of view is not entirely incompatible with the other criteria. Indeed, a model will generally be all the more stable and consistent as it will come closer to the economic reality of the phenomenon that is modeled.

6.2.1 *Local volatility*

Local volatility models rely on the hypothesis that volatility is a deterministic function of time and of the underlying asset: the constant σ of equation (6.4) is replaced by a function $(t, S_t) \to \sigma_l(t, S_t)$.

The equation of the underlying asset dynamics then becomes:

$$dS_t = S_t \times (r dt + \sigma_l(t, S_t) dW_t) \tag{6.5}$$

The function $\sigma_l(t, S_t)$ is the local volatility. In order to provide a more detailed illustration of this notion, we come back to the example of binomial trees introduced in the preceding chapter.

Let us begin by assuming that a stock does evolve according to a classical lognormal process of constant volatility σ. In other words, here, the local volatility is a constant function equal to σ. We learned that such a process may be viewed as a binomial tree with infinitesimal time steps. In this tree, the probabilities of rise (p) or fall ($1-p$) of the stock price as well as rise (u) or fall (d) amplitudes are identical for each node of the tree. The tree parameters are entirely determined by the risk-free interest rate r and the volatility σ of the process. Indeed, the formulae seen in Chapter 5, Section 3.1, states that:

$$\begin{cases} p = \frac{1}{2} + \frac{r-\sigma^2/2}{2\sigma}\sqrt{dt} \\ u = e^{\sigma\sqrt{dt}} \\ d = 1/u \end{cases} \tag{6.6}$$

Let us now imagine that we wish to modify the tree in such a way that the volatility may vary from one node to another. As each node is associated with a pair (t, S_t), this exactly reflects the hypothesis that volatility depends on time and on the levels of stocks. Unfortunately, we cannot simply keep the equation (6.6) for u, p and d and change the value of σ throughout the nodes: this would lead to a non-recombining tree. We have to impose constraints in the tree which in turn imposes constraints on the three parameters u, d and p. The three constraints in the tree are: it must be recombining, it must lead to a risk-neutral environment and the volatility at each node must be $\sigma_l(t, S_t)$. The solutions of the resulting equations will thus lead to a tree such that all its parameters vary at each node. Going from a constant volatility to a volatility which depends on time and on the stock price is thus equivalent to the transformation of a regular tree into a tree with a more flexible structure, as is sketched in Figure 6.2.

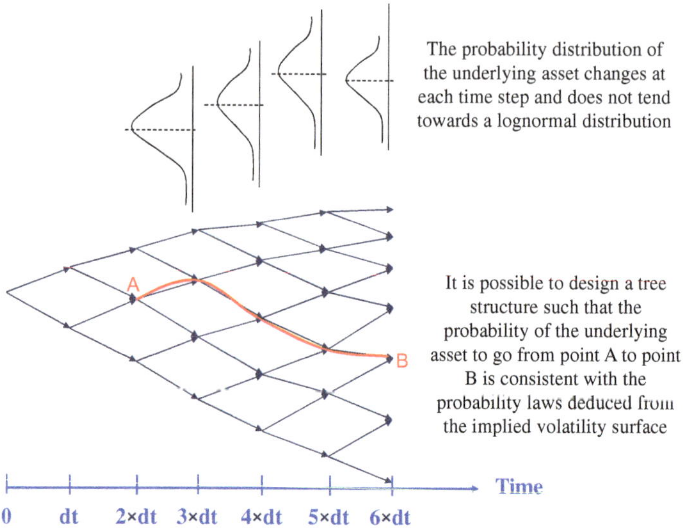

Figure 6.2: Risk-neutral binomial tree whose rise and fall amplitudes are different at each node. In this case, the volatility at each node is no longer constant, and the shape of the tree becomes irregular. This brings more flexible models which can price options consistently with prices effectively observed on markets.

Among the benefits obtained thanks to this greater flexibility, the distribution of the stock prices at time T, deduced from the model, is no longer necessarily lognormal: we may model a broader spectrum of probability laws. In particular, it is possible to fit the risk-neutral distributions that are deduced from the implied volatility surface.

Actually, [Dupire 1994] has demonstrated that there exists a unique volatility function $\sigma_l(t, S_t)$ able to ensure that the stock dynamics

$$\mathrm{d}S_t = S_t \times (r\mathrm{d}t + \sigma_l(t, S_t)\mathrm{d}W_t)$$

be consistent with the implied distributions deduced from calls and puts prices. Getting back to our binomial tree, this means that, at each node, there exists a unique set of probabilities $p(t, S_t)$ and of rise and fall amplitudes, $u(t, S_t)$ and $d(t, S_t)$, such that the tree leads to correct pricing of all calls and puts as quoted on the options market.

This being stated, it remains to explicitly determine the function $\sigma_l(t, S_t)$, or, in the case of our tree, the set of parameters $p(t, S_t)$,

$u(t, S_t)$ and $d(t, S_t)$. In order to do so, [Dupire 1994], [Derman and Kani 1994] and [Rubinstein 1994] have proposed various methods which we shall not review here. The common point of these methods is that they hinge on a discretization of time and of the underlying asset prices through binomial and trinomial trees.

Assume that we have been able to build our binomial tree by deducing the parameters $p(t, S_t)$, $u(t, S_t)$ and $d(t, S_t)$ from a sample of prices of calls and puts. What do we get from this construction?

1. We now have a modeling of the underlying asset price evolution which accounts for the prices of calls and puts as observed on markets; this model is the same whatever the expiry date and the strike of the option to be valued. We no longer have to choose different parameters to value different options on the same underlying asset. Furthermore, as the model allows one to compute the prices of all the calls and puts observed on markets, it accounts for the probability distribution of the underlying asset prices at any date T, and consequently it prices correctly all European options.
2. Contrary to the probability distributions deduced from the implied volatility surface, the local volatility model gives information on the probabilities for the underlying asset to follow a given path: indeed, as we know the probabilities to pass from one node to another one, we are able to compute the probability for the underlying asset of going from point A to point B, as illustrated in Figure 6.2. It is then possible to use this model to value options other than European ones.
3. The model as constructed is complete: within the model, there exists a unique non-arbitrable price for all financial products.
4. The model gives an interpretation of the volatility smile dynamics, that is, the way the volatility smile evolves over time. This element is important, as it leads to the computation of the options' delta,[1] in a manner more precise and more consistent than in the framework of lognormal models invalidated by the reality of

[1]We recall that the delta is the (mathematical) derivative of the option price with respect to the price of the underlying asset.

markets. The hedging of option portfolios should then become more efficient.

Box 6.1. Static hedging, dynamic hedging. Hedging a financial product means canceling or reducing the risks by purchasing or selling other financial products. In an ideal configuration, no loss is possible on the portfolio built from the financial product and its hedge. Two cases are possible. In the simplest, but also rarest case, hedging is implemented once and for all; risk is neutralized until the expiry date. One then speaks of static hedging, as the implemented hedge will stay the same during the whole lifetime of the product. In the most general case, the hedge will have to be modified regularly, and this is the reason why one then speaks of dynamic hedging. The delta-hedging of options provides a typical example: it is necessary to adjust constantly the hedge. Let us recall that hedging is done by purchasing $-\Delta$ underlying stock where Δ is the delta of the option which varies over time following the changes in stock price and implied volatility. A dynamic hedging is fully efficient only if the reaction time of the trader is infinitesimal and if there are no transaction charges. It is equally important to emphasize that the validity of the hedging strategy depends on the computational model which is used: not only Δ depends on the model used, but the capability to entirely neutralize the risk with the delta-hedge is not a feature of all models. For example, this hedging technique is not sufficient to neutralize the risks in the theoretical framework of stochastic volatility models. Thus, models are used not only to value a product, they also implicitly underlie a hedging strategy.

In order to make this point more explicit, let us make a short digression on the computation of the delta given a volatility smile. This parameter is essential, as it is the key parameter of hedging strategies. However, in the presence of a smile, the implied volatility σ_{imp} may depend on the price of the underlying asset. Consequently, the delta as computed naïvely with the Black-Scholes formulae, $\partial\text{Call}/\partial S$, is not accurate, because the contribution of the sensitivity of the implied volatility is to be taken into account:

$$\Delta = \frac{\partial \text{Call}}{\partial S} + \frac{\partial \text{Call}}{\partial \sigma_{\text{imp}}(S)} \times \frac{\partial \sigma_{\text{imp}}(S)}{\partial S} \tag{6.7}$$

The sole observation of call and put prices, by construction at $t = 0$, only allows to compute the implied volatility surface $\sigma_{\text{imp}}(S)$ for $S = S_0$. Without further modeling of volatility, we cannot compute $\partial\sigma_{\text{imp}}(S)/\partial S$. By contrast, local volatility leads to a full modeling of the smile dynamics and hence to a corrected calculus of the delta. The methods for determining local volatility proposed by [Dupire 1994], [Derman and Kani 1994] and [Rubinstein 1994] thus seem to be the key to all the questions raised by the existence of implied volatility surfaces. Unfortunately, the outcome of these methods is not as favorable as it may appear.

First of all, from a practical point of view, it must be pointed out that the determination of local volatilities from a sample of calls and puts necessitates the use of numerical methods liable to generate unstable results and with a dubious economic meaning. The interested reader may refer to [Rebonato 2004] for an in-depth analysis of these problems and their possible solutions.

From a theoretical point of view, the whole set of local volatility models relies on the hypothesis according to which volatility depends only on time and on the level of the underlying asset. [Dupire 1994] has shown that, were this assumption verified, then there would exist a unique model of evolution for the underlying assets consistent with the prices of European options observed on markets. Accepting the hypothesis of local volatility, we can demonstrate that there exists a unique possible price for all options, even exotic ones. If, on the contrary, the hypothesis is erroneous, local volatility models are only one particular case, among others, of models consistent with market prices of calls and puts. These models will end up with the same prices for European options, which, as we have seen, are deduced without ambiguity from the implied volatility surfaces, but may lead to different prices for exotic options. As a consequence, prices of exotic options computed under the local volatility model may turn out to be inconsistent with market prices.

Finally, [Hagan *et al.* 2002] have shown that the smile dynamics as predicted by the local volatility models could contradict the configurations observed on markets. The illustration of this phenomenon, presented below, is a serious questioning of the plausibility of the hypotheses of local volatility models.

Empirical studies of the smile dynamics showed that the volatility smile evolves schematically between two boundary behaviors when the level of the underlying asset varies. According to the first behavior, the implied volatility depends only on the level of the strike. In this configuration, the smile is insensitive to any variation of the underlying asset. According to the second behavior, the implied volatility is a function of the vicinity between the underlying asset price and the strike. In this case, the smile will tend to follow the evolution of the underlying asset price. These two boundary behaviors are presented in Figure 6.3. The real historical smile dynamics lie somewhere in between these boundary behaviors. Now, the local volatility models which we described imposes smile dynamics which do not correspond to behaviors which are empirically observed: [Hagan *et al.*] shows that the smile as deduced from the local volatility model will have a tendency to drift toward the right when the price of the underlying asset decreases, while empirical studies show the opposite phenomenon (see Figure 6.3).

These results show that the smile dynamics induced by local volatility models is incompatible with some generally observed market characteristics, and more particularly those observed for options on stocks and on foreign currencies. Moreover, other studies assert that local volatility models may anticipate a flattening of the smile, which contradicts the observation of its persistence with time.These elements are of a particular importance for the trader who wishes to hedge his options portfolio. Indeed, if the impact of the variation of the underlying asset price on the shape of the smile is incorrect,

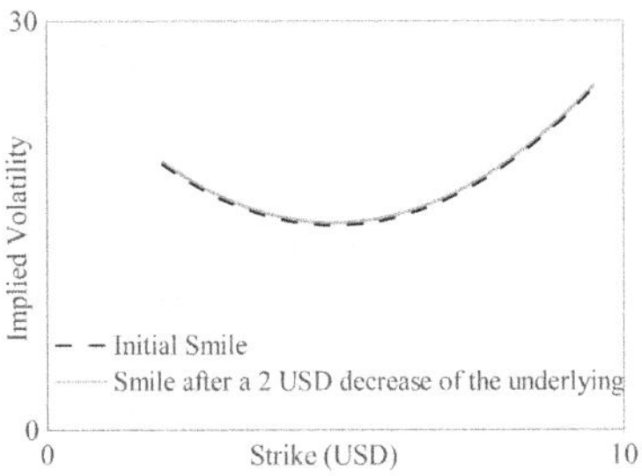

(a) Volatility smile independent from the underlying

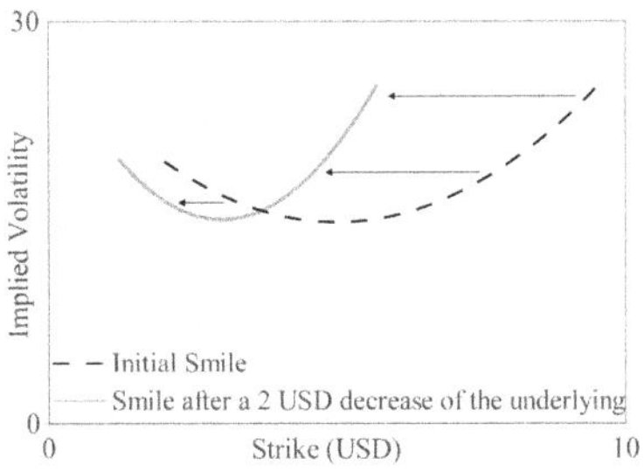

(b) Volatility smile shifting along side the underlying

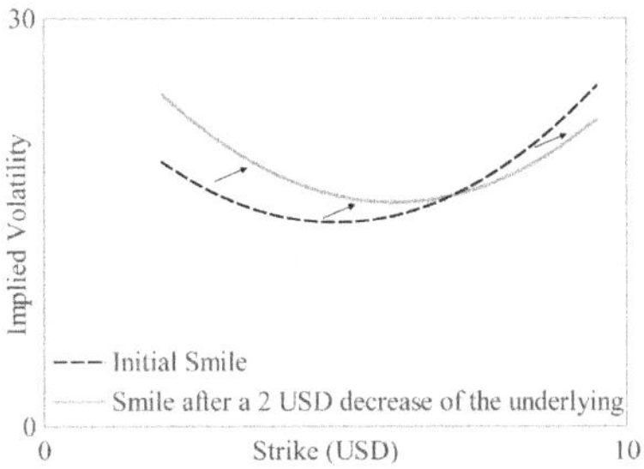

(c) Volatility smile dependence on the underlying implied from the local volatility model

Figure 6.3: The local volatility function of [Dupire 1994], [Derman and Kani 1994] and [Rubinstein 1994] imposes that the smile moves in the direction opposite to that of the underlying asset price (Figure (c)), which is inconsistent with the dynamics of volatility smiles observed in practice. This dynamics lies in general between the two limiting behaviors presented in Figures (a) and (b): in Figure (a), the smile is independent of the underlying asset price, while in Figure (b) the smile follows this price.

equation (6.7) will lead to the wrong value of delta and hence to an inadequate hedging strategy.

To sum up, the determination of a local volatility function from prices of puts and calls leads to interesting results and is still much used by many practitioners, but its relevance seems to be called into question by the fact that the basic hypothesis is disproved: the dependence of the volatility upon the two sole parameters, time t and underlying asset price S_t. This hypothesis leads to a dynamical model which is not consistent with reality.

We have presented the local volatility models deduced from the implied volatility surfaces. There exist other local volatility models for which the function $\sigma_l(t, S_t)$ is not fully deduced from market data, but is parametrized from a predetermined function. The choice of the function $\sigma_l(t, S_t)$ is then generally dictated by considerations linked to the historical behavior of volatility and to the simplicity of valuation formulae deduced from it. Among models of this kind, CEV (Constant Elasticity of Variance) models are the most widely spread. The interested reader may find details in [Rebonato 2004].

6.2.2 *Stochastic volatility*

In stochastic volatility models, which we address in the present subsection, the volatility dynamics are governed by a new random factor in addition to the random factor W_t of local volatility models (equation (6.5)). Let us define a Brownian motion Z_t independent of W_t. Starting from two independent random factors W_t and Z_t, the diffusion models of an underlying asset S_t termed "with stochastic volatility" are generally specified by the following equations:

$$\begin{cases} \mathrm{d}S_t = r\, S_t \mathrm{d}t + \sigma_t\, S_t \mathrm{d}W_t \\ \mathrm{d}\sigma_t = p(\bullet)\mathrm{d}t + q(\bullet)\left(\rho \mathrm{d}W_t + \sqrt{1-\rho^2}\,\mathrm{d}Z_t\right) \end{cases} \tag{6.8}$$

The first line is the classic log-normal equation of the underlying asset S. The second line indicates that, in contrast to the Black-Scholes model, the volatility σ_t is no longer constant, but is also subject to a diffusion with a drift $p(\bullet)$ and a volatility $q(\bullet)$. The function $q(\bullet)$ is then the volatility of the volatility. The two functions $p(\bullet)$ and $q(\bullet)$ are, for the time being, expressed in a very general way, and we shall examine later a specific example of such a model. The stochastic component of the volatility dynamics comes from the random term $\rho \mathrm{d}W_t + \sqrt{1-\rho^2}\,\mathrm{d}Z_t$ which represents a standard Brownian motion composed of two independent Brownian motions. Similarly to what was defined in Chapter 2, ρ represents the correlation between the price of the underlying asset and its volatility: it describes the tendency of these two variables to evolve in a joint manner. For example, if $\rho = 1$, $\rho\,\mathrm{d}W_t + \sqrt{1-\rho^2}\mathrm{d}Z_t$ becomes

$\mathrm{d}W_t$, hence the two processes S_t and σ_t will be linked in a deterministic manner; if $\rho = 0$, $\rho\,\mathrm{d}W_t + \sqrt{1-\rho^2}\mathrm{d}Z_t$ becomes $\mathrm{d}Z_t$, hence the two processes S_t and σ_t will be independent; finally if $\rho = -1$, $\rho\,\mathrm{d}W_t + \sqrt{1-\rho^2}\mathrm{d}Z_t$ becomes $-\mathrm{d}W_t$, hence the two processes evolve in opposite directions.

Stochastic volatility models exhibit a crucial difference with local volatility models and the Black-Scholes model: volatility becomes a source of uncertainty in the same way as the price of the underlying asset is. Arguments which were used in Chapter 5 to ensure the uniqueness of options prices do not hold anymore. Indeed, we showed in Chapter 5 that, in the framework of the Black-Scholes model, it is possible to neutralize the risk of a portfolio Π thanks to the delta hedge. This technique simply amounts to holding at each instant, besides the portfolio Π, the quantity $-\partial\Pi/\partial S$ of underlying asset S. The capability of fully neutralizing the risk ensures the uniqueness of the price, since, in the absence of arbitrage opportunity, a risk-free portfolio can only yield the risk-free interest rate r: this is what is called the completeness of models.

Adding a new random component, such as stochastic volatility, invalidates this perfect hedging construction. Indeed, as volatility is not directly exchangeable on markets, it is not possible to buy or sell it in order to cancel the risk which it generated on the options prices. Therefore, it is no longer possible to build a risk-free portfolio with the sole underlying asset; the model is no longer complete and the price of any portfolio is, in theory, sensitive to the risk appetite of traders. This loss of completeness has two impacts:

- Stochastic volatility models defined by equations (6.8) lead to a consistent pricing of various financial products; however, these models do not exclude that other prices are equally valid within the no-arbitrage framework.
- Hedging options require the use of other options. In other words, in order to hedge the risk of a portfolio, we shall not only have to neutralize its delta, but also to neutralize the sensitivity of the portfolio to volatility, which can be done thanks to other options.

Equations (6.8) which we have presented describe a quite general class of models, since the functions $p(\bullet)$ and $q(\bullet)$ have not yet been specified. The choice of these functions is influenced by various criterias.

First of all, they must make the model consistent with the real behavior of the underlying asset. In particular, it is often required that the volatility dynamics include a constraint of return towards an equilibrium situation. This constraint is important, as it guarantees that volatility will tend to stay confined within a reasonable interval and in line with the traders' intuition and observation. Second, models whose parameters are time independent may also be preferred. Indeed, the shape of the smile observed on markets since 1987 has been relatively stable. Allowing the parameters modeling smile evolution to depend on time would generate future shapes of smiles structurally different from the present ones, in contradiction with reality.

Furthermore, the choice of the functions $p(\bullet)$ and $q(\bullet)$ is generally made in order to allow a simple calculation of option prices. These models are generally designed to be parametrized in order to obtain option prices as close as possible to those observed on markets. This step requires that one uses numerical optimization methods which are all the more efficient as options prices are simply expressed as a function of the parameters that one attempts to estimate. This simplicity constraint is often criticized in the professional literature, as it is bound to entail choices whose main motivation is their simplicity of implementation on computers, to the detriment of their economic likelihood.

Among the most popular models of stochastic volatility, we now describe that of [Heston 1993], defined by the following equations:

$$\begin{cases} \mathrm{d}S_t = rS_t\mathrm{d}t + \sigma_t S_t \mathrm{d}W_t \\ \mathrm{d}(\sigma_t^2) = \lambda(\overline{\sigma}^2 - \sigma_t^2)\mathrm{d}t + \eta\sigma_t\left(\rho \mathrm{d}W_t + \sqrt{1-\rho^2}\,\mathrm{d}Z_t\right) \end{cases} \tag{6.9}$$

A remarkable feature, but without theoretical implication, is that contrary to the general model presented in equations (6.8), Heston does not model directly the underlying asset volatility, but rather its variance σ^2 which is simply the square of the volatility. The terms $\lambda(\overline{\sigma}^2 - \sigma_t^2)$ which governs the drift of the variance ensures the return towards an equilibrium situation. Indeed:

- If, $\sigma_t = \overline{\sigma}$, then the drift of the variance $\lambda(\overline{\sigma}^2 - \sigma_t^2)dt$ will vanish: on average, the volatility will stay constant.
- If, $\sigma_t > \overline{\sigma}$, then the drift of the variance $\lambda(\overline{\sigma}^2 - \sigma_t^2)dt$ will be negative: on average, the volatility will decrease.
- If, $\sigma_t < \overline{\sigma}$, then the drift of the variance $\lambda(\overline{\sigma}^2 - \sigma_t^2)dt$ will be positive: on average, the volatility will increase.

The formula $\lambda(\overline{\sigma}^2 - \sigma_t^2)$ does represent a restoring force towards the equilibrium $\overline{\sigma}$. The parameter λ accounts for the strength of this restoring force: the larger this parameter, the faster the return to equilibrium. Furthermore, in the framework of Heston model, an analytic formula can be established and therefore options prices can be easily computed.

The first goal of a volatility model is to value the simplest options, which amounts to rebuilding the shape of the volatility smile. Before assessing the performance of Heston model in this respect, let us study the impact of the various parameters $\lambda, \overline{\sigma}, \eta$ and ρ on the shape of the smile. As shown in Figure 6.4, $\overline{\sigma}$ influences the absolute level of implied volatilities in accordance with intuition since, by construction, $\overline{\sigma}$ is the equilibrium value of volatility. The correlation ρ defines the slope of the smile: the underlying asset and the volatility will evolve in the same direction for a positive correlation, and in opposite ways for a negative one. Again, the phenomenon is in accordance with intuition, as the higher ρ, the stronger is the link between the volatility and the underlying asset, and the more we expect the volatility to increase when the price of the underlying asset rises. The parameters η and λ impact the convexity of the smile. The higher the volatility's volatility η, the more probable are extreme values of volatility; as illustrated in the preceding chapter, this leads to amplified convexity of the implied volatility curve. Finally, the higher λ, the more the variance tends to come back rapidly to its equilibrium

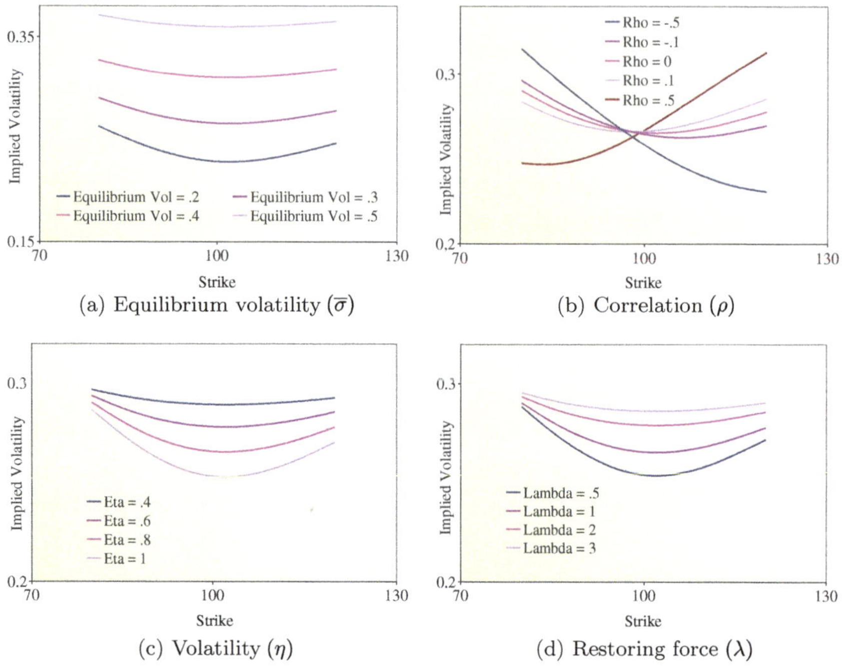

Figure 6.4: Smiles generated by Heston's model for different values of the model parameters. Prices of options with different strikes are simulated with Heston's model, the implied volatilities associated to these prices are afterward computed. The impact of the various parameters on the smile shape may be represented intuitively, which is one of the strengths of the model.

position. Thus, extreme values of the volatility are the least probable as λ is larger, which tends to flatten the smile.

Heston's model parameters allow one, in theory, to retrieve all possible shapes of the implied volatility curve. In practice, it turns out that it is difficult to reproduce a very pronounced smile for the shortest terms, while sticking to time independent parameters. Other models, such as SABR model (see [Hagan *et al.* 2002]), correct this flaw, while displaying other weaknesses. This difficulty is intimately linked with the very principle of stochastic volatility models: as the volatility and the price of the underlying asset are continuously diffused, they remain within a Gaussian framework. Therefore, they cannot predict a brutal shift of the volatility or in the underlying asset price in a very short time interval. The improvement of stochastic volatility models then lies in relaxing the Gaussian framework, which we shall study in Chapter 9.

As a conclusion, let us remember that valuation of European options requires the knowedge of the distribution of underlying assets prices at the expiry date, while valuation of other options requires to know not only the distribution at the expiry date, but also the trajectories followed by the underlying asset before the expiry date. We may invert this point of view, and note that the prices of European options give information on the probability distribution of the underlying assets prices at the expiry date, while the prices of other options also give information on the probabilities of the underlying asset trajectories before this date.

This point is important in order to understand the choices which are essential for models calibration. Let us recall that a parametric model is specified by a set of parameters, for example Heston's model (equation (6.9)) relies on $r, \rho, \overline{\sigma}, \eta, \lambda$. It is necessary to make a choice for the numerical values of these parameters: this is called calibration. Concretely, parameters are chosen in such a way that model prices are as close as possible to the market prices. The selection of options used for calibration then takes a crucial importance in order to be sure that information anticipated by markets are taken into account in the model. For example, a model dedicated to valuing non-European options calibrated on European options would have every chance to give a price far from market consensus, since it would rely only on the underlying prices probability distribution at the expiry date while the core factor of exotic options valuation is the modeling of the whole trajectories of the underlying asset before this date.

Chapter 7

Numerical Methods

Mathematical theories sometimes lead towards very abstract solutions. A trader has little interest in knowing that the price of his option is the unique solution of a partial differential equation with suitable boundary conditions: he just wants a reliable numerical price. It is quite exciting to discover that the price of a derivative is a martingale under a fictitious risk-neutral measure, but, in practice, what is the price of the derivative?

It is at this point that numerical methods come into play: widely used by physicists and engineers, they allow translation of mathematical results into numbers. We shall present the two numerical methods that are the most useful in finance: Monte-Carlo simulations and finite differences methods. The first method is used to compute prices that are expressed as mathematical expectations, which is indeed the case in finance since we showed in Chapter 4 that prices of financial products are the expectations, under the risk-neutral measure, of future cash flows. As for finite differences methods, they are built to solve numerically partial differential equations, such as the Black-Scholes equation which governs the price evolution of financial products.

We shall see that the two methods which are presented below are grounded on simple principles. However, their concrete implementation may turn out to be tricky and opens the way to many in-depth studies.

7.1 Monte-Carlo simulations

7.1.1 *Principles*

When one flips an unbiased coin a very large number of times, each face shows up half the time on average. If one counts for example the proportion, P_n, of heads after n flips, one finds that $P_n \to 1/2$: the observed percentage of heads converges towards 50%. Generally speaking, the average of a random variable may be numerically assessed by performing random simulations of this variable and by computing the average of the draws. This tautology lies at the basis of the so-called "Monte-Carlo" methods. Monte-Carlo is a neighborhood of Monaco which is home to the famous eponymous casino; it gave its name to the numerical technique which we explain in detail in the present section, since, before computers became widely available, drawing random numbers could be performed by physical methods: coin tossing, roulette, cards etc.

Naturally, the method which we just described is not very useful to compute the already known average of heads draws while flipping coins. However, it is very useful to compute averages, expectations or more complex integrals for which no exact solution is available.

Suppose, for instance, that we wish to know the value of π ($\pi = 3.1415\cdots$). A method, not very efficient but very simple, would be to randomly sample points in a square. Let us draw in this square a circle whose center is located at that of the square and which just touches its four sides. The ratio of the number of points itemized in the circle to the total number of points in the square is $\pi/4$ on average: it is the ratio of the circle surface (πR^2 if R is the circle radius) to the square surface ($4R^2$).

The reasoning is exactly the same for the valuation of financial products. We showed in Chapter 4 that, under the no-arbitrage assumption, there exists a probability measure under which discounted prices of assets are martingales. Let us recall that a martingale has no drift on average: the average value of a martingale

M_t at any date t is its initial value M_0. One consequence of this property is that the price of any asset today is the average of its discounted future prices under the risk-neutral measure. Now, prices at the expiry date of financial products are in general easy to compute. They are pre-defined functions of an underlying asset. For example, in the case of a call, we saw that the value of the call at expiry date is, by definition, $\max(S_T - K; 0)$, where S_T is the price of the underlying asset and K the strike of the option. The initial price of the call is nothing else than the discounted average value of this final function applied to the simulated underlying asset prices. If we note P the price of the call, r the continuous risk-free interest rate and $E(\bullet)$ the mathematical expectation, this sentence is translated into equation (7.1):

$$P = E\left(\max(S_T - K; 0)\mathrm{e}^{-rT}\right) \tag{7.1}$$

The numerical resolution of this equation with the Monte-Carlo method simply consists in performing random samplings of S_T, computing the final discounted value of the option $\max(S_T - K; 0)e^{-rT}$ and taking the average of the results. In a simple Black-Scholes model, S_T follows, under the risk-neutral measure, a lognormal law with drift $(r - \sigma^2/2)$ and volatility $\sigma\sqrt{T}$. In the more refined volatility models which we examined in the preceding chapter, there is in general no simple characterization of the risk-neutral probability law of S_T. On the other hand, we know the diffusion equation of the asset, for example in Heston's model (introduced in the previous chapter, Section 6.2.2):

$$\begin{cases} \mathrm{d}S_t = r\, S_t\, \mathrm{d}t + \sigma_t\, S_t\, \mathrm{d}W_t \\ \mathrm{d}\sigma_t = \lambda(\overline{\sigma}^2 - \sigma_t^2)\mathrm{d}t + \eta\sigma_t\left(\rho\, \mathrm{d}W_t + \sqrt{1-\rho^2}\, \mathrm{d}Z_t\right) \end{cases} \tag{7.2}$$

In this equation, $r, \lambda, \overline{\sigma}, \eta$ and ρ are model parameters and W_t and Z_t are two independant Brownian motions. The computation of the call price in Heston's model amounts to the following:

1. Simulating trajectories of the two Brownian motions W_t and Z_t. This simulation is done with a discrete time step $\mathrm{d}t$. In this way,

the increments $\mathrm{d}W_t$ and $\mathrm{d}Z_t$ of this time step are simulated thanks to a centered normal law of volatility $\sqrt{\mathrm{d}t}$.
2. Deducing from this, for each simulation, the trajectory of the asset S_t and of the variance σ_t^2. As the increments of the Brownian motions $\mathrm{d}W_t$ and $\mathrm{d}Z_t$ have been computed at the preceding step, it is sufficient to apply equation (7.2).
3. Deducing from each simulation the value of S_T.
4. Evaluating for each simulation the discounted final value of the call, which is defined in equation (7.1).
5. Computing the average of the results.

The Monte-Carlo method thus amounts to simulating various random events and to compute averages. This conceptual simplicity, which leads to simplicity in programming and in implementation, is a definite advantage of the method. It can easily be adapted to many situations and be implemented without difficulty even in the case of complex models such as stochastic volatility models.

Among the diversity of financial options which we presented in the preceding chapter, only American options raise a problem for the Monte-Carlo method. Indeed, for all other options, however exotic they may look, simulating the stock trajectory during the whole lifetime of the product is sufficient to exactly know what the product will finally be worth. We leave the verification of this statement to the reader. A problem arises for American options, because these options assume a decision from their holders: at what time will the holder choose to exercise the option? What is the optimal instant for exercising the option? This problem is not insoluble, and it can even be solved in the framework of Monte-Carlo simulations (*cf.* [Longstaff & Schwartz 2001]).

7.1.2 *Monte-Carlo hedging*

The random samplings of Figure 7.1 lead to very scattered results. The call payoff is zero in half of the simulations; it rises up to more

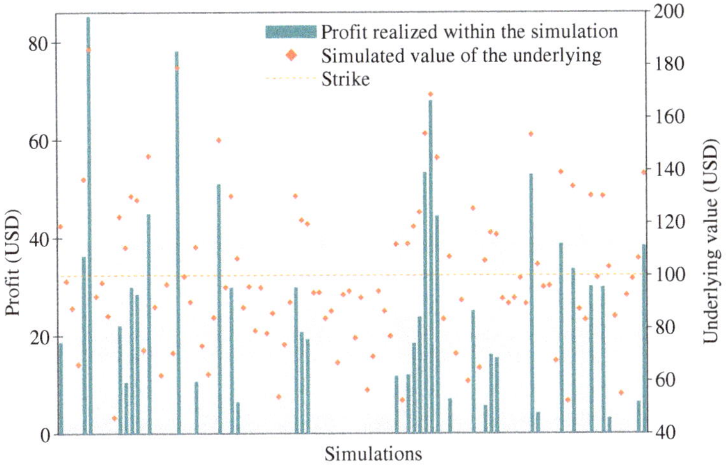

Figure 7.1: Implementation of the Monte-Carlo method in order to value a call of strike 100: each point represents the simulated price at expiry date of the underlying asset following Heston's model. If the simulated price lies below the option strike, the achieved gain is zero, if not, the gain is given by the difference between the simulated price and the strike. The average gain calculated over the 100 performed simulations is \$10.58, while, taking into account the chosen parameters, the exact model price is \$11.69. A better accuracy would have been obtained with more simulations.

than \$85 in one of the simulations. Those results are supposed to reproduce the various possible market situations: the dispersion of the results directly reflects the risk taken by traders on valued positions. As was mentioned in the preceding chapters, reducing the risk proceeds through hedging strategies, among which the delta hedge plays a prominent role.

In the Black-Scholes model, protection through a delta hedge is theoretically perfect: the hedged portfolio should not present any risk. Let us recall that delta hedging amounts to holding at any instant $-\Delta_t$ underlying stocks, where $\Delta_t = \partial \Pi_t(S)/\partial S$ is the (mathematical) derivative of the portfolio price with respect to the underlying asset. Implementing this strategy in practice is however far from being perfect, as hedging cannot be adjusted continuously but only at regular intervals. The strategy thus leaves us with a residual risk which can be simulated thanks to the Monte-Carlo method. In practice, to study the hedging of a call with strike K, we can proceed in the following way:

- For each simulation, we randomly sample the evolution of asset $S_{t_1}, S_{t_2}, S_{t_3} \cdots$ at chosen regular time intervals $t_1, t_2, t_3 \cdots$ and according to a specified model.
- At each time t_i, we compute the delta, Δ_{t_i}, of the hedged asset and re-adjust hedging. This re-adjustment assumes that we re-invest $-(\Delta_{t_i} - \Delta_{t_{i-1}}) \times S_{t_i}$ in the hedge.
- At the due payment date t_n of the option, we unwind the hedge and exit the option, for an amount $[\max(S_{t_n} - K; 0) - \Delta_{t_{n-1}} \times S_{t_n}]$. This latter cash flow, reduced by the capitalized re-adjustment costs of hedging, exactly corresponds to the strategy result.

If the hedging strategy was perfect, the result of the strategy computed would be the same across all simulations, so that there would be no risk. All possible market conditions would lead to the same result. This result would thus correspond to the gain achieved by the sale of the call, in other words, to the price of the call. In the case of an imperfect hedge, the result of the strategy depends on the simulation and the price of the call may be estimated as the average of the various simulated results. The reasoning is presented in Figure 7.2. While not perfect, the hedging techniques reduce in a significant way the risk taken by the trader; simultaneously, they can be used to reduce the dispersion of the Monte-Carlo draws, and thus to ensure a better accuracy of numerical results.

However, the approach we just followed suffers from a major flaw: it requires that we know the delta, and therefore the price, while our Monte-Carlo simulations have as their primary goal the computation of this price. As was shown by [Potters *et al.* 2001], it is possible to use Monte-Carlo simulations to compute at the same time the price and the optimal hedging. Let us now address this technique for the determination of the price and of the optimal hedging strategy with Monte-Carlo simulations.

Suppose first that we know at any time t the price $P_t(S_t)$ of a call. We are going to search for the hedge which minimizes the risk; more

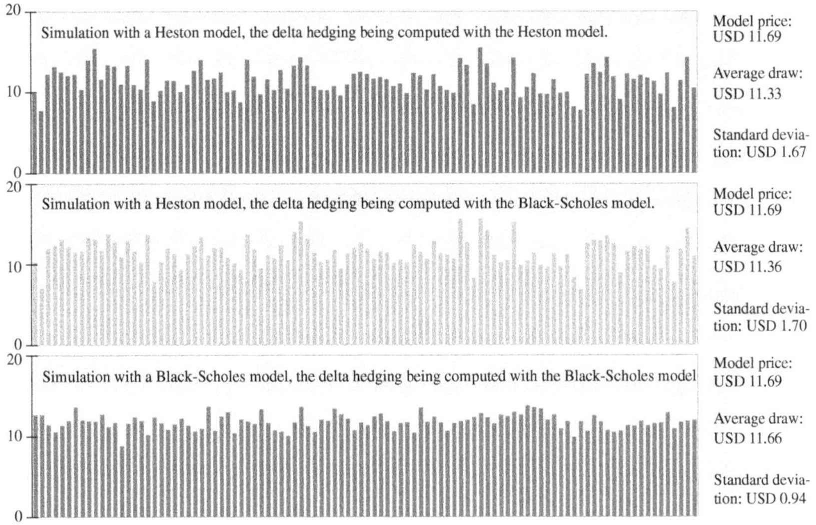

Figure 7.2: Implementation of the Monte-Carlo method in order to value a hedged call. Simulations are performed in the same conditions as in Figure 7.1: hedging does not modify the theoretical price of the portfolio, but it strongly reduces the total risk, and thus the dispersion of the samplings. This risk is measured by the standard deviation of the samplings. In the Black-Scholes model, the impossibility of hedging continuously leads to a residual risk on the hedged portfolio. However, it is less important than in Heston's model where risk originates in two distinct sources of randomness, one of which cannot be hedged by the delta hedge. On the middle graph, we observe that a delta computed with the wrong model increases the risk with respect to the correct computation of the delta (upper graph), without nevertheless substantially questioning the hedging efficiency. In a general way, using a delta computed with the Black-Scholes model will remain roughly efficient in any quasi-Gaussian model, but it will become all the more powerless as the modeling of the underlying asset will drift further apart from this framework.

precisely, we wish to minimize the variance of the Monte-Carlo simulations. Other measures of risk could have been contemplated, but we shall restrict ourselves here to associating the risk with volatility. As for the delta hedge, the hedging technique studied now consists simply in holding at time t some proportion h_t of the underlying asset (h stands for hedge).The quantity of hedge which is held will of course depend on the price of the asset S, and thus h_t is a function of S_t. It is this function $h_t(S_t)$ which we wish to optimize in order to reduce the risk to its minimum.

The evolution of the portfolio price between t and $t + \mathrm{d}t$, neglecting interest rates, is given by the formula:

$$P_{t+\mathrm{d}t}(S_{t+\mathrm{d}t}) - P_t(S_t) + h_t(S_t) \times (S_{t+\mathrm{d}t} - S_t) \qquad (7.3)$$

Indeed, our gain results from the evolution of the call price and of the hedge price. Here, we are interested in the variation of the assets value, and not in the incoming/outgoing money flows entailed by the hedging re-adjustments. Both lead to the same final result, since after the liquidation of the portfolio, the sum of the generated cash flows exactly equals the variation of the portfolio value. The advantage of the vision presented here is that it captures at every instant the variations of the call value, while, in the cash flow vision presented earlier, the impact of the call is visible at the due payment date only, when it is exercised.

In compliance with our aim, the function $h_t(S_t)$ is chosen in order to minimize the variance of the hedged portfolio; this variance is estimated as the average through all the Monte-Carlo simulations of the square of equation (7.3). Noting N the number of Monte-Carlo samplings, this last sentence is translated into the equation:

$$\frac{1}{N} \sum_{N \text{ draws of } S_t \text{ and } S_{t+\mathrm{d}t}} \left[P_{t+\mathrm{d}t}(S_{t+\mathrm{d}t}) - P_t(S_t) + h_t(S_t)(S_{t+\mathrm{d}t} - S_t)\right]^2 \qquad (7.4)$$

Then, at each instant t, the function $h_t(\bullet)$ is chosen in order to minimize the expression defined in equation (7.4). This construction leads to a function $h_t(\bullet)$ which is not very different from the delta of the option. It represents indeed the average sensitivity of the option price to the variation of the stock price over the time step $\mathrm{d}t$. In the models studied up to now, $h_t(S_t)$ converges towards $\Delta_t(S_t)$ when $\mathrm{d}t \to 0$. However, models which predict wilder variations of S_t, $h_t(S_t)$ and $\Delta_t(S_t)$ diverge, even when the time step approaches zero. Actually, the delta captures the sensitivity to an infinitesimal variation, while the hedge captures an average sensitivity through all the possible variations over the time step $\mathrm{d}t$: if these variations $\mathrm{d}S_t$ remain infinitesimal, the two notions will be identical, but if dS_t happens to be large even over a small time step, the two sensitivities will be different.

Up to now, we only solved half of the problem, since we computed the hedge of the portfolio, but not yet its price. Let us begin with the case where there is only one time step $T = dt$ and let index our N Monte-Carlo samplings by i. The hedge $h_0(S_0)$ is chosen in order to minimize the following quantity, provided we already found $P_0(S_0)$:

$$\frac{1}{N}\sum_{i=1}^{N}\left(P_T(S_T^i) - P_0(S_0) + h_0(S_0) \times (S_T^i - S_0)\right)^2 \qquad (7.5)$$

Since we work under the risk-neutral measure and have neglected the interest rates, the price of the call at time $t = 0$ is necessarily the average of the prices at T. Let us, for the moment, note this price Π. One can prove mathematically that the quantity defined by equation (7.5) is minimal when $P_0(S_0) = \Pi$, and this property is true whatever the value of $h_0(S_0)$. It is remarkable that the price Π of the call is equal to the quantity which, when injected in equation (7.5), minimizes the variance of the hedged portfolio.[1] It is important to notice that the use of a measure other than the variance to assess the risk would not have allowed such a short cut. Therefore, in the framework of our study, the two quantities $P_0(S_0)$ and $h_0(S_0)$ may be searched for in a single step: we don't need the price to compute the hedge nor the hedge to compute the price as they can be found at the same time by looking for the paramaters $P_0(S_0)$ and $h_0(S_0)$ that minimize equation (7.5).

[1]The mathematically minded reader will note that, when $N \to \infty$, the quantity $P_0(S_0)$ which minimizes the quantity defined in equation (7.5) is the expectation value:

$$E(P_T) + h_0(S_0) \times (E(S_T) - S_0)\,.$$

Now, under the risk-neutral measure and without interest rates, S_t is a martingale and $E(S_T) = S_0$.

This property is true at any instant t of the simulation: the price and optimal hedge may be both computed by minimizing the quantity defined in equation (7.4). Lingering on this equation, the reader will notice that this reasoning requires the knowledge of the price at time $t + \mathrm{d}t$. This is not a problem, as we have set in advance $P_T(\bullet)$ at the due payment date of the option: it is by definition the payoff of the call. We may then compute $P_{T-\mathrm{d}t}$ and $h_{T-\mathrm{d}t}$ by minimizing the quantity defined in equation (7.4) at time $T - \mathrm{d}T$. After this calculation, we know $P_{T-\mathrm{d}t}$ and we may pursue at time $T - 2\mathrm{d}t$, and so forth until $t = 0$. Starting from the latest time, we can thus go back in time in order to compute at any instant t the call price and its optimal hedge.

Results of applying this method in the same conditions as those of Figure 7.2 are summarized in Table 7.1 below.

Table 7.1

	Basic Monte-Carlo	Monte-Carlo with Black-Scholes hedge	Monte-Carlo with optimal hedge
Exact model price		11, 69	
Simulated price	10, 58	11, 36	11, 05
Standard deviation of the simulations	18, 53	1, 70	1, 46

In [Potters *et al.* 2001], the authors apply this same method while leaving the risk-neutral framework. Although we shall not enter the details of this discussion, we shall emphasize that this approach leads us to a remarkable alternative provided by Monte-Carlo methods: the use of real historical data rather than simulated data. This alternative is very useful if one wishes to leave theoretical modelings and to study financial products and models on actual data. Figure 7.3 illustrates this kind of applications.

7.1.3 *Convergence of the method**

The techniques which we just described substantially improve the accuracy of the Monte-Carlo simulations, and even use the lack

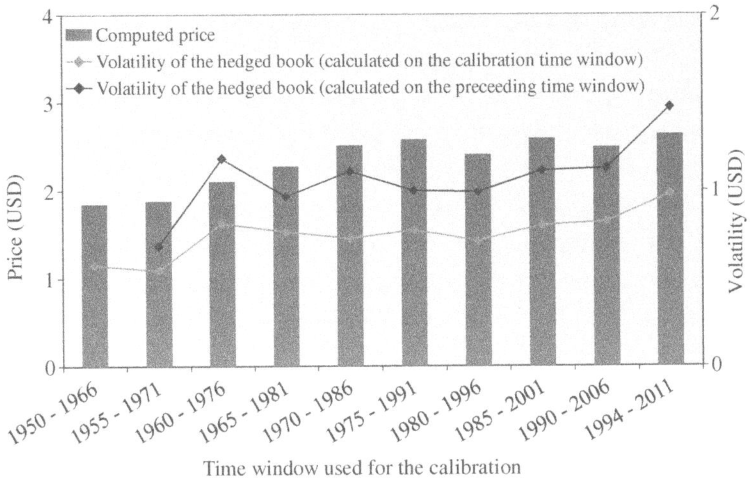

Figure 7.3: Computation of a call price from Dow Jones time series. Ten 15 years windows of history are used, each one is used to reconstruct 100 paths for the Dow Jones level (1,000 simulations in total). In each time window, the call price and the hedge are computed by minimizing at each instant the variance of the hedged portfolio. The volatility of the hedged portfolio is estimated over the whole lifetime of the call. It is computed in two ways: in the first one, the optimal hedge function is directly used on the sample which was used for its calibration; in the second one, the hedge function calibrated on the preceding period is used to simulate the results of the hedging technique. The aim of this second method is to account for the fact that the strategy is calibrated on past data in order to be applied to future situations. Two elements are highlighted here to quantify the robustness of the optimal hedging strategy: the time evolution of computed prices and the increase of their volatility between the calibration sample and the application sample. Indeed, stable prices indicate that it will be possible to use past prices in order to compute future ones; the less the volatility deteriorates from a sample to another one, the more the hedge calibrated in the past will stay optimal in the future.

of accuracy to quantify the residual error of hedging strategies. However, the computing time necessary to implement Monte-Carlo methods remains a major handicap insofar as the convergence of the simulation is very slow; many of the computations performed in banks use up to one night of computational resources. We shall address in what follows some theories meant to reduce the necessary computing time and to increase the accuracy of numerical results.

Box 7.1. Convergence speed. The convergence speed of a numerical method is defined here as the order of magnitude of how the accuracy is enhanced by the number of computational steps. For example, a $1/n^2$ convergence means that the accuracy of the calculation is multiplied by 100 if the number of steps is multiplied by 10. Thus, a $1/n^2$ convergence is much faster than a $1/n$ convergence, as $1/n^2$ tends to zero much more rapidly than $1/n$ when $n \to \infty$. We are only interested in orders of magnitude, so that multiplicative constants are irrelevant: convergences in $1/n$, $3/n$ or even $50/n$ are considered equivalent.

The question of the convergence is formulated in the following way: given a required level of accuracy, how many computational steps are necessary? Equivalently, given a number of computational steps, what is the expected accuracy of our results? The answer to these questions points to the convergence speed of the numerical method. In the framework of Monte-Carlo simulations, statistics allow to precisely assess this speed. Schematically, when we compute the mean value of n random samplings, the estimated mean value (computed by taking the average of results) diverges from the theoretical mean value (the true mean value which we attempt to evaluate) by $1/\sqrt{n}$. The mean value of the samplings results is itself a random variable: it is equally possible to find by chance the exact searched value, or to find a complete outlier. Theory tells us that, in general, the error will be on order $1/\sqrt{n}$, where n is the number of random samplings. This result is illustrated in Figure 7.4.

This statistical convergence is very slow: to improve the accuracy by a factor of 10, we must multiply by 100 the number of samplings. In its applications to financial equations resolution, the Monte-Carlo method can actually be even slower because it may require the calculation of the asset price at any instant before the due payment date. Each random sampling will then use N computational steps to define the evolution of the underlying asset between the initial time $t = 0$ and the due payment date $t = T$. Indeed, we must discretize time, that is, divide a continuous time in the interval $t \in [0, T]$ into

Computation of Π's value with Monte Carlo simulations:
For each simulation, a number of points are randomly drawed within a square. After each simulation, the average number of points that were drawed within the inner circle is calculated and multiplied by 4: the result should tend towards Π.

	10 draws	50 draws	100 draws	500 draws	1,000 draws	10,000 draws
Simulation 1	3.6	3.04	3.24	3.200	3.108	3.1372
Simulation 2	2.8	2.96	3.24	3.184	3.168	3.1380
Simulation 3	4.0	3.20	3.08	**3.200**	3.172	3.1192
Simulation 4	2.4	3.20	3.20	3.048	3.220	3.1184
Simulation 5	2.8	3.28	3.32	3.160	3.168	3.1312
Average theoritical estimation error	.519	.232	.164	.073	.052	.016

Real value of Π: 3.14159...

Focus on the 500 first draws of simulation 3

Each mark is the result of a random draw within the square. There are 400 points drawn within the innercircle, that is 80% of the total number of draws. This induces an estimation for Π of 4×80%=3.2

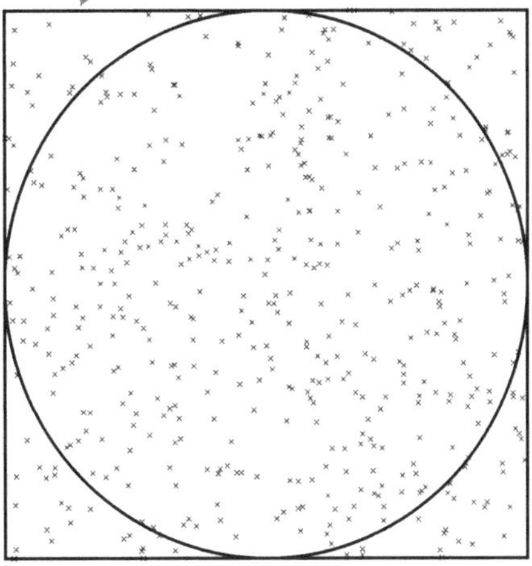

Figure 7.4: Estimating π with the Monte-Carlo method. The average statistical error of the estimate decreases as $1/\sqrt{n}$: when we go from 100 to 10,000 samplings, the error on the estimate has only been divided by 10 (it is reduced from 0.16 to 0.016).

N instants, $0, T/N, 2T/N, \ldots$. The final results will then be subject to two sources of uncertainty:

- the statistical error linked to the number of random samplings, n, which is on order $1/\sqrt{n}$;
- the error linked with the discretization of the time interval $[0;T]$ into N time steps, and we shall admit that this error is generically on order $1/N$.

The total number of computational steps is, in this configuration, of order $N \times n$: for any of the n simulations, we must compute the asset trajectories over the N time steps. In order to minimize the number of computational steps, we must cleverly choose n and N with respect to each other: as the two sources of uncertainties add up, it would not be wise to have an extreme precision on the one side while having a large uncertainty on the other. It is possible to show that the best choice is to have errors of the same order of magnitude $1/\sqrt{n} \simeq 1/N$, that is, $n \simeq N^2$.

In the end, for an error approximately of $1/N$, we must divide the time scale into N points and perform N^2 samplings, that is N^3 computational steps. For an accuracy to increase 10 times, we must perform 1,000 times more computational steps. The convergence is extremely slow, and could prove to be impracticable in some situations. The techniques for speeding up the convergence of Monte-Carlo methods are, therefore, of crucial importance. We now address one of these techniques, which uses quasi-random series. The interested reader may go deeper into the subject and discover other methods in [Jäckel 2002].

Look at the details of one of the Monte-Carlo simulations which were used to compute π in Figure 7.4. The points are far from being uniformly distributed in the square: some zones are densely populated, while others are rather empty. This phenomenon is a burden for Monte-Carlo estimates because zones with a large concentration of points will be overweighted compared to the ones with a low concentration. The idea of quasi-random series is, on the contrary, to occupy space in a way that is more efficient than sheer randomness in order to obtain a better convergence of Monte-Carlo estimates.

We shall address this problem by concentrating on the random sampling of points in the hypercube $[0;1]^n$, each point of the hypercube representing one sampling of n random variables $(X_1, X_2, \ldots, X_n)$ independent and uniformly distributed in $[0;1]$. For example, for $n = 1$, it amounts to randomly choosing one point in the $[0;1]$ interval; for $n = 2$, to randomly choose one point in the square

$[0;1] \times [0;1]$, as we did to estimate π. Mathematicians know how to transform n independent random variables uniformly distributed in $[0;1]$ into n random variables distributed according to any possible law and with any possible correlations. We shall not detail this computation, and we simply retain that the results which we shall illustrate with uniform samplings in $[0;1]^n$ hypercubes are easily generalized to any kind of random variable, in particular Gaussian and lognormal laws.

Let us come back to our issue: how may we best succeed in choosing points uniformly distributed and dense in space? In dimension 1, the best way to occupy the $[0;1]$ interval is of course to divide the interval into regularly spaced points $0, 1/N, 2/N, \ldots, (1-1/N), 1$. Thanks to this partition into $N+1$ points, we have obtained a grid such that no point of the interval $[0;1]$ is further than $1/2N$ from some point of the grid. Assume we wish to estimate an expectation $E(f(u))$ where u is a random variable uniformly distributed in $[0;1]$, and where f is a function of which we want to compute the average. Using a brute force Monte-Carlo method, we would perform n random samplings $t_1, \ldots, t_n$ in $[0,1]$ and we would estimate $(1/n)\sum_i f(t_i)$: this method leads to the desired result with a $1/\sqrt{n}$ convergence. If instead of using our n random samplings we started from a grid on $[0;1]$, we would compute $(1/n)\sum_i f(i/n)$: under the assumption that the function f is regular enough, this method is substantially more efficient and converges with a $1/n$ speed towards the desired result.

In dimension 2, the problem is more complicated, as covering the square with a grid requires N^2 points; because of this, such a simple partition of the square will not give better results than the Monte-Carlo method. In dimension d, where d may take any positive integer value, the partition becomes completely inefficient as it requires N^d points for an $1/N$ accuracy, while the Monte-Carlo method gives an $1/N$ accuracy with N^2 points.

Covering with a simple grid is thus a good idea in dimension 1, but cannot directly be generalized. In order to solve the problem, we will build different series in $[0;1]$, each of them occupying space almost as well as the regular partition of the one-dimensional interval, and which seems independent from one another: the Van der Corput Series.

Van der Corput Series in a basis p is built by partitioning the $[0;1]$ interval into p sub-intervals, and repeating the partitioning. The base 2 Van der Corput Series is built as follows:

1. Divide the interval into two and put the first point in the middle $u_1 = 1/2$.
2. Divide the two sub-intervals $[0;u_1]$ and $[u_1;1]$ into two and put the second point in the middle of the first sub-interval ($u_2 = 1/4$) and the third point in the middle of the second subinterval ($u_3 = 3/4$).
3. Divide into two the four sub-intervals $[0,u_2]$, $[u_1;u_3]$, $[u_2;u_1]$ and $[u_3;1]$, which leads to: $u_4 = 1/8, u_5 = 5/8, u_6 = 3/8$ and $u_7 = 7/8$.
4. And so forth.

Thanks to this technique illustrated in Figure 7.5, the series $u_1, \ldots, u_{2^n-1}$ covers the $[0;1]$ interval with a grid of 2^n sub-intervals of size $1/2^n$. The method may be used starting from a base 2 as in our example, but also from bases 3, 4, etc. The Van der Corput Series in base 10 is as follows[2]:

$$.1\,;.2\,;.3\,;.4\,;.5\,;.6\,;.7\,;.8\,;.9\,;.01\,;.11\,;.21\,;\ldots$$

The use of a Van der Corput Series is almost as efficient as that of a regular partition of the $[0;1]$ interval. These series, which occupy space in a dense and regular manner are termed *series with a low discrepancy*. Concretely, to perform the Monte-Carlo simulations, a quant must replace the random samplings $t_1, \ldots, t_N$ in $[0;1]$ by the successive values $u_1, \ldots, u_N$ of a series with low discrepancy. This method is termed quasi Monte-Carlo, since it relies not on random sequences, but on well-chosen deterministic sequences.

[2]It amounts to a simple counting 1, 2, 3, ..., 10, 11, 12, etc. where the order of figures has been inverted and where a decimal point was added; for example, the 1040th term of a Van der Corput Series in base 10 is .0401.

$u_1 = .5$
$u_2 = .25$
$u_3 = .75$
$u_4 = .125$
$u_5 = .625$
$u_6 = .375$
$u_7 = .875$
$u_8 = .0625$
$u_9 = .5625$
$u_{10} = .3125$
$u_{11} = .8125$
$u_{12} = .1875$
$u_{13} = .6875$
$u_{14} = .4375$
$u_{15} = .9375$

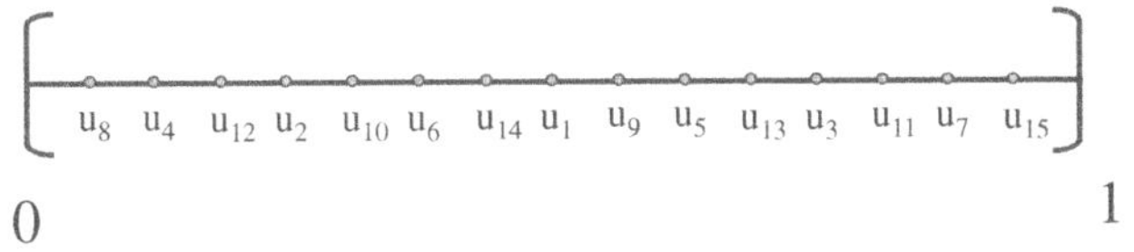

Figure 7.5: Representation of the first 15 values of the Van der Corput Series in base 2. The first 15 draws achieve a perfect partition (in 16 identical pieces) of the [0; 1] interval. Van der Corput Series may be used to speed up the convergence of Monte-Carlo simulations.

A very simple method to build sequences with low discrepancy in any dimension d is to use directly d Van der Corput Series of distinct bases. In dimension 2, for example, we may create the series (x_n, y_n) where x_n is a Van der Corput of base p and y_n a Van der Corput Series of base q. In this way, the series x_n is distributed in an optimal way on the abscissa axis and y_n on the ordinate axis. In order to ensure that the pair (x_n, y_n) properly occupies space, we need one last condition, which originates in number theory: the integers p and q must be coprime, they must not have a common divisor. In this case, the series x_n and y_n are endowed with all the necessary independence properties which allow the pair to properly occupy space. In the case where p and q are not coprime, the sequences x_n and y_n exhibit similarities and they are concentrated in specific zones. Figure 7.6 provides examples of how couples of Van der Corput Series occupy space. In the most extreme case where $p = q$, we have $x_n = y_n$ and the sequence (x_n, y_n) is confined to the diagonal $x = y$ (which is then occupied in a perfectly dense and regular manner, but this is not what we were looking for!). In order to avoid being bothered by independence questions, sequences are in general built starting from bases p_1, p_2 and so on where the p_is are primes. Series built in this way are called Halton series.

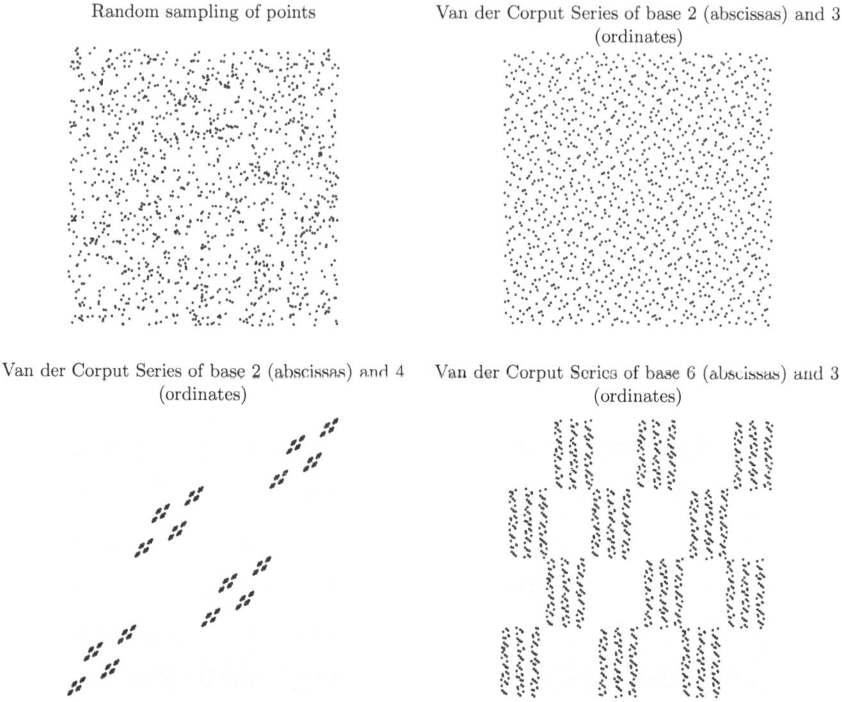

Figure 7.6: Examples of covering space with a grid. The upper left-hand graph corresponds to random samplings: the points are not optimally distributed in space, which slows down the convergence of Monte-Carlo simulations. On the contrary, the upper right-hand graph which represents samplings using a Halton series (Van der Corput Series in base 2 for the abscissas and base 3 for the ordinates) displays a dense and regular occupation of space. The lower graphs represent sampling performed from Van der Corput Series with bases which are not coprime; they display non-occupied zones.

Thanks to low discrepancy series, as illustrated in Figure 7.7, we achieved to substantially speed up the convergence. It has been conjectured that the limiting speed of convergence is $\ln^d(n)/n$, where d is the number of dimensions. However, confirmation of this conjecture is still waiting for a proof! Anyway, the Halton series which we have mentioned, and its variants, are the series which empirically bring good convergence speed. The Halton series are however not very efficient in high dimension.

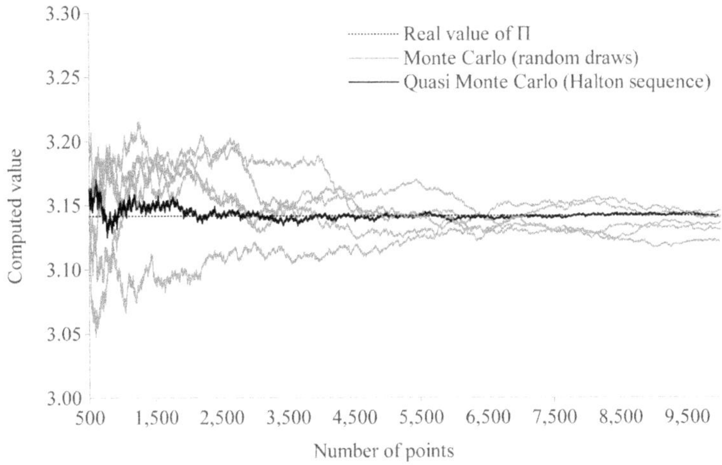

Figure 7.7: Convergence of the Monte-Carlo method (use of random sampling) and of quasi Monte-Carlo (use of a Halton series) for the estimate of π. The superiority of the Halton series for the estimate of π is blatant on this graph: the estimate converges much faster.

7.2 Finite Differences Method*

This section is devoted to the numerical resolution of a partial differential equation. The reader who is not familiar with such equations may skip it and proceed directly to the next chapter; the notions which are developed below are somewhat technical and are not used further in the book.

We introduced in Chapter 5 the Black-Scholes equation:

$$\frac{\partial \Pi_t}{\partial t} + rS_t \frac{\partial \Pi_t}{\partial S} + \frac{1}{2}\sigma^2 S_t^2 \frac{\partial^2 \Pi_t}{\partial S^2} = r\Pi_t \tag{7.6}$$

In the Black-Scholes model, this equation must be obeyed by any financial product whose price $\Pi_t(S_t)$ depends at time t on the value S_t of an underlying asset. Recall that, in this model, S_t follows a log-normal motion of yearly volatility σ (regardless of its drift) and the risk-free interest is constant and noted r.

To be specific, we shall from now on limit ourselves to the example of a call on a stock S of due payment date T and of strike K. The price

$\Pi_t(S_t)$ will have not only to obey equation (7.6), but also the final boundary condition:

$$\Pi_t(S_t) = \max(S_T - K; 0) \tag{7.7}$$

The two equations (7.6) and (7.7) are sufficient to characterize the price Π_t: under hypotheses which are almost not restrictive, there exists a unique function $\Pi_t(S_t)$ which obeys both equations. This property is not specific to calls, any final boundary condition may be used instead of equation (7.7). However, in order to keep it simple, we shall stay with the example of the call, which should, at this point, be familiar to the reader.

The method of finite differences is a technique which allows to numerically solve the combination of equations (7.6) and (7.7), that is, to explicitly compute the values of $\Pi_t(S_t)$ given the parameters r, σ, K, T. The underlying idea is very simple.

- Equation (7.6) may be discretized: as in the framework of binomial trees, we return to a discrete time (0, $\mathrm{d}t$, $2 \times \mathrm{d}t$, $\ldots, N \times \mathrm{d}t = T$) and discrete values for S (0, $\mathrm{d}S$, $2 \times \mathrm{d}S$, $\ldots, N \times \mathrm{d}S, \ldots$).
- Once it is discretized, equation (7.6) links the values of Π_t to those of $\Pi_{t+\mathrm{d}t}$.
- Now, values of Π_T at time T are known, thanks to equation (7.7). It is then sufficient to go back in time, starting from T, then $T - \mathrm{d}t$, $T - 2\mathrm{d}t$ etc., down to 0.

Let us implement this and fix $\mathrm{d}t$ and $\mathrm{d}S$, the time and stock price increments. To first order, partial derivatives may be expressed, by the following ratios:

$$\begin{cases} \dfrac{\partial \Pi_t}{\partial t} = \dfrac{\Pi_t(S_t) - \Pi_{t-\mathrm{d}t}(S_t)}{\mathrm{d}t} + \mathcal{O}(\mathrm{d}t) \\ \dfrac{\partial \Pi_t}{\partial S} = \dfrac{\Pi_t(S_t + \mathrm{d}S) - \Pi_t(S_t - \mathrm{d}S)}{2\mathrm{d}S} + \mathcal{O}(\mathrm{d}S^2) \\ \dfrac{\partial^2 \Pi_t}{\partial S^2} = \dfrac{\Pi_t(S_t + \mathrm{d}S) - 2\Pi_t(S_t) + \Pi_t(S_t - \mathrm{d}S)}{\mathrm{d}S^2} + \mathcal{O}(\mathrm{d}S^2) \end{cases} \tag{7.8}$$

In the preceding equations, $\mathcal{O}(\mathrm{d}t)$ and $\mathcal{O}(\mathrm{d}S^2)$ mean that discretization entails errors on order of $\mathrm{d}t$ and $\mathrm{d}S^2$. Note $\mathcal{O}(\mathrm{d}t)$ and

$\mathcal{O}(\mathrm{d}S^2)$ are infinitesimal quantities; we will see later on that the discretization of time (the fixing of dt) and the discretization of the asset price (the fixing of dS) should ensure that $\mathcal{O}(\mathrm{d}t)$ and $\mathcal{O}(\mathrm{d}S^2)$ are of the same order.

The smaller the discretization steps, the smaller the approximation error will be. In this set of equations, all expressions are defined from the function $\Pi_t(\bullet)$, with the exception of a single term which is written from the function $\Pi_{t-\mathrm{d}t}(\bullet)$. As a consequence, plugging approximations (7.8) into equation (7.6) and reorganizing the various terms, it is possible to express $\Pi_{t-\mathrm{d}t}(\bullet)$ from $\Pi_t(\bullet)$. The result of the calculation is:

$$\begin{aligned}\Pi_{t-\mathrm{d}t}(S_t) = {} & \Pi_t(S_t - \mathrm{d}S) \times \left(\frac{\sigma^2 S_t^2 \mathrm{d}t}{2\mathrm{d}S^2} - \frac{rS_t \mathrm{d}t}{2\mathrm{d}S}\right) \\ & + \Pi_t(S_t) \times \left(1 - r\mathrm{d}t - \frac{\sigma^2 S_t^2 \mathrm{d}t}{\mathrm{d}S^2}\right) \\ & + \Pi_t(S_t + \mathrm{d}S) \times \left(\frac{\sigma^2 S_t^2 \mathrm{d}t}{2\mathrm{d}S^2} + \frac{rS_t \mathrm{d}t}{2\mathrm{d}S}\right) \\ & + \mathcal{O}(\mathrm{d}t \times \mathrm{d}S^2) + \mathcal{O}(\mathrm{d}t^2)\end{aligned} \tag{7.9}$$

This equation is long and cumbersome, but it does not present any technical difficulty. It states that the value of $\Pi_{t-\mathrm{d}t}(S_t)$ is computed by adding and multiplying various terms, and, among them, the parameters of the model $(\sigma, r, \mathrm{d}t, \mathrm{d}S)$ and the values of $\Pi_t(\bullet)$ at $(S_t - \mathrm{d}S)$, at S_t and at $(S_t + \mathrm{d}S)$. This calculation generates two approximation errors, whose magnitudes are respectively on order $\mathrm{d}t^2$ and $\mathrm{d}t \times \mathrm{d}S^2$. Thus, if we may forget about the errors $\mathcal{O}(\mathrm{d}t \times \mathrm{d}S^2)$ and $\mathcal{O}(\mathrm{d}t^2)$, the finite differences method hinges on the propagation equation:

$$\begin{aligned}\Pi_{t-\mathrm{d}t}(S_t) = {} & \Pi_t(S_t - \mathrm{d}S) \times \left(\frac{\sigma^2 S_t^2 \mathrm{d}t}{2\mathrm{d}S^2} - \frac{rS_t \mathrm{d}t}{2\mathrm{d}S}\right) \\ & + \Pi_t(S_t) \times \left(1 - r\mathrm{d}t - \frac{\sigma^2 S_t^2 \mathrm{d}t}{\mathrm{d}S^2}\right) \\ & + \Pi_t(S_t + \mathrm{d}S) \times \left(\frac{\sigma^2 S_t^2 \mathrm{d}t}{2\mathrm{d}S^2} + \frac{rS_t \mathrm{d}t}{2\mathrm{d}S}\right)\end{aligned} \tag{7.10}$$

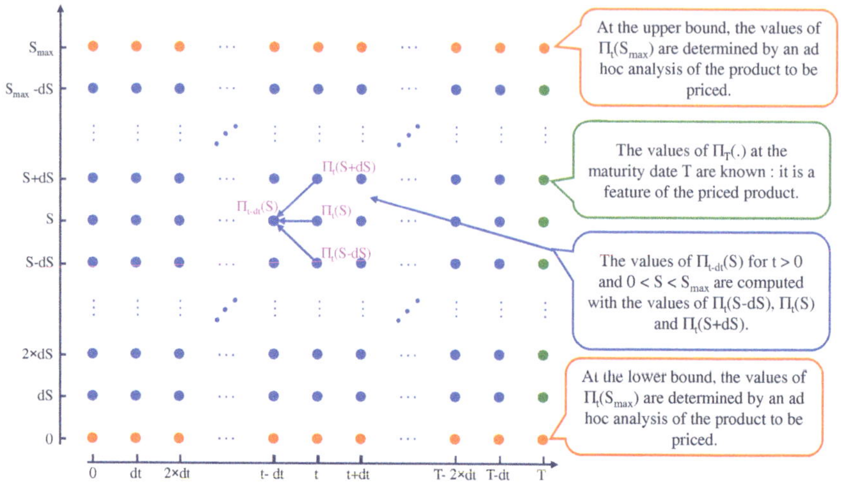

Figure 7.8: Illustration of the finite differences method. The goal is to fill at each point of the grid the price of the option $\Pi_t(S)$ which one wishes to value. At $t = T$, the price is given by the final condition. At $S = 0$ or $S = S_{\max}$, a good approximation of the prices $\Pi_t(0)$ and $\Pi_t(S_{\max})$ can generally be identified by a theoretical analysis of the product to be priced. For the other points, one propagates equation (7.10).

By choosing as a starting point the known value at T of $\Pi_T(S_T)$ — it is by definition equation (7.7) — a numerical program can sequentially compute all the values of $\Pi_T(\bullet)$, then those of $\Pi_{T-\mathrm{d}t}(\bullet)$, $\Pi_{T-2\mathrm{d}t}(\bullet)$ and so forth, the result of all these iterations being $\Pi_0(\bullet)$, which is the initial price of the call.

Thus, the finite differences method amounts to covering a grid, such as represented in Figure 7.8. By construction, this grid contains $T/\mathrm{d}t$ abscissa points and $S_{\max}/\mathrm{d}S$ ordinate points. Actually, a computer cannot build an infinite grid, and in practice it will be necessary to limit the upper value of the stock to a sufficiently large figure. This raises the issue of boundary conditions: how do we compute the values of $\Pi_t(S)$ when S reaches the boundaries of the graph? Equation (7.10) cannot be evaluated at $S = 0$ and at $S = S_{\max}$. However, in these limiting cases, and under the assumption that $S_{\max}$ is large, it is in general possible to compute explicit formulae which approximate $\Pi_t(0)$ and $\Pi_t(S_{\max})$. The solution chosen thus depends on the derivative to be valued; in the case of a call, we shall admit for example that $\Pi_t(0) = 0$ and

$$\Pi_t(S_{\max}) \simeq S_{\max} - Ke^{-r(T-t)}$$

Thus, the finite differences method amounts to filling the grid of Figure 7.8 in the following way.

1. Fill the last column thanks to equation (7.7).
2. Fill the first and last lines thanks to the computed boundary conditions:

$$\Pi_t(0) = 0 \text{ and } \Pi_t(S_{\max}) \simeq S_{\max} - Ke^{-r(T-t)} \text{ in the case of a call}.$$

3. Fill the interior of the grid by propagating equation (7.10).

The principle for applying the finite differences method is simple; however, it is much more complicated to prove that the method does lead to the solution of equation (7.6). As the verification of the convergence is the major issue of the finite differences method, we are going to address it. We shall see, by the way, that the convergence is not always guaranteed, and that instabilities may arise in some situations. Two questions define the problem of convergence.

1. What is the error made at each point of the grid?
2. How does this error propagate through the grid?

If we can show that the error created at each node and propagated through the grid remains under control, and that it tends to zero when the discretization steps tend to zero, we shall have demonstrated the convergence. The answer to the first question is contained in the term $\mathcal{O}(\mathrm{d}t \times \mathrm{d}S^2) + \mathcal{O}(\mathrm{d}t^2)$, which is the error resulting from the approximation of partial derivatives in equations (7.8). From the very definition of the symbol $\mathcal{O}(\bullet)$, there exists a constant M such that[3]:

$$\mathcal{O}(\mathrm{d}t \times \mathrm{d}S^2) + \mathcal{O}(\mathrm{d}t^2) \leq M(\mathrm{d}t \times \mathrm{d}S^2 + \mathrm{d}t^2) \qquad (7.11)$$

[3] The mathematically minded reader will note that we implicitly assume that the values of the partial derivatives are bounded on the whole grid.

The quality of the approximation at each node is not sufficient to ensure the convergence of the computations. It is also necessary that this error is not amplified during the propagation process. Let us note ε_t the maximal error made at each time step. Formally

$$\varepsilon_t = \max_{0 \leq 0 \leq S_{\max}} (|\Pi_t(S) - \Pi_t^*(S)|)$$

where $\Pi_t(\bullet)$ is the price computed with the grid and Π_t^* the exact theoretical price, solution of equation (7.6). Using equations (7.9) and (7.11) and some intermediate algebraic manipulations, we can bound the propagation of the error as follows:

$$\begin{aligned}\varepsilon_{t-\mathrm{d}t} \leq \varepsilon_t & \left(\left| 1 - \sigma^2 S_{\max}^2 \frac{\mathrm{d}t}{\mathrm{d}S^2} - r\mathrm{d}t \right| + \sigma^2 S_{\max}^2 \frac{\mathrm{d}t}{\mathrm{d}S^2} + rS_{\max} \frac{\mathrm{d}t}{\mathrm{d}S} \right) \\ & + M(\mathrm{d}t \times \mathrm{d}S^2 + \mathrm{d}t^2)\end{aligned} \tag{7.12}$$

The term multiplying ε_t represents the rate of the error increase. If it is bigger than 1, the error made at the first time step $\varepsilon_{T-\mathrm{d}t}$ is amplified exponentially: there is a risk that our numerical scheme diverges. How then can we control this amplification factor?

The first step is to keep the ratio $\mathrm{d}t/\mathrm{d}S^2$ under control: if the discretization step of the stock is too small compared to the time step, this quantity becomes infinite, as well as the amplification factor of the error. Figure 7.9 clearly shows that this condition is not only a theoretical one, and if the increment $\mathrm{d}S$ is too small, the method does not converge. Let us assume that $\mathrm{d}S^2$ is chosen large enough compared to $\mathrm{d}t$, in such a way that $\mathrm{d}t/\mathrm{d}S^2$ remains bounded, and let us look more precisely at the other terms of the amplification factor in equation (7.12). The terms

$$rS_{\max} \frac{\mathrm{d}t}{\mathrm{d}S} = \mathrm{d}S \times rS_{\max} \frac{\mathrm{d}t}{\mathrm{d}S^2}$$

and $r\mathrm{d}t$ will tend to zero, when the discretization steps $\mathrm{d}t$ and $\mathrm{d}S$ tend to zero: they have a negligible influence on the error, and, for simplicity, we shall forget about these terms. We can hence simplify

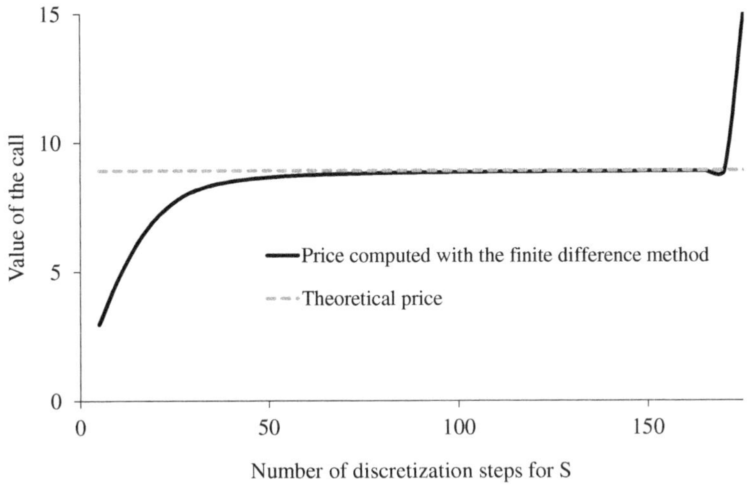

Figure 7.9: The black curve represents the price of a call computed by the finite differences method as a function of the number of discretization steps of the stock (the number of time steps being fixed at 1,000 and $S_{\max} = 500$). The method is more and more precise from 0 to 150 discretization steps and it diverges beyond 160.

the equation of the error propagation:

$$\varepsilon_{t-\mathrm{d}t} \leq \varepsilon_t \left(\left| 1 - \sigma^2 S_{\max}^2 \frac{\mathrm{d}t}{\mathrm{d}S^2} \right| + \sigma^2 S_{\max}^2 \frac{\mathrm{d}t}{\mathrm{d}S^2} \right) + M(\mathrm{d}t \times \mathrm{d}S^2 + \mathrm{d}t^2) \tag{7.13}$$

Thus, in order to avoid an amplification factor bigger than 1, we must have:

$$\sigma^2 S_{\max}^2 \frac{\mathrm{d}t}{\mathrm{d}S^2} \leq 1 \iff \sqrt{\mathrm{d}t} \leq \frac{\mathrm{d}S}{\sigma S_{\max}} \tag{7.14}$$

This is the main condition of convergence for the finite differences method applied to the Black-Scholes equation (7.6). Without this condition, nothing guarantees that our calculations effectively lead to the correct solution, as illustrated in Figure 7.9.

If this condition is satisfied, equation (7.13) simplifies and propagates in a straightforward way. The error at the edge of the grid, at

$t = 0$, can hence be bounded:

$$\begin{aligned}
\varepsilon_0 &\le \varepsilon_{\mathrm{d}t} + M(\mathrm{d}t \times \mathrm{d}S^2 + \mathrm{d}t^2) \\
&\le \varepsilon_{2*\mathrm{d}t} + 2M(\mathrm{d}t \times \mathrm{d}S^2 + \mathrm{d}t^2) \\
&\le \cdots \\
&\le \frac{M}{\mathrm{d}t}(\mathrm{d}t \times \mathrm{d}S^2 + \mathrm{d}t^2) = \mathcal{O}(\mathrm{d}S^2) + \mathcal{O}(\mathrm{d}t)
\end{aligned} \tag{7.15}$$

Thus, if we chose $\mathrm{d}S^2$ on order $\mathrm{d}t$, while obeying the stability condition (7.14), we just showed that the convergence error of the numerical scheme is on order $\mathrm{d}t$. Schematically, if we wish an accuracy $1/N = \mathrm{d}t$, we must divide time into N intervals and the stock into $\sqrt{N}$ ones. In the end, we thus count $N^{3/2}$ points in the grid: the method is much more efficient than the Monte-Carlo simulations where we required N^3 computational steps for the same $1/N$ accuracy.

However, when the number of dimensions increases, the finite differences method lacks interest. Indeed, one can prove that the number of computational steps necessary for a $1/N$ accuracy is $N^{1+d/2}$, where d is the number of dimensions. As for the Monte-Carlo method, it requires $d \times N^3$ computational steps: the latest quickly becomes more efficient when the number of dimensions increases.

The finite differences method does not directly give the probability distribution of the assets' prices. Consequently, it will be less useful than Monte-Carlo simulations in order to compute various risk indicators such as the probability that a loss exceeds $x\%$ (also known as the *value at risk* which we will address in the next chapter).

However, a big advantage of the finite differences method is that one solves in a single calculus the whole valuation function $\Pi_t(S_t)$ for any t and S_t. With the Monte-Carlo method on the contrary, the simulations must be re-iterated at each point (t, S_t) where one wishes to value $\Pi_t(S_t)$. With the finite differences method, the computation of the delta, $\partial\Pi/\partial S$, which is very useful for hedging strategies, may be realized without any additional effort. The other partial derivatives may be computed as well at each point of the grid. This overview of the whole valuation grid also gives opportunities to easily refine the modeling: one could introduce time and stock dependent parameters $\sigma(t, S)$ or $r(t)$, add jumps at different points of the grid, take into account an uncertainty on a parameter, etc.

Within the same logic, finite differences methods are very efficient to compute prices of American options. Recall that an American call provides its holder with the option to claim from the seller the amount $\max(S_t - K; 0)$ at any instant during the lifetime of the option, the claim being allowed only once. The central issue is then the following: what is the best time to exercise the option; that is, to claim the amount $\max(S_t - K; 0)$? This question is addressed naturally in a finite differences grid: at each node (t, S_t) of the grid, the calculation of the propagation equation (7.10) gives the continuation value of the option, that is, its price if one decides not to exercise it at this precise time. This continuation value should be compared to the exercise value, that is, the price of the option if one chooses to exercise it, which is by definition $\max(S_t - K; 0)$. The rational choice is then obvious: if the exercise value is larger than the continuation one, one must claim the option, and in this case $\Pi_t(S_t) = \max(S_t - K; 0)$; otherwise, one must keep the option and in this case $\Pi_t(S_t)$ is computed thanks to the propagation equation (7.10). Applying this methodology not only provides the price of the American option, but also its optimal time of exercise.

As in the case of Monte-Carlo methods, the method described above must be refined to improve the convergence, to better take into account the multiple dimensions, to reduce and control instabilities, to optimize calibration, etc. We went into some detailed refinements of the Monte-Carlo method, and we let the reader study more in depth the various finite differences methods in [Wilmott 2006] or [Duffy 2006].

Chapter 8

Value at Risk (VaR)

Capital Market activities involve various products and risk types: stocks, interest rates and currencies account for an important part of these activities, as well as commodities (energy, agricultural products, metals etc.). Other domains of application, such as real estate or climatic hazards, may also be encountered. To measure, in a synthetic and homogeneous way, risks generated by the build up of these activities is obviously of great interest and difficulty. The financial industry and regulators have equipped themselves with key risk indicators, among which *Value at Risk* is the most prominent one. Widely used by the banking industry, Value at Risk is also used by banking control authorities in the calculation of the minimum equity capital that banks must hold. This Value at Risk, which we generally denote by its acronym, VaR, will be addressed in the present chapter.

We shall begin with the theoretical definition of the VaR. Then, the issues relating to its practical implementation will be examined: selection of the risk factors, choice of their diffusion models, and modeling of their impact on the prices of financial products. As a conclusion, we shall address the limits of this indicator; some of these limits were highlighted during the 2007–2009 financial crisis. Although the present chapter only introduces a limited number of new theoretical concepts, the issues developed here are quite close to the real problems faced by market risk professionals.

8.1 General principle

Capital Market activities of an international bank are generally composed of many sub-activities without direct links and acting on very different types of risks. Some of their functions may be to provide their customers with financial products. In this case, the bank mainly acts as an intermediary. The traders are then focused on hedging the positions resulting from customer transactions. Other activities are dedicated to speculation: their goal is to elaborate investment strategies in order to make the most of its investment capacities, although such activities are becoming scarcer due to recent regulation such as the Volcker Rule which aims at banning the so-called proprietary trading from the US Banking Industry. In all cases, these activities may happen to generate losses when asset prices vary. These risks are termed market risks.

As financial crises went by, the banking industry has little by little equipped itself with standards in terms of measuring and monitoring market risks. Thus, there exists in any bank a department in charge of ensuring that the risk measurement is relevant and that the measured level of risk is in line with the financial structure and strategy of the institution. In order to correctly master the risk, the action of this department must be exercised at two levels.

- At an individual level, it must ensure that the risks taken by each trader individually are contained within reasonable limits. It will check, for example, that a trader dealing with options on stocks has correctly hedged the delta.
- At a global level, it must control that the sum of all the traders' investments is not liable to put the institution at too important a risk.

The level of individual control requires, once the risks generated by the Capital Market activities are correctly identified, to put in place suitable individual indicators. The level of global control requires building a synthetic indicator able to aggregate all the individual risks. Indeed, without such an indicator, how could one evaluate the global risk resulting from investments made on underlying as different as the Dow Jones index (DJ) and copper? Is a portfolio composed of \$10 M of copper and of a short selling[1] position of \$5 M on the DJ, less risky than a simple buying position of \$7 M of copper? The VaR, a universally used indicator, has the ambition to answer this kind of questions, given of course a number of hypotheses and approximations which we shall make precise in what follows.

Let us assume that we know the probability distribution of the daily profits of a portfolio. VaR with a 1-day horizon and a 90% confidence threshold is then defined as the amount K such that the probability that the daily loss does not exceed K be equal to 90%. It will be convenient to simply denote it as the 1-day 90% VaR. In

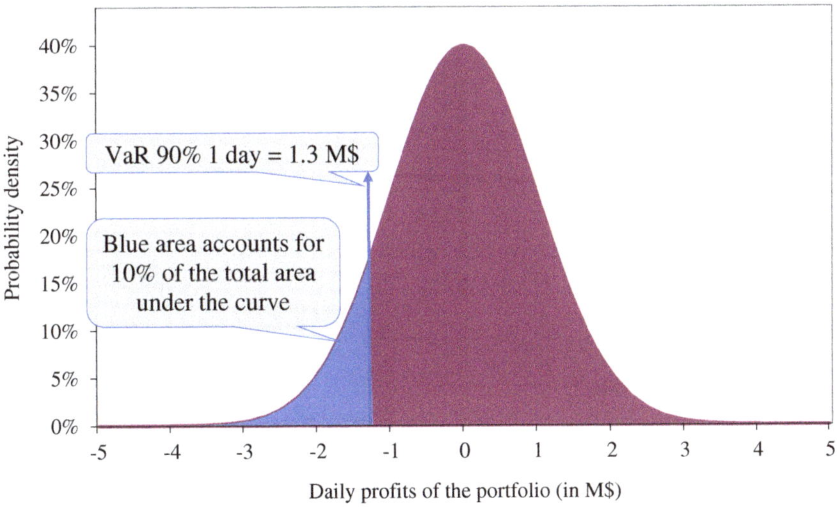

Figure 8.1: VaR with a one day horizon and a confidence threshold of 90%. Generally speaking, VaR is a negative gain, and thus a loss of \$1.3 M in the above example. In practical terms, it means that the probability of earning more than $-$\$1.3 M in one day is 90%. Equivalently, the probability of losing more than \$1.3 M is 10%.

[1]Short selling consists in holding a negative proportion of an asset, that is to gain money when the asset price falls.

mathematical terms, the 1-day 90% VaR is defined as follows:

$$\text{Probability(losses in one day} > \text{VaR)} = 10\% \tag{8.1}$$

Naturally, we could as well have written: Probability(Profits$\geq$ $-$VaR)=90%. The same procedure could have been followed for the profit distribution with a different time horizon: 10 days, 1 month, 1 year, etc. Generally speaking, potential profits are all the more volatile as the time horizon is longer. Thus, VaR will be all the more important as the time horizon is longer.

In most cases, the VaR calculation will be done not from a probability distribution such as presented in Figure 8.1, but rather from a finite number of possible scenarios for the variations of the portfolio values. As a matter of fact, it is generally easier to compute, using historical data or Monte-Carlo simulations, a set of scenarios of changes in the portfolio value, rather than a continuous probability distribution of these variations. Sorting these scenarios from the

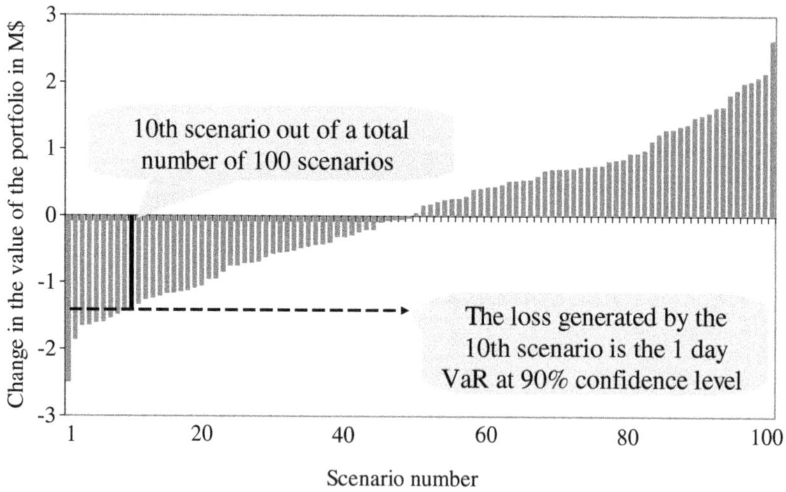

Figure 8.2: Determination of the 1-day 90% VaR from a set of 100 scenarios of daily change in the portfolio value. Each bar represents the gains obtained in one day in one of the 100 equiprobable scenarios which are simulated; these scenarios are sorted according to the size of the gains. The 1-day 90% VaR is the loss (on the ordinate axis) of the 10th scenario.

worst loss to the highest profit, one can obtain an estimate of the portfolio VaR. The 1-day 90% VaR will then be:

- the loss associated with scenario #10 when using a total of 100 scenarios, as indicated in Figure 8.2;
- the loss associated with scenario #100 if we had used 1,000 scenarios;
- the loss associated with scenario $\#n/10$ if we had used n scenarios.

The amount of 1-day 90% VaR indicates that, on average, losses larger than this value should occur only once in 10 days. It is illustrated in Figure 8.3, with VaR = \$1.3 M as in the example of Figure 8.2. This kind of verification, termed *backtesting*, is commonly used in order to check that the hypotheses used for the calculation of the scenarios are suitable. Indeed, up to now, we have taken for granted the knowledge of this set of scenarios. However, in practice, their computation requires formulating numerous hypotheses, and is at the heart of the practical implementation of VaR, which will be taken up in the next section.

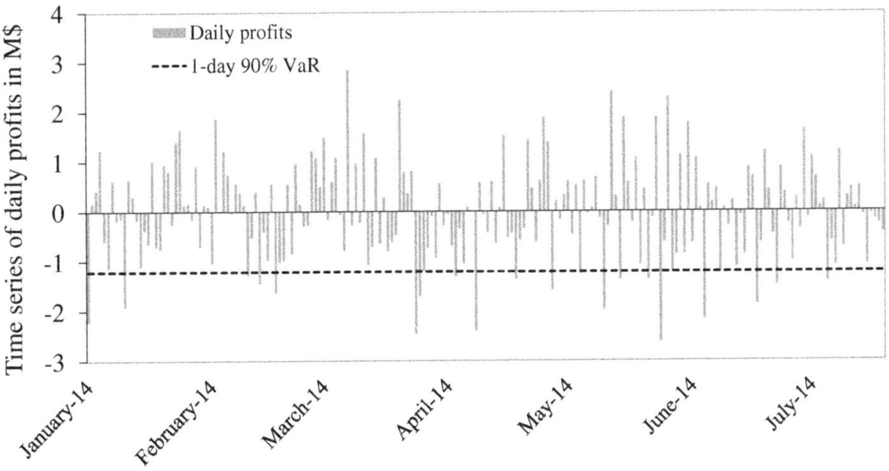

Figure 8.3: Daily gains generated by a fictitious portfolio over 200 days. The losses exceed the amount of the 1-day 90% VaR about 20 times, that is, in 20/200=10% of the cases, as expected.

8.2 VaR construction in practice

8.2.1 *Selection of the risk factors*

Computing the VaR of a portfolio requires an estimate of scenarios representative of potential profits and losses. A first but somewhat simplistic method could be to directly estimate the profit profile from the history of changes in the value of the portfolio. However, such a method would not comply with good statistical practices, according to which it is wiser to model the cause of a phenomenon rather than its consequences. For a quant who computes a VaR, the modeled consequence is the variation of the portfolio value, and the causes of this variation are the evolution of the market parameters: stock prices, interest rates curves, implied volatilities, credit spreads, etc. Going against this principle is likely to generate biases and instabilities in the modeling. First, the composition of the portfolio may vary over time, either resulting from the action of the trader, or because differences in the assets returns will naturally modify their respective weights in the portfolio. Second, some of the assets will converge over time towards a limit value, all things being equal: it is in particular the case for bonds whose value will converge towards the face value, or of options whose prices will converge towards the payoff. Because of these two phenomena, it is not adequate to directly use a history of portfolio values for VaR computation. When computing VaR, one cannot be satisfied with a global modeling of the portfolio: it is necessary to analyze, and then model, the different sources of the risks attached to the portfolio.

What do we mean by "sources of risks"? The Capital Market activity of an investment bank may be seen as a portfolio composed of various financial products, whose values depend on quite diverse parameters, such as stock prices, interest rates curves, foreign exchange rates, commodities prices, volatility surfaces associated with each of these data, dependency parameters such as the correlation between assets etc. In all rigor, each parameter liable to influence the value of the portfolio should be taken into account in building the scenarios. In practice, proceeding in such a manner generally turns out to be ineffective. Indeed, the multiplication of parameters is likely to lead to significant increase in human and computational resources without any noticeable gain in precision. Thus, it is generally mandatory to select the most important parameters. The parameters which are thus selected are the risk factors of the portfolio, that is, those which are the most likely to have a significant impact on the valuation of the portfolio.

Selecting these risk factors originates globally in an arbitrage between the gain in accuracy and the additional cost generated. In order to do so, it requires that one takes into account the strategies of the different sub-portfolios. For example, a bond price depends on the full interest rates curve and on its credit spreads curve. Is it however necessary to keep all the points of these curves in the VaR calculation? Is it not better to use only the main factors of the interest rates curve dynamics as determined from the principal component analysis presented in the first chapter? The answer to these question is not straightforward and it will depend in particular on the strategy which is applied to the portfolio whose VaR we attempt to calculate. Thus, for a traditional investment activity on government bonds, taking only into account the three main deformations of the interest rates curve is sufficient to capture the main part of the risk. However, in the case of a more sophisticated activity where the trader attempts to exploit what he or she thinks to be a market anomaly, such as a too important gap between the prices of two bonds of close maturity, this selection of risk factors will be completely unsuitable as it will not allow him or her to capture the main risk of the strategy, that is, the reality of the identified anomaly. A second example, presented in Figure 8.4, also illustrates how the strategy is decisive in choosing risk factors.

Lastly, one must note that for some parameters, such as credit spreads, data available from history may not be sufficient to be exploited in a statistically significant way. Consequently, their integration in the risk factors will likely require the use of

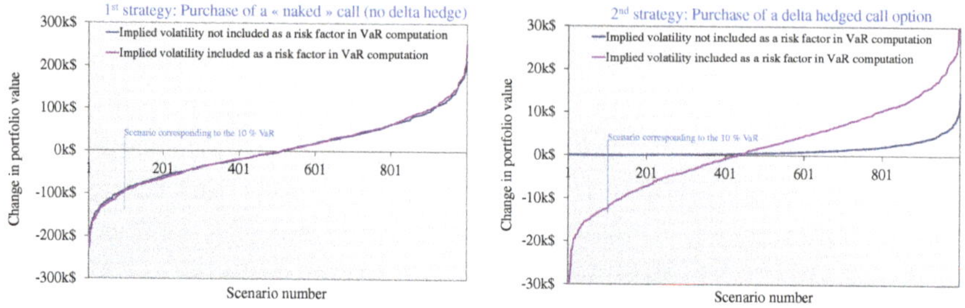

	Strategy 1: Purchase of a « naked » call (no delta hedge)	**Strategy 2:** Purchase of a delta hedged call
Risk factors: Only the underlying stock price	VaR 90% 1 day 98 k$	VaR 90% 1 day -0.02 k$
Risk factors: Both the underlying stock price and the implied volatility	VaR 90% 1 day 99 k$	VaR 90% 1 day 12 k$

Figure 8.4: The two graphs represent the results of simulating 1,000 scenarios for assessing the value of a portfolio composed, respectively, of a naked call (without delta hedge) and of a delta hedged call. Let us recall that delta, noted Δ, is the sensitivity of the option price to the variation of the stock price. As we saw in Chapter 5, delta hedging means holding the option and $-\Delta$ stocks; this should neutralize the risk linked to the option sensitivity to the stock price. The profile of the profit distribution of the first strategy is relatively insensitive to selecting or not the implied volatility as a risk factor: the main risk on a call which is not hedged is the variation of the underlying asset price, and not the volatility. This is no longer the case for the second strategy, for which the main risk originates in the implied volatility. Not selecting this parameter as a risk factor thus amounts to denying the existence of the main risk of this strategy. The visual feeling given by these two graphs is confirmed by the computation of the 1-day 90% VaR.

approximations or of additional hypotheses. This feature must also be taken into consideration when selecting risk factors.

8.2.2 *Modeling the risk factors*

Once risk factors have been identified, the next step is to model their evolution. The most natural approach is to use the history of the risk factor variations, without any specific assumption on the form they may take. This way of computing VaR is commonly called historical VaR. It does not rely on any hypothesis for modeling risk factors, but nevertheless assumes that their distribution is stationary.

This means that the expression of their laws is time independent. A historical VaR may be computed for any portfolio composed of complex products, such as exotic options. In this case, the history will have to contain data relating to all the selected risk factors: this step might prove to be a hurdle as some of the factors can be difficult to observe (for example, volatility of volatility). Computing VaR from these historical data will next require the use of a valuation model in order to account for the impact of risk factors variations on the portfolio value.

As an alternative to the calculation of historical VaR, it is quite possible to assume a predetermined shape for risk factors distribution. Similarly to the problem of having to model multiple defaults, as encountered in Chapter 2, we face here a multidimensional case, since we have not only to model the individual distribution of risk factors, but also their joint probabilities of evolution. In the most classical case, we will assume that risk factors follow a multidimensional Gaussian distribution; or, said differently, that they form a Gaussian vector. In Chapters 2 and 5, the one-dimensional Gaussian distribution was discussed. Its multidimensional version includes what is termed a correlation structure. The main asset of this structure lies in its simplicity: the joint evolution probability of random variables following a multidimensional Gaussian law only depends on averages, variances and on a single parameter for each pair of variables, named correlation coefficient. Thus, in the case of two risk factors, five parameters will be enough to describe their joint distributions: their averages (two parameters), their variances (two parameters) and a single correlation coefficient. For three-risk factors, we shall need nine parameters; for n risk factors, $2n+n(n-1)/2$ parameters (n pairs average/variance and $n(n-1)/2$ correlation coefficients).

A widespread misunderstanding states that n Gaussian random variables build a n-dimensional Gaussian vector. In the case of a Gaussian vector, any linear combination of its components follows a normal (or Gaussian) law. This last condition determines the correlation structure and allows the description of the full dependence between the two variables thanks to a single correlation parameter.

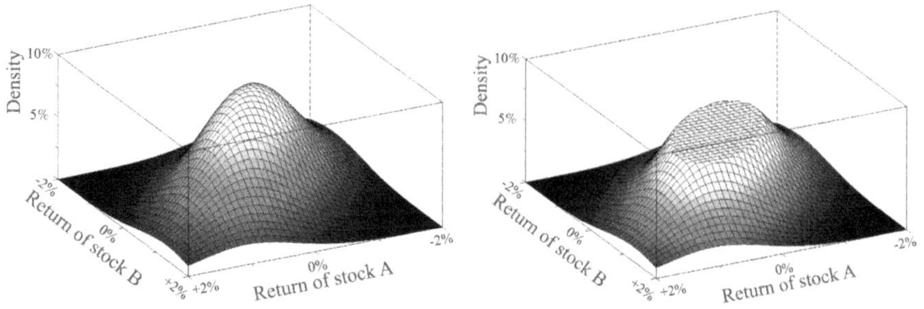

Figure 8.5: Density of a two-dimensional Gaussian vector. The correlation structure associated with this Gaussian model is relatively rigid. For example, as is shown on the right-hand graph, the curves defined by the intersection of the surface with horizontal planes are necessarily concentric ellipses.

As a consequence of this parametrization simplicity, the shape of a Gaussian vector is rather rigid. As an example, Figure 8.5 presents the density of a 2-dimensional Gaussian vector. The curves defined by the intersection of the surface with horizontal planes trace concentric ellipses which represent the regions where the realization of the Gaussian vector is the most likely. The correlation coefficient acts on the flattening of the ellipse and its orientation, as shown in Figure 8.6 which represents the realization of Gaussian vectors with various correlation values. We shall come back in the last section of this chapter on the implications and limitations of this Gaussian modeling.

8.2.3 *Impact of risk factors on the portfolio*

At this point, we have at our disposal a list of risk factors and their distributions, either empirical or modeled (by a Gaussian vector, for example). It remains to translate these variation probabilities of risk factors into scenarios of evolution of the portfolio values.

The case of historical VaR seems simple: one can use the value the portfolio would have had in previous market conditions for each day of the considered time window. In the case of a modeled distribution of risk factors, it is possible to simulate market conditions via the

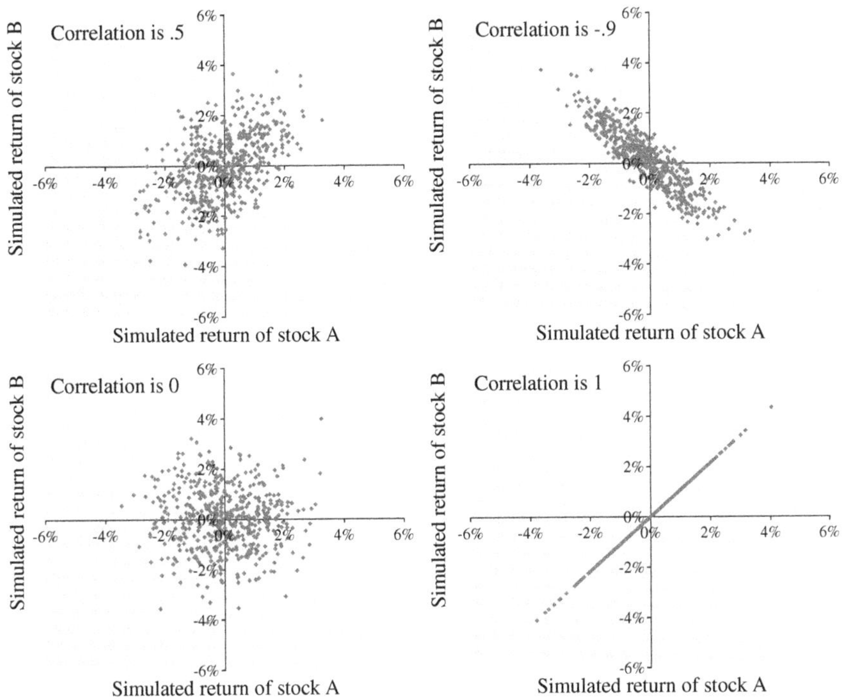

Figure 8.6: Random sampling of 2-dimensional Gaussian vectors for various values of the correlation. If the correlation coefficient is close to 0, the variables forming the vector are independent and the four quadrants are symmetrical. If this coefficient is close to +1 or −1, the cloud collapses along a line whose slope is the ratio of the standard deviation of each stock return.

Monte-Carlo technique described in the preceding chapter. A set of scenarios for the joint evolution of the risk factors is simulated and can be used for the calculation of the VaR, called in this case Monte-Carlo VaR. Nevertheless, a big difficulty lies behind this apparent simplicity. How can we compute thousands of values of a portfolio composed of complex derivative products whose valuation requires material computation time and memory space. Can we consider recalculating for each financial product and each scenario a new value? The answer to this question clearly depends on many parameters among which the number and complexity of the products to be dealt with and the available computing resources.

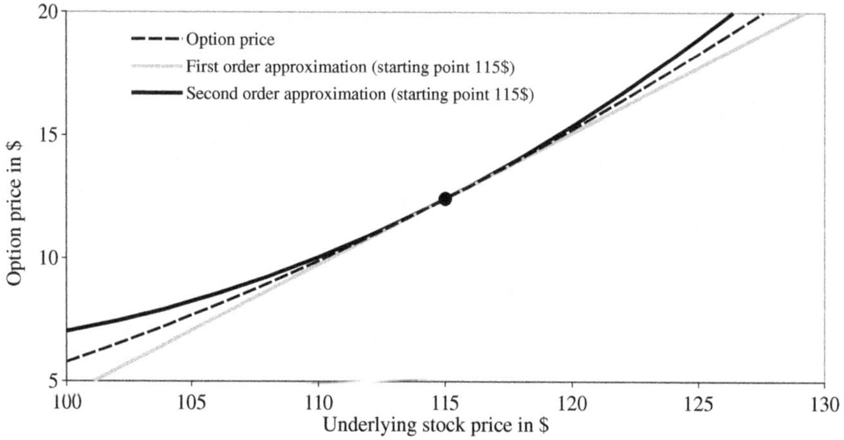

Figure 8.7: Expansions to first and second order of the price of a call option on a stock: the dotted curve is the option price within a Black-Scholes model; the solid curves are the first and second order approximations around the underlying price \$115. The two approximations are fairly good in the vicinity of the initial point, but deteriorates when the variation of the price of the underlying stock is too large. One also observes that the second order approximation always lies higher than the call price.

In many cases, a systematic re-calculation is not conceivable. An alternative solution is then to use the sensitivities of the portfolio to each risk factor. Let us illustrate this technique with a simple example: the case of a portfolio composed of a single call option on a stock. The value of such a product mainly depends on the price of the underlying stock and on the level of implied volatility. Using the sensitivities of the option prices to these two risk factors, it is possible to approximate the new value of the option after a shock on these two parameters. As Figure 8.7 shows, the approximation will be acceptable only if the applied shocks are not too important. This sensitivity may be taken into account to first order, that is, by using first derivatives of prices with respect to parameters. The expansion of sensitivities to second order, that is, taking second derivatives into account, is often used to refine the approximation. However, Figure 8.7 shows that this does not necessarily guarantee a better accuracy nor a more conservative approach.

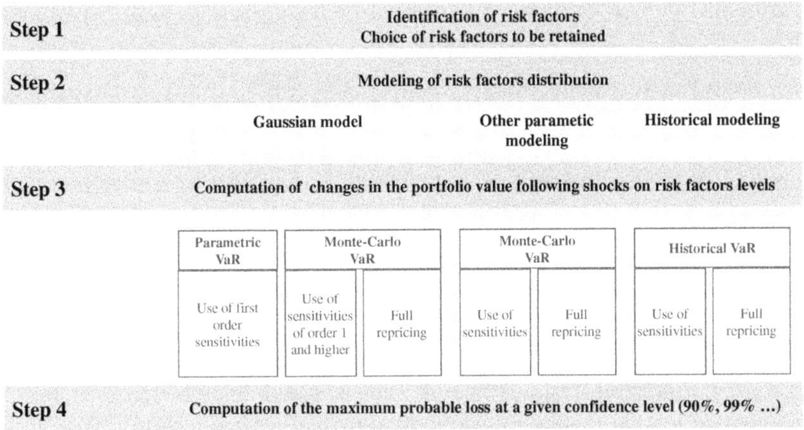

Figure 8.8: Flow chart highlighting the necessary steps for VaR computation. Risk managers generally identify three kinds of VaR: parametric VaR, Monte-Carlo VaR and historical VaR.

In addition to saving computation time, portfolio linearization, that is, first order approximation, displays another advantage: it allows one to compute VaR by a direct mathematical formula, without resorting to Monte-Carlo simulations. This method is termed parametric VaR. This VaR is computed in a framework where all the variations are approximated to first order and follow Gaussian laws and Gaussian correlation structures. In this configuration, let us recall that any linear combination of the variations follows itself a normal law. Thus, calculated portfolio variations follow a Gaussian law, and, thanks to this property, one can compute VaR without Monte-Carlo simulations.

8.3 Practical and theoretical VaR limitations

8.3.1 *Diversification and sub-additivity*

The definition of the risk to which a portfolio is sensitive is a theoretical issue, but it is one with strong practical implications. The risk measured by VaR indicates the level of losses which will be reached with a given frequency. However, the indicator does not inform on how serious the losses can be beyond the VaR. Imagine two portfolios A and B such that:

➲ portfolio A has a level of 1-day 90% VaR of \$2 M and an average estimate of losses beyond VaR of \$5 M;
➲ portfolio B has a level of 1-day 90% VaR of \$2 M and an average estimate of losses beyond VaR of \$2.5 M.

If we only take VaR into consideration, these two portfolios seem to bear an equivalent risk. However, the second indicator, that is, the average of losses larger than VaR, states that portfolio A is more risky. Let us somewhat modify the example:

➲ portfolio C has level of 1-day 90% VaR of \$1.5 M and an average estimate of losses beyond VaR of \$3 M;
➲ portfolio D has a level of 1-day 90% VaR of \$2 M and an average estimate of losses beyond VaR of \$2.5 M.

Which of these two portfolios is more risky? This question does not admit a universal answer, as it depends on the measure of risk that is used.

In order to build up a consensus for the properties a risk indicator should satisfy, the notion of consistent risk measure has been defined. However there exist many consistent risk measures, so that there is no universal criterion that favors one among the others. Then, as illustrated in the preceding examples, the risk hierarchization is necessarily an arbitrary process.

On the other hand, VaR has often been criticized on the ground that it does not comply with one of the founding properties of consistent risk measure, namely, sub-additivity. This property implies that any portfolio diversification will necessarily lead to a decrease of the risk measure. Its translation into a mathematical language is as follows. Let us note $M(\bullet)$ the risk measure, X and Y two different financial assets; sub-additivity imposes that:

$$M(X+Y) \leq M(X) + M(Y) \tag{8.2}$$

This property seems rather natural and agrees in particular with the portfolio theories which we addressed in Chapter 3: diversification reduces risk. However, it turns out that VaR does not satisfy this property in all circumstances. Nevertheless, this criticism relating to the fact that VaR is not sub-additive, seems to us of secondary importance. Indeed, in most cases, portfolio diversification will be translated into a decrease in the VaR level; this behavior will even be systematic in the case of a Gaussian VaR. Moreover, the counter examples built to illustrate this flaw usually display potential losses profiles very atypical with respect to portfolios encountered in practice.

8.3.2 *Stationarity of risk factors*

The hypothesis related to risk factors stationarity is key to legitimate any VaR calculation. Indeed, when computing VaR, future behavior is inferred from the observation of the past. All the same, practitioners agree that this hypothesis is unfounded. Observing the evolution of S&P 500 variances and correlation coefficients between Goldman Sachs and JP Morgan stock returns presented in Figure 8.9 illustrates it.

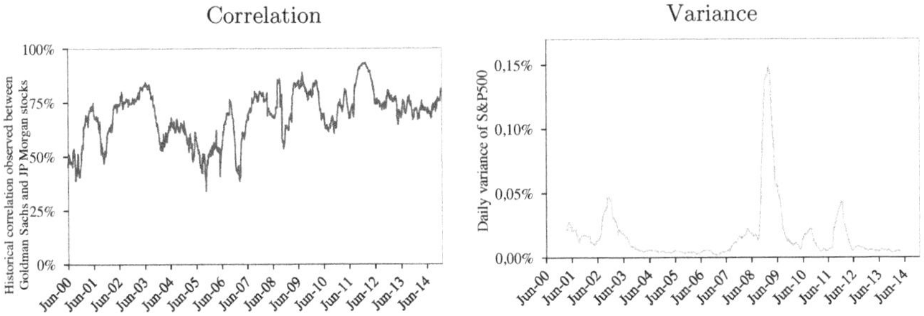

Figure 8.9: Evolution of S&P 500 variances and correlation coefficients between Goldman Sachs and JP Morgan stock returns calculated on a moving time window of 100 days. This graph illustrates the absence of stability of variances and correlations.

Because of this instability, computed VaR will never be able to predict with certainty future losses levels. However, the existence of periods with a relative stability of the variance balances this statement. Moreover, VaR may be interpreted, not as an estimator predicting potential future losses, but rather as a synthetic indicator informing on the evolution of the portfolio risk. This evolution may be the result of traders' actions, in which case the computational mode must be stable enough to highlight changes in the investment strategy. VaR evolution can also be the result of variations of assets' volatilities. One of the crucial issues of the computation is thus to carefully choose the period over which parameters are estimated. The estimation window must be:

- long enough in order to account for the background trend while maintaining some stability of the estimators;
- responsive enough in order to reflect the change of market conditions and volatility.

The non-stationarity of risk factors represents a major flaw of VaR when considered as a predictive indicator of future losses; however, it is not prohibitive when one uses the VaR framework for the purpose of assessing changes in the risk profile of a given portfolio. Thus, if the period chosen for parameters estimation is suitable, VaR is able to detect risks stemming from a change in the traders' investment strategy or from variations in market conditions.

8.3.3 *Limitations of the Gaussian modeling of risk factors*

Gaussian modeling of the evolution of risk factors displays many advantages: simplicity of calibration and simplicity of calculation. However, as is often the case, these advantages are balanced by major flaws. We shall see in the next chapter that Gaussian modeling does not account well for variations in stock prices: in particular, extreme variations are under-represented in this modeling. This is particularly problematic in the framework of the VaR calculation when one attempts to model extreme variations in financial assets prices.

Let us recall Figures 8.5 and 8.6. The random sampling of Gaussian vectors will result in a cloud of points building more or less an ellipse. The resulting cloud of points displays a central symmetry with respect to the center of the ellipse. Indeed, in the clouds drawn for the Figure 8.6, the lower-left and the upper-right quadrants are symmetrical: this implies that the dependency between assets is identical in a situation of losses (lower-left quadrant) and in a situation of profits (upper-right quadrant). Now, the representation by a cloud of points of the real history of stock returns leads to a different conclusion (Figure 8.10). One observes on this graph that, in the case of a fall of one stock, the other one will have a tendency to fall with a comparable magnitude. This occurrence is not as obviously clear in the case of a rise of stock prices. This observation corresponds to a phenomenon which is classically observed for the whole of financial

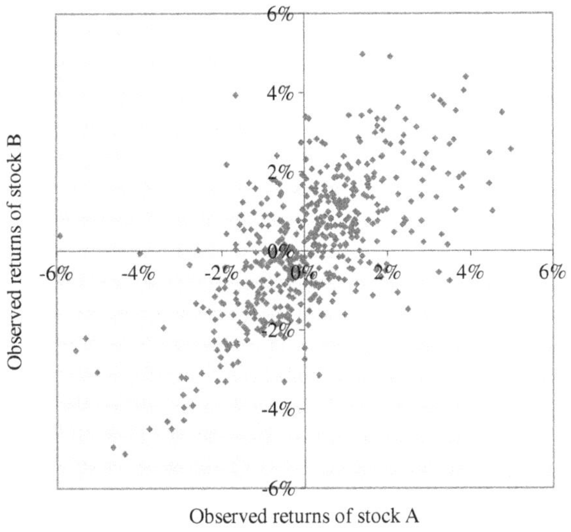

Figure 8.10: Joint representation of the historical returns of two stocks. When returns are negative (lower left quadrant), points tend to align along the diagonal, which shows a stronger dependency. On the contrary, in the case of positive returns, the dependency is weaker as the cloud of points is more scattered (upper right quadrant).

assets: correlations increase in a crisis situation. The Gaussian correlation structure is unable to model such a phenomenon, which may be considered as a sizeable flaw of this modeling.

Gaussian modeling of risk factors presents a number of flaws, which were the object of much criticism during the 2007–2009 financial crisis. The use of such a modeling is not always adapted and its relevance must be checked. However, we think that the main criticisms phrased against VaR should go beyond technical debates and involve the understanding and use of the measure. This subject is dealt with in the next sub-section.

8.3.4 *Stress tests and stressed VaR*

VaR calculations are used by banking control authorities in order to estimate the minimum capital requirements; that is the minimal equity capital banks are required to have. Now, in a crisis period, the VaR indicator tends to strongly increase due to the growth in volatility of risk factors. By doing so, it reduces the room for manoeuvre of banks, which must sometimes sell part of their assets, thus speeding up all the more the downfall of Capital Markets. VaR may thus be qualified as being pro-cyclic in the sense that it amplifies economic tendencies. As a consequence, rather than helping global risk management, VaR may have contributed to undermine the system.

In particular, this is the reason why regulators of banking institutions have imposed the use of another indicator, termed stressed VaR, in addition to the traditional VaR. Its calculation relies on a history including a crisis period likely to provoke major losses for the institution. By construction, this indicator is insensitive to economic cycles and incorporates the effect of an economic crisis on the distribution of risk factors. In order to avoid pro-cyclicity, regulators have also introduced a mechanism which allows them to adjust the capital requirements during an economic crisis period.

By its very nature, the modeling of extreme events is a perilous exercise bound to be criticized. It is impossible to attribute probabilities to events very rare and as sudden as financial crises. This is the reason why VaR used as an estimator of extreme losses is bound to fail.

- VaR will never be able to anticipate very rare events which did not occur within a relatively recent past, and if this is the case, the probability of occurrence of such an event may well be overestimated and would, then, bias the calculation.
- Computing a 1-day 90% VaR is meaningful, as events leading to losses higher than predicted by this indicator occur, on average, 10 days over a 100-day history. By contrast, it is useless to compute a 1-year 99% VaR as events leading to losses higher than predicted by this indicator will occur on average once every 100 years.

The interest of VaR lies thus in its capacity to model events which are rare but still frequent enough so that they may be statistically exploited. Criticizing VaR for its inability to model and predict events which are statistically unobservable is irrelevant.

Box 8.1. The Basel Committee. The Basel Committee is composed of control authorities from many countries, mainly from Europe and North America; it proposes standards for risk measurement and monitoring, risk management and minimum capital requirements. Recommendations of the Basel Committee are generally published as rules: Basel I (published in 1988), Basel II ([Basel Committee 2006]), Basel 2.5 ([Basel Committee 2009b]) and Basel III ([Basel Committee 2010]). These recommendations are then meant to be transposed into legislations of each jurisdiction.

This is the reason why the array of risk measurement is generally supplemented with indicators representative of stressed market conditions. These indicators, termed *stress tests*, pre-existed the 2007–2009 financial crisis, but even the most pessimistic scenarios finally turned to be overtaken by its magnitude. Among the reasons of this relative failure identified by [Basel Committee 2009a], let us quote:

- A too radical simplification, if not the overlooking, of risk factors such as basis risks. Basis risks are generated by the imperfect hedging of an asset by another one: for example, hedging the credit risk of a 5-year bond by a 10-year CDS will generate a basis risk. The core issue is to correctly identify risk factors.
- A shyness in stress scenario building, as bank managers considered unlikely the most pessimistic stress tests.
- An excessive approximation of derivative products which concealed potential risks.
- Taking into account inefficiently the so-called *wrong way risk*, such as the correlation between the default of an issuer and the default of an insurance provider on this issuer. Generally speaking, this wrong way risk is the situation when the default of a counterparty is all the more likely to occur as a derivative contract signed with it becomes in our favor.
- Underestimating the duration of stress market conditions.
- A reluctance to consider correlation schemes different from those observed in the past.
- But also an insufficient involvement of managers in building and analyzing these indicators; insufficient transversality of information within banking organizations; information systems not reliable and not interconnected enough...

Some of these shortcomings are in the process of being corrected, but building relevant stress tests remains a complex task. In particular, in elaborating crisis scenarios, it remains difficult to free oneself from the influence of past history and past crises, while the goal of complementarity with VaR indicators should precisely impose it.

Chapter 9

Non-Gaussian Models

The models which we studied from Chapter 5 onwards were all based on Gaussian probability laws. In Chapter 6, we refined and adapted this Gaussian framework to the anticipations of real market prices through volatility models. Many researchers and professionals propose to abandon these Gaussian paradigms and to explore other kinds of models. To achieve this goal, the first step is to study the historical behavior of financial markets, to draw useful lessons and to understand at which points Gaussian modelling fails; this reasoning will be presented in the first section.

Among the very active schools, let us mention the econophysicists whose reasoning starts from an empirical, and even physical, analysis of the markets. Traditional quants are also very active in the exploration of non-Gaussian models and they keep on developing classes of models with a broader scope and more fitted to observed time series, such as Lévy processes or multi-fractal processes.

As early as 1963, Mandelbrot questioned the use of Gaussian laws in finance, as they underestimate the frequency of extreme changes in stock prices; these extreme values being termed "distribution tails". [Mandelbrot 1963] proposes an alternative model based on Pareto-stable laws which, by contrast and given the most recent analyses, overestimate distribution tails. Nevertheless, this modelling opens

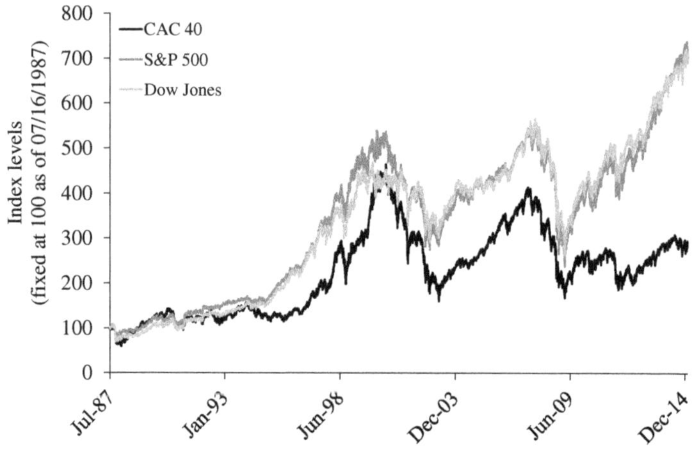

Figure 9.1: History of CAC 40 (French stocks market main index), S&P 500 and Dow Jones indices in base 100 as of July 16th, 1987.

two avenues for in-depth studies which we shall review in the second and third sections:

➲ extreme variation modeled by a power law;
➲ evolution modeled by Lévy processes.

9.1 Submitting Gaussian models to the test

Up to the preceding chapter, we assessed the relevance of models according to their ability to fit market prices — this is what led us to the concept of volatility smile. We shall now come back to empirical observations in order to confront our models to the historical reality of stock prices.

The conclusion that one must draw from Figure 9.2 is that the Gaussian model does not fit reality. The most blatant phenomenon is that the historical distribution of log-returns[1] is less flat than the normal distribution: the core of the historical distribution is sharper,

[1]We recall that the log-returns are the quantities $\ln(S_{t+1}/S_t) \simeq (S_{t+1} - S_t)/S_t$. They follow a Gaussian law in the Black-Scholes model.

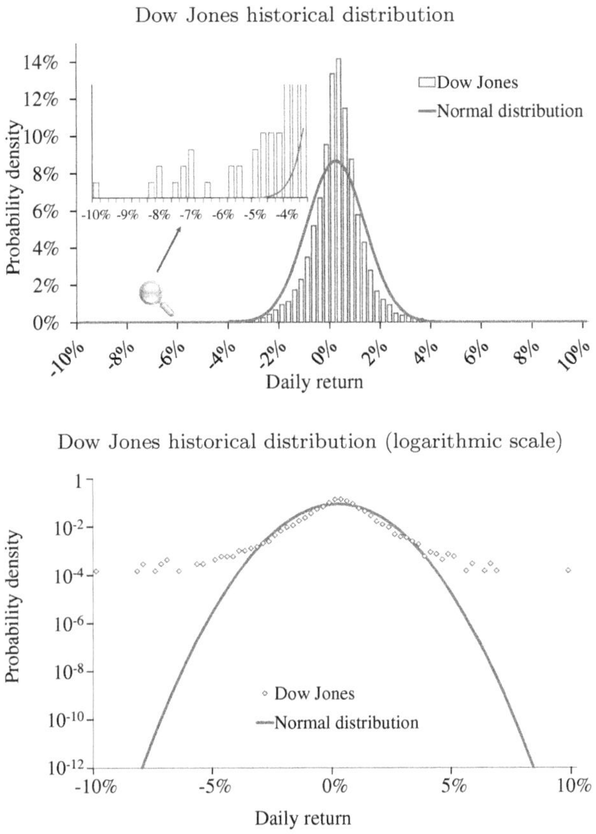

Figure 9.2: Historical distributions of the daily log-returns of the Dow Jones index and comparison with the distribution of a centered normal law with the same volatility. The two graphs display the same data, only the ordinate scale differs from one graph to the other. This figure demonstrates that the daily log-returns of historical prices do not follow a Gaussian law. Distributions are narrower and extreme variations (less than 4% for example) are more likely: mathematicians speak of heavy distribution tails. The phenomenon is blatant if observed with a logarithmic scale, it requires a zoom otherwise.

more concentrated, and the distribution tails are heavier. In concrete terms, it means that, in the historical distribution, usual variations, of lesser magnitude, are more probable (sharp shape of the core distribution), while extreme values are also much more likely than predicted by the Gaussian law (heavy distribution tails).

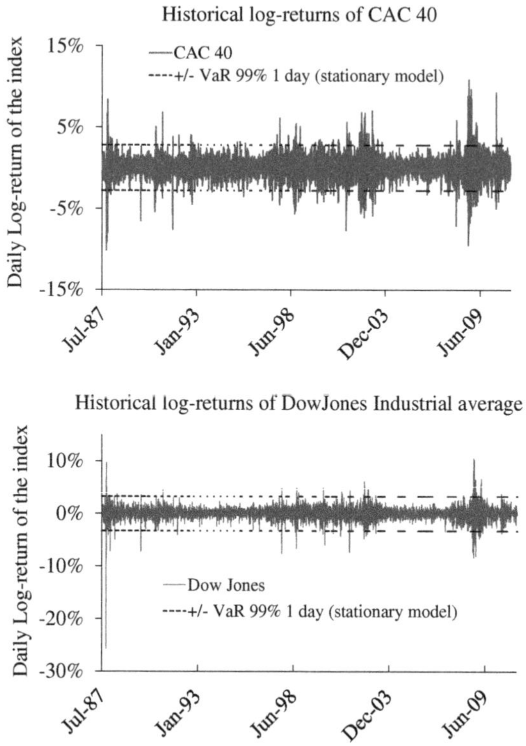

Figure 9.3: Historical log-returns of CAC 40 and *DowJones Industrial average* are compared here to the 1st and 99th Gaussian percentiles. These thresholds are, by definition, the levels crossed on average once every 100 times by independent log-Gaussian returns (Black-Scholes model). By contrast, one notices that threshold crossings by real returns are much more frequent and occur in clusters during periods corresponding to a greater instability of stock prices.

In other words, the Gaussian model under-evaluates such rare events as crises or exceptional profits and losses. According to [Haug 2007b], the first identification of heavy-tailed distributions belongs to [Mitchell 1915], almost 60 years before the Black-Scholes model. In order to give more details on this phenomenon, we have reproduced in Figure 9.3 the daily variations of CAC 40 and Dow Jones indices, identifying the variations beyond the 1st and 99th Gaussian percentiles. In theory, within a lognormal model, crossing each of these thresholds should occur about once in a 100 times, that is, about 60 crossings per threshold over the 5,980 days of the history displayed.

Now, Figure 9.3 shows 104 overshootings downwards and 84 upwards. These overshooting rates are more than 30% over what was predicted by the Gaussian model. Let us zoom on some variations:

- On October 19th 1987, the CAC 40 index lost 10% and the Dow Jones index lost 25%.
- On October 13th 2008, CAC 40 and Dow Jones indices both rose by 10%.
- On October 28th 2008, the Dow Jones index rose by 10% and the CAC 40 index rose by 9% the following day.

Such variations are complete outliers in a Gaussian model, where their expected frequency is less than once every 30 million years. Figure 9.3 shows another very interesting phenomenon: there exist different regimes for return amplitudes. History shows that calm periods, with small variations, alternate with hectic periods where amplitudes of returns are much higher. Furthermore, one observes that overshootings of our Gaussian percentiles may occur in series: in the examined period, one finds eight occurrences of consecutive overshootings of the 99th Gaussian percentile. Were daily changes really independent, the probability of observing two consecutive overshootings over the period would be $(104/5{,}980)^2 \simeq 0.03\%$, while the observed rate is four times larger ($8/5{,}980 \simeq 0.13\%$).

Thus, it appears that the independence of returns assumption is as unjustified as the Gaussian assumption. Figure 9.4 traces these historical correlations between July 1987 and January 2015. The conclusions which may be drawn from this figure are the following:

- There does not seem to exist correlation between log-returns (correlations remain close to zero irrespective of the lag). In other words, the value of the log-return on a given day does not add information regarding the future log-returns.
- By contrast, it is clear that absolute values of log-returns display a positive correlation. This means that, if the absolute value of the

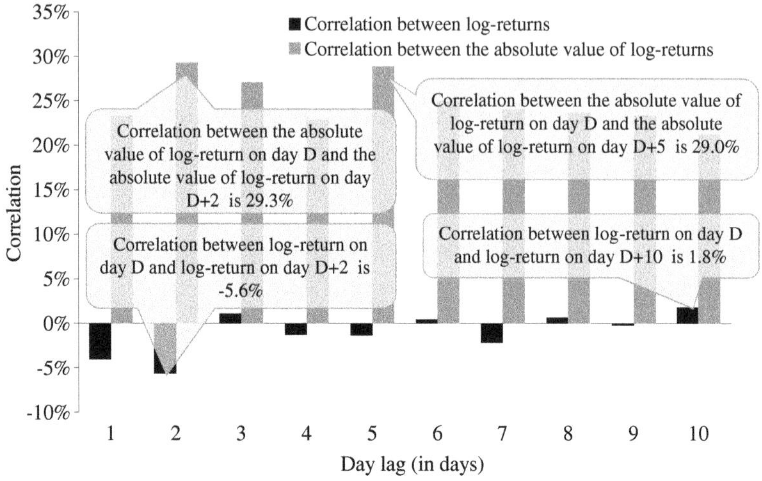

Figure 9.4: Historical autocorrelations of log-returns and of their absolute values. The graph shows that returns are uncorrelated (correlation is almost zero). Absolute values of daily log-returns, however, do seem to be correlated to each other. Hence, log-returns are not independent to each other as their magnitudes are correlated.

log-return on a given day is high, it is likely that the absolute value of returns on the following days will also be high. However, the sign of the changes remains uncertain, which ensures the absence of correlation of the log-returns.

This means that return amplitudes are linked together. Returns are uncorrelated but not independent as their absolute values are correlated. This implies that a present return value cannot be used to predict a positive or negative future average return — this is fortunate as there would be arbitrage opportunities otherwise. However, there is indeed a statistical link between past and future returns: if stocks variations are of high amplitude one day, it is probable that they are still of high amplitude the next day, but without any possibility to predict their sign.

Other phenomena may be observed in the light of historical data; they all contribute to specify the requirements that should be imposed in modelling financial assets evolution. The reader interested in an in-depth presentation of the subject is referred to [Bouchaud and Potters 2003]. In the present section, we focused on the most two striking observations: heaviness of the distribution tails and correlation of returns magnitude. It is possible to use volatility models, such as those studied in Chapter 6, in order to correct for the shortcomings of the Gaussian model. But a good understanding of those phenomena requires to leave the Gaussian framework and its many disguises.

9.2 Power laws

In 1963, Benoît Mandelbrot published a paper demonstrating the inadequacy of the use of Gaussian models in finance. He proposed a family of alternative laws, the Pareto-stable laws, also called α-stable laws. Gaussian laws obey the remarkable property that the sum of two independent Gaussian variables is a Gaussian variable: α-stable laws are, by definition, those which also obey this kind of property (the sum of two α-stable laws is α-stable). We shall concentrate on two properties of α-stable laws without a detailed presentation.

- They generally exhibit, with the exception of the Gaussian case, a heavy-tailed distribution which follows a power law.
- They can be modeled with Lévy processes.

The second point will be defined and dealt with in the next section, and we now focus on the distribution tails. Figure 9.5 shows an example of an α-stable distribution, the Cauchy law, which is compared with the Gaussian distribution. We exactly recover the characteristics observed in graphs of Figure 9.2: narrower distribution and more probable extreme values.

One may prove that, with the exception of some particular cases, distribution tails of α-stable laws follow a power law. For such a distribution law, the probability to observe values larger than x is, for x large enough, proportional to $1/x^{\alpha}$ with $0 < \alpha < 2$. Noting S the modeled random variable, we shall say that it follows a power

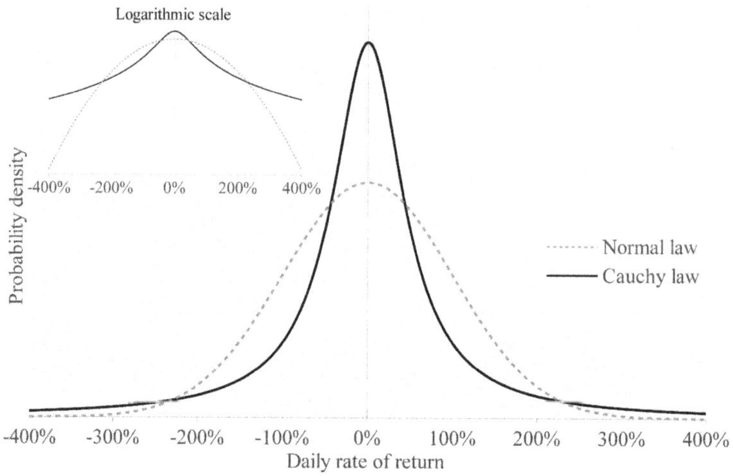

Figure 9.5: Comparison of a Gaussian law with a Cauchy law. The latter possesses a narrower distribution core and a much heavier tail than that of the Gaussian law.

law if, for x large enough:

$$\text{Prob}(|S| > x) \simeq \frac{1}{x^\alpha} \tag{9.1}$$

Historical studies (see a compilation in [Gabaix 2009] or [Bouchaud and Potters 2003]) show that this power law is a fair modelling of historical distribution tails. Figure 9.6 provides drawing of such power laws tails. These studies, performed on different markets (American, European, Asian) all seem to display a power law of parameter $\alpha = 3$:

$$\text{Prob(return larger than } n\%) \simeq \frac{p}{n^3} \tag{9.2}$$

In other words, if the probability to observe a change larger than 1% is p (the value of p depending on specific characteristics of the market) then the probability of observing a $n\%$ change will be p/n^3.

Empirical observations exhibit a $1/x^3$ power tail, and thus invalidate α-stable laws with $0 < \alpha < 2$ (for α defined as in equation (9.1)). Historical distributions of returns display tails which are clearly less heavy than α-stable laws. The $1/x^3$ law seems valid for daily returns, but over a longer period, monthly to yearly for example, returns seem to be fairly well modeled by a Gaussian law. This phenomenon is, by the way, correctly taken into account by markets and can be observed through the volatility smile and skew, which tend to fade away in the long term (as we learnt at the end of Chapter 5). One thus says that distributions of returns present a scaling effect. Modelling short-term returns through a $1/x^3$ power law is very robust, and correctly captures crisis periods. Actually, financial crises do not seem to be statistical anomalies when returns are modeled by power laws [Gabaix 2009]. In such models, crises are events which are admittedly rare but possible, while we saw that they are incompatible with Gaussian models.

However interesting such empirical observations may be, it is also necessary to explain them: which mechanisms and hypotheses could give rise to power laws on financial markets? This is the question taken up by some econophysicists, who draw their inspiration from other modelling fields. Power laws are in fact widely spread in many physical and socio-economical phenomena.

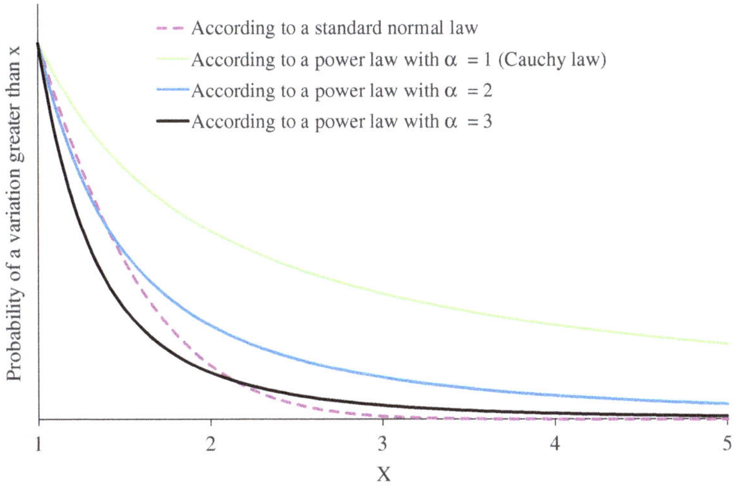

Figure 9.6: Graphic representation of the power law $\text{Prob}(|S| > x) \simeq 1/x^{\alpha}$, and comparison with the Gaussian law. The higher the parameter α, the faster the fall of the probability $\text{Prob}(|S| > x) \simeq 1/x^{\alpha}$. Thus, extreme events are less probable. As for the Gaussian function, it falls faster than any power law: power laws exhibit heavier tails.

The model by [Cont and Bouchaud 2000] uses percolation theory in order to account for the mutual influence of different market players. It represents an excellent example of physics inspired modelling of financial activities.

Percolation theory studies the properties of connection networks, similar to the interaction between small ducts in a sponge whose connectivity determines the filtering abilities of the sponge. In a simple model, if there exists a large enough number of interconnected ducts, then water will be able to cross the sponge, otherwise the sponge will be waterproof. In [Cont and Bouchaud 2009], ducts are replaced by traders and the connectivity between traders determines the gregarious effect, or herd behavior.

Let us then consider that each market participant is labelled by an index i. Two traders i and j may be connected or not; being connected means here that they have the same opinion on a given stock: it should be bought, it should be sold, or nothing should be done. The variation of the stock price is then modeled as being directly proportional to the balance between the number of buyers and sellers:

$$\Delta S_t \simeq \sum_{i=1}^{N} \phi_i \tag{9.3}$$

In this equation, i labels the trader, N is the total number of participants and ϕ_i the action of trader i: $\phi_i = -1$ if the trader sells the stock, $\phi_i = 0$ if he or she does nothing, and $\phi_i = +1$ if he or she buys. The reader familiar with the central-limit theorem (which we shall address in the next section) will immediately notice that this model leads inevitably to a Gaussian variation of prices, provided the trader opinions are sufficiently independent and that the number of participants is large ($N \gg 1$). By contrast, the Cont-Bouchaud model accounts for the gregarious effect: traders are not independent one from another and two connected traders necessarily share the same opinion (as illustrated in Figure 9.7). The opinions of two unconnected traders remain completely independent.

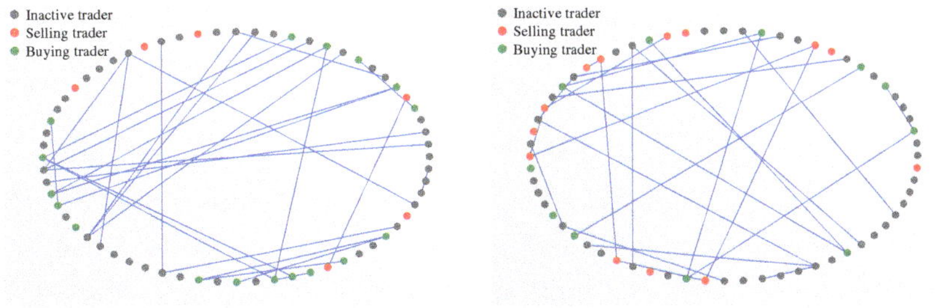

Figure 9.7: Two random samplings of the herd behavior model of [Cont and Bouchaud 2000]. Each point represents a trader, and the links between traders are randomly sampled. This allows Cont and Bouchaud to create groups of traders linked to one another, who will have the same position (buyer, neutral or seller), where the position is randomly sampled for each group. In our illustration, there are 64 traders, the parameter c is fixed at 0.8 and n_{order} at 13; this corresponds roughly to a 10% probability of selling, to a 10% probability of buying, and thus to a 80% probability for a neutral position.

This model is characterized by several variables.

- The total number of traders, N, which is assumed very large.
- The average number of connections for one trader is noted c; this number also specifies the probability $c/(N-1)$ that two traders i and j are connected.
- The average number of traders which are effectively involved in the market, that is, the traders for which $\phi_i \neq 0$, is noted n_{order}. It represents what is generally called the market depth. The probability that $\phi_i \neq 0$ is then by definition n_{order}/N.

If the average number of connections c is larger than 1, the gregarious effect prevails and the model diverges: the connection networks (the set of traders connected directly or through other traders) are of such a size that the difference between supply and demand is arbitrarily large.

Let us focus on the case when the gregarious effect stays moderate, that is, c is close but less than 1. In addition, let us assume that n_{order} remains finite, which is realistic: the number of stock exchange orders at a given instant generally stays finite. The model then leads to a power law with an exponential cut-off, of the kind:

$$\mathrm{Prob}(|S| > x) \simeq \frac{1}{x^{\alpha}}\, \mathrm{e}^{-x/A} \tag{9.4}$$

This function looks like a power law as long as $x \ll A$ as, in this case, $\exp(-x/A)$ is close to 1. By contrast, as soon as x is larger than A, the exponential fall will prevail, hence the term "exponential cut-off". Thus, when A is large enough, the law may look similar to a power law over a relatively large domain.

Cont and Bouchaud also quantified the heaviness of the distribution tail, with the following two observations.

- The larger the number of connections per trader is, the more the distribution tails are heavy.
- The smaller the market depth n_{order} is, the heavier the distribution tails are. This highlights the link observed on markets between the decrease in liquidity, that is, the decrease in the number of sellers and buyers, and the rise of the amplitudes of changes (and consequently an increase in the risks).

In conclusion, thanks to a very simple structure, based on the mutual influence of traders, this model exhibits many interesting features:

- a modelling of price which leads to power laws (with an exponential cut-off);
- a critical threshold for the gregarious effect; there is a model divergence when the threshold is exceeded;
- a sensitivity of the heaviness of distribution tails to traders' interconnection rate;
- a link between the market depth and the heaviness of distribution tails.

Of course, the structure we have used above is too simplistic to give a refined representation of price changes. It is however useful to understand various phenomena, to account for causality links and, possibly, to warn against the existence of critical thresholds which may lead to market instability. Moreover, there exist many avenues for refinement, for example, in modelling the mutual influence of traders. Indeed, instead of creating random binary links between traders, one may imagine influence structures where the choice made by a trader is dictated, not only by his or her *a priori* view of the market, but also by that of his or her neighbors, the weight of the opinions of others in the final choice depending on how much the trader is prone to be influenced, etc.

9.3 Lévy processes

Let us now quit physicists' approach and adopt mathematicians' one, where the starting point is not the past history of prices, but axiomatic. Gaussian modelling was based on the three following founding hypotheses.

- Stock prices are continuous.
- Their returns $(S_{t+s} - S_t)/S_t$ are stationary.
- Returns are independent of the stock past values.

These three hypotheses are sufficient by themselves to define the log-normal motion. Volatility models may be used to adapt modelling, by acting on the parametrization of the volatility σ, constant in the original log-normal model, but which may become dependent on the following factors: time, the asset price, and the volatility history or a random factor in more sophisticated models. Thus, the volatility models studied in Chapter 6 soften the stationarity and independence hypotheses.

The only assumption which is not challenged by volatility models is the first one: stocks are continuous functions of time. This was an assumption supposed to be of a technical aspect, without any noticeable impact on modelling. Actually, giving up this hypothesis leads to a new class of models, a much broader one: the Lévy processes. Starting from these processes and adapting them to market characteristics through the parametrization of the diffusion constants broaden our spectrum of models while relying on a clear and intuitive axiomatic basis.

In the present section, we describe Lévy processes, in order to understand their potentialities, their characteristics and their interest in modelling financial assets. Formally, a Lévy process L_t is a random process which obeys the following properties.

- Its increments $L_{t+s} - L_t$ are stationary.
- Its increments $L_{t+s} - L_t$ are independent of past values of $L_u, u \leq t$.

Modelling stock prices requires using the exponential of Lévy processes, similarly to the case of Brownian motion. The first question asked by a mathematician facing this new axiomatics is: why does relaxing the continuity constraint leads outside the Gaussian framework? The answer is that, in so doing, we leave the applicability domain of central limit theorem. What does it mean? Central limit theorem states that the average value of an infinite number of random variables, independent, not too volatile, and with an identical probability distribution, is necessarly a Gaussian law.

Let us consider a Lévy process, L_T, with the boundary condition $L_0 = 0$. We may write:

$$\begin{aligned} L_T &= L_T - L_0 \\ &= (L_T - L_{T/2}) + (L_{T/2} - L_0) \\ &= (L_T - L_{2T/3}) + (L_{2T/3} - L_{T/3}) + (L_{T/3} - L_0) \\ &= \cdots \\ &= \sum_{i=1}^{N} (L_{iT/N} - L_{(i-1)T/N}) \\ &= \left[\frac{1}{N} \sum_{i=1}^{N} N \times (L_{iT/N} - L_{(i-1)T/N}) \right] \end{aligned} \tag{9.5}$$

In this equation, we decomposed variable L_T into the sum of its increments over smaller and smaller time steps. The specificity of Lévy processes is that its increments are independent and follow the same law (for a given time step). Thus, the process is at every instant the sum of an arbitrarily large number N (N may tend to infinity) of independent random variables identically distributed. Asserting that a process is continuous amounts to assuming that its increments tend to zero when the time step goes to zero: $(L_{iT/N} - L_{(i-1)T/N})$ must go to zero when $N \to \infty$. Thus, increments $(L_{iT/N} - L_{(i-1)T/N})$ must not be too volatile. The central limit theorem then states that, under these conditions, the equation (9.5) necessarily follows a Gaussian law. Hence, continuous Lévy processes are necessarily Brownian motions.

This explains why the continuity hypothesis brings us within the applicability domain of the central limit theorem (although the rigorous proof is much more involved). This is why we were able to build Black-Scholes model from the sole assumptions of continuity, stationarity and independence.

If we give up the continuity hypothesis, we leave the applicability domain of the central limit theorem, and we enter a broader class of stochastic processes: Lévy processes. These processes may be decomposed as the sum of a Brownian motion and a process with jumps. We shall not enter the details of processes with jumps, but we shall illustrate them with some examples. A first category, the simplest one, is called *compound Poisson processes.* These are piecewise continuous processes, which can only move thanks to jumps with a fixed or random size. These jumps occur at random times. For example, one could model the number of points scored in a basketball game by a compound Poisson process whose jumps are of size 1, 2 or 3 randomly distributed. Various random samplings of compound Poisson processes are represented in Figure 9.8.

These compound Poisson processes are the building blocks of Merton's asset evolution model.[2] In this model, the evolution of asset prices S_t is defined by:

$$\ln(S_t) - \ln(S_0) = \mu\, t + \sigma\, W_t + P_t \tag{9.6}$$

[2]Merton's asset evolution model is different from Merton's credit model encountered in Chapter 2.

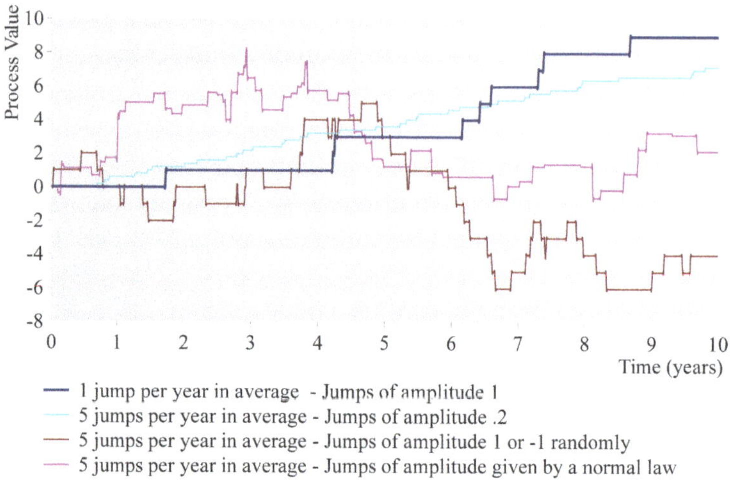

Figure 9.8: The graph illustrates compound Poisson processes. The curves only evolve through jumps of fixed (blue curves) or random magnitude. The interval between two consecutive jumps is random. On average, it is all the shorter as the jump intensity is higher.

where μt is the drift, σW_t is a Brownian motion without drift and of yearly volatility σ, while P_t is a compound Poisson process. This process will then admit two kinds of parameters.

- The jump intensity, λ, related to the frequency of jumps.
- The jump magnitude, which, by assumption, follows a normal law of average M_s and volatility V_s. The parameter M_s describes the average magnitude of jumps and V_s the dispersion of jump magnitudes around this average. For example, if we choose $M_s = 0$ and V_s large, it will mean that we consider that positive jumps are as likely as negative ones, and that jump sizes may be large and widely spread. Choosing $M_s < 0$ and V_s small will mean that we only account for negative jumps (modeling a crisis situation, for example), whose size will be fairly close to M_s.

Merton's model thus brings an additional component to the Black-Scholes model, the possibility of sudden events, of discontinuous variations, that is, jumps. This component brings heavier distribution tails, as illustrated in Figure 9.9. The increase in distribution tails

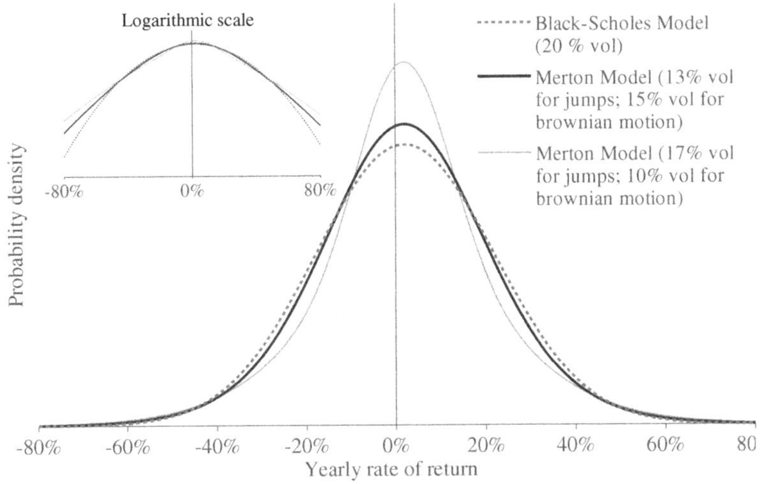

Figure 9.9: Distribution at one year of processes following Merton's model whose jumps are centered (the total volatility is kept constant so that the distributions may be compared to one another). Merton's model displays heavier distribution tails than Black-Scholes'.

thickness is modest, as jumps magnitude is accounted for by a normal law, which is an arbitrary choice. The use of stronger laws, that is, laws allowing higher probabilities for important jumps, is quite possible, in particular if one wishes to recover the power laws studied in the preceding section.

The main implication of jumps is that they add a major qualitative difference: the impossibility of continuously hedging financial products. In Chapter 5, in the framework of the Black-Scholes model, we showed that we could neutralize portfolios' risks thanks to delta-hedging. This technique only works to hedge the continuous component of the risk, and it is unable to neutralize risks induced by jumps. The theory of the Black-Scholes model relies on the idea that our reaction time is infinitely short, which allows us to manipulate assets with an infinite accuracy. Furthermore, the degree of freedom which is available to us in order to act is exactly equal to the number of degrees of freedom available to the asset for its evolution (*cf.* Chapters 4 and 5).

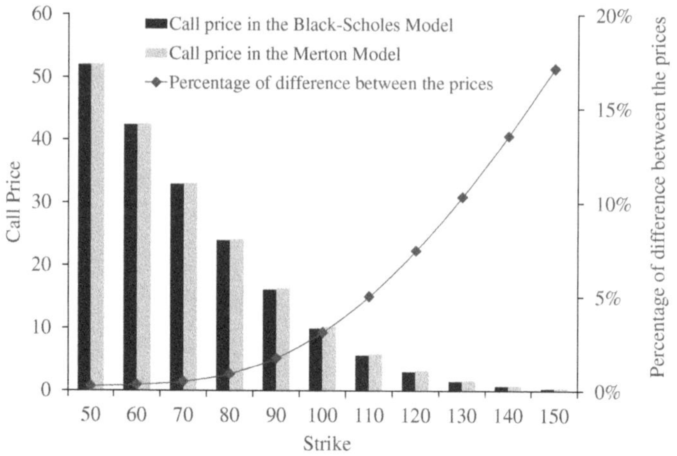

Figure 9.10: Comparison of call prices, as a function of the strike, in the Black-Scholes and Merton's models. The graph shows that the model uncertainty is all the larger as the strike is higher (in such situation, options are called "out of the money", because they are very far from the stock price supposed to be 100).

The jumps of Merton's model destroy the comfort provided by the Black-Scholes one. Whatever our theoretical reactivity, the potentiality of jumps occurrence adds an additional degree of freedom to the evolution laws and ruins any hope to neutralize risks with a simple hedging. Merton's model is not complete (*cf.* Chapter 4), and the equivalent risk-neutral measure is not unique. This implies that, in Merton's model, the risk-neutral prices are not unique; this model admits the existence of many valid prices, in the sense that they are arbitrage free.

One of the model's interests is the analysis and the evaluation of the impact of a jump. Comparing prices obtained in the Black-Scholes' and Merton's models gives the opportunity to quantify the potential impact of sudden price variations, and thus of the unrealistic assumption of instant reactivity for hedging (*cf.* Figure 9.10). Furthermore, some financial products and constructions are particularly sensitive to this jump risk, such as the CPPIs (Constant Proportion Portfolio Insurance) presented in Figure 9.11; studying these products in the framework of a Black-Scholes model would amount to simply denying the existence of the risk.

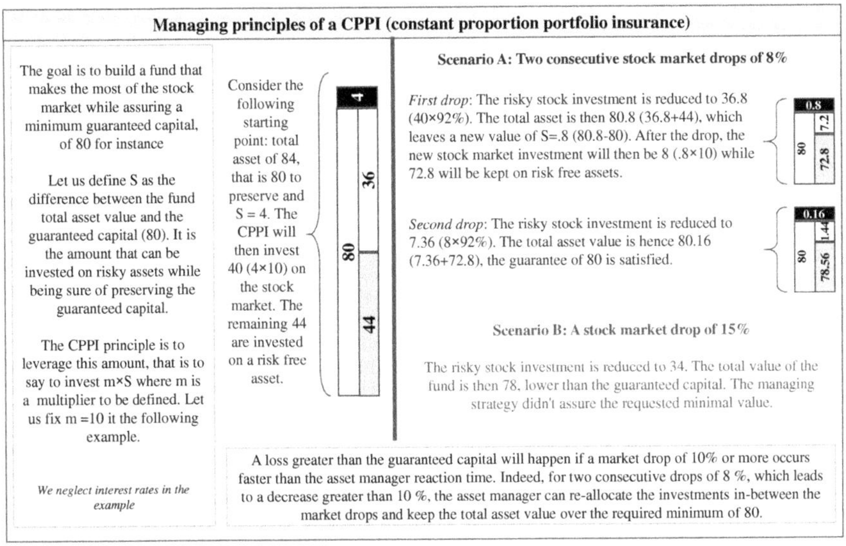

Figure 9.11: Example of management strategy of a CPPI. The strategy is designed to take advantage of the stock dynamics, thanks to leverage, while attempting to guarantee a minimum capital. In a model of continuous evolution of assets, of the Black-Scholes type, the strategy never loses as all the asset variations are infinitesimal and the reaction time is infinitely short. Actually, all these strategies bear some risks that can be evaluated, for example, by the use of a jump model, where the price variations may be sudden and lead to overshooting the safety cushion.

This line of thought shows that a model is not intrinsically better than another one; everything depends on the way we wish to use it. If our goal is to sell a traditional financial product by protecting it with a delta hedge, it is important to study the strategy in the framework of the two modelings we have analyzed: the Black-Scholes model (possibly augmented with a volatility model) which is adapted to find out a relevant market price, even though the model does not capture all the risks, and jump models which better assess the risks of sudden price variations and can help quantifying model risk, for example.

There exist other kinds of Lévy processes in the details of which we shall not enter. More difficult to intuitively picture, they may have

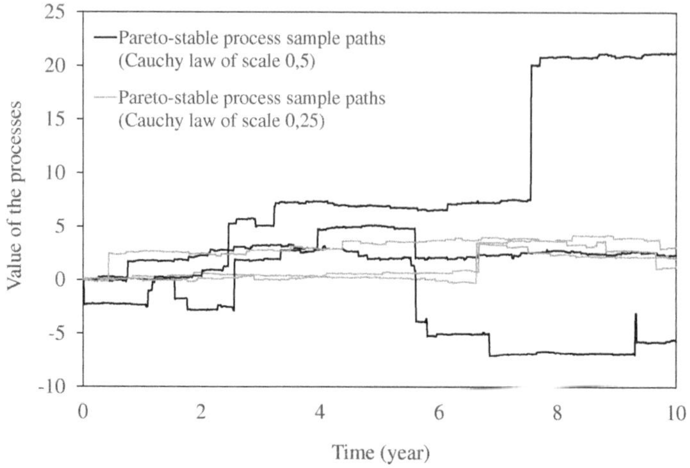

Figure 9.12: Example of trajectories of α-stable processes (Cauchy laws). The process evolution is built with an infinity of quasi-infinitesimal jumps and of some jumps with a big amplitude which occur in the same way as the jumps of compound Poisson processes.

an infinite intensity of jumps, that is, between two instants, there always exists an infinite number of jumps. These processes can be used to build evolution laws such as the α-stable processes proposed by Mandelbrot, an illustration of which is presented in Figure 9.12.

Lévy processes open new windows for the risk analysis and bring new mathematical tools for the improvement of models. Taking jumps into account allows us to thicken distribution tails, in small proportions (Merton's model), or as far as giving an infinite variance to diffusions (case of α-stable laws). The two founding assumptions of these processes are the stationarity of the processes and the independence of the returns. As in the case of Black-Scholes model, these two constraints may easily be bypassed by using time-dependent parameters or new random factors as in the volatility models.

Conclusion

Financial markets show a natural propensity to the construction of mathematical models, as they produce a large amount of numerical data. Among the most abundant data, we find the prices of financial products. These prices are often expressed using parameters which may be given an intuitive meaning:

- interest rates and yields;
- default probabilities;
- volatility;
- volatility of volatility;
- correlations.

Whatever the model, the usual mechanism for computing the price of a financial product is always the same: (i) one postulates a model; (ii) one chooses the input parameters which allow the model to be consistent with the prices of financial products listed on markets; this step is the calibration of the model, and the parameters determined are termed "implied parameters"; (iii) one uses the model thus calibrated to compute prices of financial products not available on markets.

Implied and economic parameters can only be compared when the model has, at least, some economic meaning and consistency with reality. However, it may then turn out that the parameters values used as input of the models has nothing in common with the real value of the economic or financial data it is supposed to represent.

These parameters often incorporate a risk premium which leads, for example, to implied default probabilities larger than the real ones.

In this regard, it is important to notice that the valuation process described above always operates whatever the model, complex or simplistic, economically justified or entirely preposterous. Provided the chosen model displays enough degrees of freedom, it is always possible to find parameters which give the right price on a sample of products, and then to use the calibrated model to compute the prices of other financial products. Consequently, there exists no *a priori* safeguard that prevents practitioners from using inappropriate models; only their expertise allows them to guarantee, as far as possible, the quality of modelings. Then, how can we distinguish between a good model and a bad one?

There is no textbook answer to this question, besides the prerequisite of the no-arbitrage property. If a model offers arbitrage possibilities, other market participants may take advantage of it. This no-arbitrage requirement essentially imposes that the anticipated rate of return of all assets be the risk-free rate. This leaves room for many competing models whose quality must be assessed.

The most explored property is the ability of the model to be in line with the market. It is quite easy to check the consistency of the model by applying it to listed products. For the prices which are not directly available, traders know the competition practices and can thus check the calibration of their model. From this sole point of view, it would follow that any model which achieves a consensus is a good one.

Nevertheless, there are other ways to assess a model quality. The time stability of implied parameters is a very important aspect, which is termed the robustness of the model. The more stable the parameters are, the more their interpretation will be meaningful and the more the follow-up of the ensuing risk will be relevant. Furthermore, parameters stability is also crucial for the efficiency of hedging strategies. Indeed, the model indicates how to hedge an asset, or an asset portfolio, in particular through the computation of sensitivities; each significant change in the parameters leads to a modification of the hedging portfolio, which generates risks and costs. Schematically, the more artificial and far from reality a model is, and the more frequently it needs to be re-calibrated; on the contrary, a model whose parameters are stable is endowed with a good predictive power and is likely to lead to dynamics consistent with prices evolution.

What about the physical relevance of the model and how consistent is it to the actual underlying asset prices history? Clearly, the evolution of implied parameters must be in line with the market behavior: a model whose implied correlation decreases, while in reality one observes an increase of correlations between values, naturally deserves to be reviewed.

However, the fact that models should fit histories often takes a back seat. Valuation models are not calibrated on prices histories. This is, by the way, quite fortunate because such a calibration would require the stationarity of the calibration sources or, in other words, would assume that the past be representative of the future. Figure 2 of Chapter 2 gives an excellent example of the devastating effects that an incorrectly formulated stationarity hypothesis would generate. However, without being calibrated on histories, it is more than desirable that models calibrated on market prices account for probability laws consistent with prices histories; Chapter 9 showed the extent to which distribution tails are under-estimated in Gaussian modelings. Now, financial crises generally arise when market participants massively correct for a past judgment mistake; the latter can involve the validity of an assumption, of a model or of an economic environment (solvency of Governments, prospects of an activity sector etc.). Histories of prices are, in this respect, the sole statistical elements available in order to assess the relevance of mathematical models and their underlying hypotheses.

In the end, is it better that the model be in phase with today's market prices or with the lessons learned from historical observations? The answer is far from obvious. If the valued product is perfectly hedged by other product bought from competitors, it is important to agree with market prices. John Maynard Keynes reminds us that "Markets can remain irrational a lot longer than you and I can remain solvent". In practice, hedging strategies are not perfect and the risk borne by investors depends on the real behavior of stock prices.

After having computed prices, we face another issue: the risk measurement which is the evaluation of the risks borne by Capital Market activities. Risk measures are much less constrained by the need of consistency with market prices, and much more by the consistency with historical reality. For example, simplistic correlation structures resulting from Gaussian vectors may turn out to be totally inappropriate. The most important step is identifying the sources of risk. This step, which proceeds through an analysis which is more financial than mathematical, should lead, for example, to identify whether a simple modeling of the correlation is sufficient, or whether a more sophisticated modeling is required, in particular to account for wrong way risk. The quantitative risk measurement requires that one evaluates the actual, and not the implied, probability driving the assets dynamics. It necessarily relies on the stationarity hypothesis and historical data. Consequently, it is not aimed at predicting events which are statistically unobservable. It must be supplemented by economic analyses which may require a crisis simulation (stress tests). On the other hand, risk measures give birth to other issues, which are completely external to the intrinsic quality of risk evaluation, but which result from systemic risks which they contribute to feed because of their pro-cyclicity. This point is today well identified by the banking control authorities which attempted to solve it within the latest financial reforms.

Bibliography

[Alexander, 2001] Alexander, C. (2001). *Market Models: A Guide to Financial Data Analysis*. John Wiley & Sons.

[Ayache et al., 2004] Ayache, E., Henrotte, P., Nassar, S., and Wang, X. (2004). Can anyone solve the smile problem? *Wilmott Magazine*.

[Bachelier, 1900] Bachelier, L. (1900). *Théorie de la spéculation*. Gauthier-Villars.

[Bacry et al., 2001] Bacry, E., Delour, J., and Muzy, J.-F. (2001). Multifractal random walk. *Physical Review E*.

[Bacry and Muzy, 2003] Bacry, E. and Muzy, J.-F. (2003). Log-infinitely divisible multifractal processes. *Communications in Mathematical Physics*.

[Basel Committee, 2006] Basel Committee (2006). International convergence of capital measurement and capital standards — a revised framework (comprehensive version).

[Basel Committee, 2009a] Basel Committee (2009a). Principles for sound stress testing practices and supervision.

[Basel Committee, 2009b] Basel Committee (2009b). Revisions to the basel 2 market risk framework.

[Basel Committee, 2010] Basel Committee (2010). Basel 3: A global regulatory framework for more resilient banks and banking systems.

[Black, 1972] Black, F. (1972). Capital market equilibrium with restricted borrowing. *The Journal of Business*.

[Black and Scholes, 1973] Black, F. and Scholes, M. (1973). The pricing of options and corporate liabilities. *The Journal of Political Economy*.

[Bouchaud, 2001] Bouchaud, J.-P. (2001). Power laws in economics and finance: Some ideas from physics. *Quantitative Finance*.

[Bouchaud and Potters, 2003] Bouchaud, J.-P. and Potters, M. (2003). *Theory of Financial Risk and Derivative Pricing: From Statistical Physics to Risk Management*. Cambridge University Press, 2nd edition.

[Brigo et al., 2010] Brigo, D., Pallavicini, A., and Torresetti, R. (2010). *Credit Models and the Crisis: A Journey into CDOs, Copulas, Correlations and Dynamic Models*. John Wiley & Sons.

[Calvet and Fisher, 2008] Calvet, L. and Fisher, A. (2008). *Multifractal Volatility: Theory, Forecasting, and Pricing.* Academic Press.

[Cont and Bouchaud, 2000] Cont, R. and Bouchaud, J.-P. (2000). Herd behavior and aggregate fluctuations in financial markets. *Macroeconomic Dynamics.*

[Cont and Tankov, 2003] Cont, R. and Tankov, P. (2003). *Financial Modelling with Jump Processes.* Chapman & Hall.

[Delbaen and Schachermayer, 1994] Delbaen, F. and Schachermayer, W. (1994). A general version of the fundamental theorem of asset pricing. *Mathematische Annalen.*

[Delbaen and Schachermayer, 1998] Delbaen, F. and Schachermayer, W. (1998). The fundamental theorem of asset pricing for unbounded stochastic processes. *Mathematische Annalen.*

[Delbaen and Schachermayer, 2005] Delbaen, F. and Schachermayer, W. (2005). *The Mathematics of Arbitrage.* Springer Verlag.

[Derman, 2003] Derman, E. (2003). The boy's guide to pricing and hedging. *Risk.*

[Derman and Kani, 1994] Derman, E. and Kani, I. (1994). Riding on a smile. *Risk.*

[Derman and Kani, 1998] Derman, E. and Kani, I. (1998). Stochastic implied trees: Arbitrage pricing with stochastic term and strike structure of volatility. *International Journal of Theoretical and Applied Finance.*

[Derman et al., 1996] Derman, E., Kani, I., and Chriss, N. (1996). Implied trinomial trees of the volatility smile. *The Journal of Derivatives.*

[Duffy, 2006] Duffy, D. (2006). *Finite Difference Methods in Financial Engineering: A Partial Differential Equation Approach.* John Wiley & Sons.

[Dumas et al., 1998] Dumas, B., Fleming, J., and Whaley, R. (1998). Implied volatility functions: Empirical tests. *The Journal of Finance.*

[Dupire, 1994] Dupire, B. (1994). Pricing with a smile. *Risk.*

[El Karoui, 2003] El Karoui, N. (2003). Couverture des risques dans les marchés financiers. *Université Paris VI.* http://www.cmap.polytechnique.fr/elkaroui/.

[Engle and Granger, 1987] Engle, R. and Granger, C. (1987). Co-integration and error correction: Representation, estimation, and testing. *Econometrica.*

[Fama, 1965] Fama, E. (1965). The behavior of stock-market prices. *The Journal of Business.*

[Fama and French, 1992] Fama, E. and French, K. (1992). The cross-section of expected stock returns. *The Journal of Finance.*

[Fouque et al., 2000] Fouque, J.-P., Papanicolaou, G., and Sircar, K. (2000). *Derivatives in Financial Markets with Stochastic Volatility.* Cambridge University Press.

[Gabaix, 2009] Gabaix, X. (2009). Power laws in economics and finance. *Annual Review of Economics.*

[Gatheral, 2006] Gatheral, J. (2006). *The Volatility Surface: A Practitioner's Guide.* John Wiley & Sons.

[Hagan et al., 2002] Hagan, P., Kumar, D., and Lesniewski, A. (2002). Managing smile risk. *Wilmott Magazine.*

[Harrison and Kreps, 1979] Harrison, J. and Kreps, D. (1979). Martingales and arbitrage in multiperiod securities markets. *Journal of Economic Theory.*

[Harrison and Pliska, 1981] Harrison, J. and Pliska, S. (1981). Martingales and stochastic integrals in the theory of continuous trading. *Stochastic Processes and their Applications.*

[Haug, 2007a] Haug, E. (2007a). *The Complete Guide to Option Pricing Formulas.* McGraw-Hill Professional, 2nd edition.

[Haug, 2007b] Haug, E. (2007b). *Derivatives: Models on Models.* John Wiley & Sons.

[Heston, 1993] Heston, S. (1993). A closed-form solution for options with stochastic volatility with applications to bond and currency options. *The Review of Financial Studies.*

[Hull, 2011] Hull, J. (2011). *Options, Futures and Other Derivatives.* Pearson Education, 8th edition.

[Jäckel, 2002] Jäckel, P. (2002). *Monte Carlo Methods in Finance.* John Wiley & Sons.

[Jarrow and Turnbull, 1995] Jarrow, R. and Turnbull, S. (1995). Pricing derivatives on financial securities subject to credit risk. *The Journal of Finance.*

[Joshi, 2008] Joshi, M. (2008). *The Concepts and Practice of Mathematical Finance.* Cambridge University Press, 2nd edition.

[Kreps, 1981] Kreps, D. (1981). Arbitrage and equilibrium in economies with infinitely many commodities. *Journal of Mathematical Economics.*

[Le Gall, 2011] Le Gall, J.-F. (2011). Mouvement brownien, martingales et calcul stochastique. *Université Paris Sud.* http://www.math.u-psud.fr/ jflegall/.

[Lewis, 2000] Lewis, A. (2000). *Option Valuation Under Stochastic Volatility.* Finance Press.

[Lintner, 1965] Lintner, J. (1965). The valuation of risk assets and the selection of risky investments in stock portfolios and capital budgets. *The Review of Economics and Statistics.*

[Lipton and McGhee, 2002] Lipton, A. and McGhee, W. (2002). Universal barriers. *Risk.*

[Litterman and Scheinkman, 1991] Litterman, R. and Scheinkman, J. (1991). Common factors affecting bond returns. *The Journal of Fixed Income.*

[Longstaff and Schwartz, 2001] Longstaff, F. and Schwartz, E. (2001). Valuing American options by simulation: A simple least-squares approach. *The Review of Financial Studies.*

[Mandelbrot, 1963] Mandelbrot, B. (1963). The variation of certain speculative prices. *The Journal of Business.*

[Markowitz, 1952] Markowitz, H. (1952). Portfolio selection. *Journal of Finance.*

[Markowitz, 1959] Markowitz, H. (1959). *Portfolio Selection: Efficient Diversification of Investments.* John Wiley & Sons.

[Martellini and Priaulet, 2004] Martellini, L. and Priaulet, P. (2004). *Produits de taux d'intérêt: méthodes dynamiques d'évaluation et de couverture.* Économica, 2nd edition.

[Merton, 1973] Merton, R. (1973). Theory of rational option pricing. *The Bell Journal of Economics and Management Science.*

[Merton, 1974] Merton, R. (1974). On the pricing of corporate debt: The risk structure of interest rates. *The Journal of Finance.*

[Merton, 1976] Merton, R. (1976). Option pricing when underlying stock returns are discontinuous. *Journal of Financial Economics.*

[Mitchell, 1915] Mitchell, W. (1915). The making and using of index numbers. *Bulletin No. 173 of the US Bureau of Labor Statistics (reprinted in 1921, Bulletin No. 284 and in 1938, Bulletin No. 656).*

[Mossin, 1966] Mossin, J. (1966). Equilibrium in a capital asset market. *Econometrica.*

[Nelson and Siegel, 1987] Nelson, C. and Siegel, A. (1987). Parsimonious modeling of yield curves. *The Journal of Business.*

[Potters et al., 2001] Potters, M., Bouchaud, J.-P., and Šestović, D. (2001). Hedged Monte-Carlo: Low variance derivative pricing with objective probabilities. *Physica A.*

[Rebonato, 2004] Rebonato, R. (2004). *Volatility and Correlation: The Perfect Hedger and the Fox.* John Wiley & Sons, 2nd edition.

[Ross, 1976] Ross, S. (1976). The arbitrage theory of capital asset pricing. *Journal of Economic Theory.*

[Rubinstein, 1994] Rubinstein, M. (1994). Implied binomial trees. *Journal of Finance.*

[Schönbucher, 2003] Schönbucher, P. (2003). *Credit Derivatives Pricing Models: Models, Pricing and Implementation.* John Wiley & Sons.

[Sharpe, 1964] Sharpe, W. (1964). Capital asset prices: A theory of market equilibrium under conditions of risk. *The Journal of Finance.*

[Sharpe *et al.*, 2000] Sharpe, W., Alexander, G., and Bailey, J. (2000). *Fundamentals of Investments.* Prentice Hall, 3rd edition.

[Taleb, 2008] Taleb, N. (2008). *Le cygne noir: La puissance de l'imprévisible.* Les Belles Lettres.

[Tankov, 2009] Tankov, P. (2009). Calibration de modèles et couverture de produits dérivés. *Université Paris VII.* http://www.math.jussieu.fr/ tankov/.

[Tobin, 1958] Tobin, J. (1958). Liquidity preference as behavior towards risk. *The Review of Economic Studies.*

[Wilmott, 2006] Wilmott, P. (2006). *Paul Wilmott on Quantitative Finance.* John Wiley & Sons, 2nd edition.

Index

www.ingramcontent.com/pod-product-compliance
Ingram Content Group UK Ltd.
Pitfield, Milton Keynes, MK11 3LW, UK
UKHW020311150926
8624IPUK00014B/515

9 789813 142107